The Book of Iowa Films

Marty S. Knepper
and
John Shelton Lawrence

The Book of Iowa Films Press
Berkeley, California, and Sioux City, Iowa

Credits

Cover pictures:

"Will Rogers and Blue Boy," *State Fair* (1933), Fox Film publicity still; collection of Marty S. Knepper and John S. Lawrence

"Ghost Players" © Dream Catcher Productions, by permission

"The Roseman Bridge of Madison County," 2008 Wikimedia Commons; Sanjay-Fays, photographer

A Place for Heroes poster image © My Town Pictures, by permission

Marty Knepper and John Lawrence photo by Gail Ament

Interior pictures:

p. vi, *State Fair* (1933) special edition book jacket (color); collection of Knepper and Lawrence

p. 234, *The Strange Woman* (1918), Fox Film lobby card; Knepper and Lawrence

p. 254, "They Did Their Part—the five Sullivan Brothers missing in action off the Solomons," 1943, poster (color), Library of Congress Digital Collections

Cover art: Bob Ng

Book design: Mark McDermott

The Book of Iowa Films Press
758 Spruce Street, Berkeley, CA 94707 /
2715 Ross Street, Sioux City, IA 51103

The Book of Iowa Films /
Marty S. Knepper and John Shelton Lawrence
ISBN 978-0-9904289-1-6
Lulu perfect bound paperback edition, 2014

Information about the electronic edition of this book is available at bookofiowafilms.com.

To John L. Knepper,
who found many films for us,

and

To Morningside College students, faculty,
and staff who also shared their
Iowa film finds

Table of Contents

State Fair (1933), book jacket
Phil Stong's bestselling novel, published in May 1932, became a film by 10 February 1933. This special edition cover displays the stars and their part of the story. Stong followed this speedy conversion with three more Hollywood screenplays based on quickly written books.

Preface and Acknowledgements

How did *The Book of Iowa Films* come about? Our script for that answer ranges over nearly two decades and includes a large cast of supporting actors. As the principals in this production, our opening scenes were played out during the 1980s as colleagues at Morningside College in Sioux City, Iowa. In a team-taught, interdisciplinary seminar for our curious and creative undergraduates, we examined American popular culture. We always included segments of Hollywood films that illustrated class and gender stereotypes, teen fascination with horror, heroism, and mythologies of success, failure, family, and romance. Until the early 1990s we taught with little consciousness of how Iowa or the Midwest was portrayed in popular culture.

Then came a pair of popular novels and blockbuster films, both made in Iowa, which presented Iowa culture in a way that launched and sustained a new kind tourism. *Field of Dreams* (1989) and *The Bridges of Madison County* (1995) surprised many Iowans whose "dream vacations" would take them to beaches, mountains, or urban centers with famous museums and live theatrical performances, not to small town Iowa. We began to discuss this phenomenon with our students, many of whom came from towns like Dyersville and Winterset. In the later 1990s Marty began teaching an Iowa Film seminar, which eventually evolved into an Iowa Film tour of the state for her students, who interviewed filmmakers and visited film tourist sites. These early circumstances spurred us to write a series of articles on Iowa films. More recently, the State Historical Museum of Iowa's "Hollywood and the Heartland" exhibition, scheduled for June 2014 to June 2017, led us to update our research and create this book.

And now for some credits. We wish to acknowledge our Morningside College students, faculty and staff colleagues, friends and family members, and several other audiences that gave us a sympathetic hearing for our interests, interpretations, and calls for help. Our first public outings were "Films about Iowa," a paper for an international meeting of the Popular Culture and American Culture Association at Oxford University (July 1995), and "The Iowa Romance Formula," a presentation at the Great Plains Popular Culture and American Culture Association Conference at Morningside College (Oct. 1995).

Our first publication, assisted greatly by skillful assistance from Editor Ginalie Swain, came as a handsomely illustrated essay "Visions of Iowa in Hollywood Film" in *Iowa Heritage Illustrated* 79.4 (Winter · 1998): 156-69. That article was followed by "Iowa Filmography: 1918-2002," *Annals of Iowa* 62.1 (Winter 2003): 30-100, improved by Marvin Bergman's astute, helpful editorial hand. Since we continue to use some formulations that first appeared in both of these publications of the State Historical Society of Iowa (SHSI), we publish the materials here with their permission and point out that the issue containing the beautifully produced "Visions of Iowa in Hollywood Film"is still available for purchase from *Iowa Heritage Illustrated*, SHSI, 402 Washington Street, Iowa City, IA 52240. It is a wonderful supplement to the textual rendering of film in this book. Our next publication was a book chapter: "World War II and Iowa: Hollywood's Pastoral Myth for the Nation" in *Representing the Rural*, edited by Catherine Fowler and Gillian Helfield (Detroit: Wayne State UP, 2006, 323-40). We include that chapter as Appendix C in this book and publish it by permission of the Wayne State University Press.

Bob Ford of Long Beach, California, known since the 1950s as "Iowa by the Sea," hosted an Iowa film festival for a number of years and shared his film list with us. More recently Timothy Lostetter, author of *Iowa in the Movies* (Boscobel, WI: Flat Bridge Media, 2013), led us to some previously unknown titles, especially films that merely mention Iowa. Christopher Rossi, Executive Director of Humanities Iowa, regularly updated us on Iowa films funded by their organization. The Sioux City Public Library staff and the Morningside College Library staff helped with interlibrary loans and reference questions. Dani Dahlkoetter and Sarah Munson both offered precision research assistance in keeping our dates and titles in order. Carrie Rice and Marcie Ponder of the Morningside English Department offered invaluable assistance over the years.

Wendol Jarvis and Tom Wheeler, Directors of the Iowa Film Office, gave us definitive lists of films shot in Iowa. Liz Gilman, Director of Produce Iowa, the new manifestation of the Iowa Film Office, continues to assist us. John Knepper was especially helpful in identifying and watching films for us over a long period of years. Timothy Orwig and John McGarrahan were important for the original Appendix C publication. Robert Birkby loaned us a rare DVD. Gail Ament, Robert Jewett, and Timothy Steele have offered excellent editorial advice. Mark

McDermott has solved many formatting problems. Bob Ng designed our print edition book jacket as well as our bookofiowafilms website. Tony Thompson and Greg Welker assisted with lobby card reproductions. Grace Linden of the Sioux City Historical Museum has archived our collection of Iowa videotapes and DVDs. Erv Sandlin provided some marketing direction. All these helpers deserve our profound thanks.

Marty Knepper has had opportunities to speak about Iowa films throughout the state, learning much from those audiences. She is also currently a consulting scholar for the "Hollywood in the Heartland" exhibit, a public programming partnership among Preservation Iowa, the State Historic Preservation Office, Main Street Iowa, the Iowa Tourism Office, and the State Historical Museum of Iowa. Members of the Advisory Council for the exhibit—especially Kristian Day, Liz Gilman, Andrew Harrington, Leo Landis, and J. Douglas Miller—have helped us make contacts and shared their knowledge of the history of Iowa films and the current scene in production.

Iowa filmmakers have also assisted us: Rick Amundsen, Scott Beck and Bryan Woods, Kimberly Busbee, Joe Clarke, Sean Gannon, George Lindblade, Stuart Pepper, Kelly and Tammy Rundle, Insane Mike Saunders, Joe Scherman, A. J. Schnack, Don Thompson, and Scott Thompson. Lisa Eddy of the Appanoose County Historical Museum allowed Marty to see the hard-to-find silent film *The Wonderful Thing*. John Lawrence, who moved to Berkeley, California, retiring after thirty-two years of teaching at Morningside, regrettably missed interactions with state actors on the Iowa film scene. But he has been ideally located to use the University of California-Berkeley's libraries and Pacific Film Archives. It is also a fine place to spy on West Coast sophisticates who talk about "flyover country" and proudly advertise their ignorance of the Midwest.

As we completed our manuscript, we were privileged to attend the opening of the "Hollywood in the Heartland" exhibit at the State Historical Museum of Iowa, 600 E. Locust Street, Des Moines. The exhibit features film clips from the most popular Iowa films along with commentary by Marty Knepper and theater owner Bob Fridley. The exhibit conveys the theater-going experiences of Iowans from the time of opera houses, silent films, and drive-in movies to the present. Ingenious, bulky projectors from the past highlight the dominance of today's diminutive digital systems. Movie posters, reviews, and display ads show how movies were promoted when print was still supreme. The exhibit reminds viewers about the importance of snacks at the movies, showing soda fountain menus and popcorn machines. The stories of Iowa movie stars are told, highlighting famous Iowa performers like Donna Reed and John Wayne and others whose Iowa roots are less well known. Iowa filmmakers such as Oscar Micheaux receive their due as well. We recommend this colorful, lovingly created exhibit, scheduled to run until 2016 or 2017, as a visual complement to our book.

Marty S. Knepper, Sioux City, Iowa
John S. Lawrence, Berkeley, California
July 2014

Introduction: The History of Iowa Films, 1918-2013

Iowans have been in the movies since 1921, when First National Pictures arrived in Centerville to shoot scenes from *The Wonderful Thing* with Norma Talmadge, a marquee star. Filming took place at a local hog farm, which the *Centerville Journal* celebrated with the headline, "1000 Hogs See Norma." After nine months of waiting for the edited film, the community had two days of screenings in the Majestic Theater. According to Lisa Eddy, Curator at the Appanoose County Museum, one newspaper enthusiastically urged readers to "See actual Appanoose County hogs on the screen."[1]

The "Look at us!" sentiment in Centerville was perhaps accompanied by the anxious question, "How do we look?" The desire to be thought well of by others plays a role in film viewing when we Iowans find ourselves on the screen. This depiction of Iowa identity lured us as scholars to engage with these films. Iowans, we have learned, occupy a special place in the national cinematic imagination.

Iowans are accustomed to stereotypes that treat them as inhabitants of "flyover country," characterized by Cary de Wit as "a term of playful condescension toward rural America from an urban perspective."[2] We spotted a mild version of this "playful condescension" in a *Texas Monthly* ad for Savane jeans: "THIS IS BEN. He grew up on a farm in Iowa. When we discovered him at a strip mall near Ames, he was wearing nothing but overalls and a baseball cap. We hosed him down and gave him some new clothes—including a pair of Savane Deep Dye Pants. Last we heard, he had changed his name to Paolo and was running for mayor of Palm Springs."[3] One of the best known sneers at Iowa came through Harold Ross's famous dismissal. Formulating his prospectus for *The New Yorker* magazine, he announced that no thought originating in Dubuque could possibly matter.

> *The New Yorker* will be the magazine which is not edited for the old lady in Dubuque. It will not be concerned in what she is thinking about. This is not meant in disrespect, but *The New Yorker* is a magazine avowedly published for a metropolitan audience and thereby will escape an influence which hampers most national publications.[4]

His "old lady in Dubuque" became part of bicoastal provincialism's lexicon of insults aimed at the heartland.

Iowa place and character stereotypes are not all negative, however. *The Promised Land* (2012) features Steve Butler (Matt Damon), whom we call in this book a "traveling Iowan." He left rural Iowa in despair about its future and now works for a global corporation that buys leases for fracking gas. When he discovers his employer's manipulative deceptions, he resigns and declares his allegiance to the Pennsylvanians he came to exploit. Steve Butler's Iowa-positive aura is also shown in *Saving Private Ryan* (1998), where Private Ryan was played by Matt Damon in a role that echoed a host of World War II films with patriotic Iowans. Beyond the simple "Iowa-negative" and "Iowa-positive" portrayals, there are more complex patterns in films, some of which display genuine Iowa people, places, and events. This introductory essay maps the Iowa cinematic territory before offering detailed film listings.

Our Preface indicates that we began our Iowa filmography project almost two decades ago. A short version of our findings with 42 entries appeared in *Iowa Heritage Illustrated* (1998). An expanded version, with entries on 165 films through 2002, was published in *The Annals of Iowa* (2003). Anticipating the State Historical Museum of Iowa's 2014 "Hollywood in the Heartland" exhibition, we felt it timely to update our survey of Iowa films.

Our research in 2013 brought several surprises. In scale, our filmography grew from considerably less than two hundred films in 2002 to four hundred plus and counting in 2013. Partly accounting for the larger numbers were improved databases and our expanded categories to include films that merely mention Iowa or were shot in Iowa. But the major factor was the upsurge in films produced by independent filmmakers like Scott Beck and Bryan Woods from Bettendorf and by small companies such as Scott Thompson's My Town Pictures. These films—made on low budgets with relatively inexpensive technology—found the market for new films that can be distributed on websites or by downloading from sites such as Amazon Instant Video, YouTube, and IPTV's *Iowa Stories*. Many filmmakers screened their movies at small film festivals around the state. These independent filmmakers almost totally replaced Hollywood studios as sources of Iowa films. For the most part, prominent twentieth-century themes did not cross the divide to the new millennium. The older fictional films portrayed Iowa either as a pastoral place celebrated for its patriotism, integrity, and love of family and community—or, alternatively, as a comically old-fashioned place with its farmers and small town residents preserved in a time capsule dated 1912. In contrast, the post-millennial filmmakers experimented with a wider range of genres including horror and social realism. They portrayed Iowa's past historically rather than mythically and its present as part of the US mainstream.

The newest edition of our Iowa filmography in Chapter 2 is obviously a work in progress since we continue to make fresh discoveries about the past and encounter the new. More Iowa films are coming, many encouraged by Produce Iowa, the new incarnation of the Iowa Film Office services, which earlier helped birth so many films. This introductory essay provides our vision of the Iowa film tradition's past century and our sense of new directions in the twenty-first century. Perhaps this essay and filmography will increase knowledge of Iowa's cultural history, spark further scholarship, and provide pleasure to Iowans who seek out movies about the Hawkeye State for their own entertainment.

Twentieth-Century Patterns and Sources

At the beginning of our study, we and many other Iowans were intrigued by the huge impact on Iowa tourism of *Field of Dreams* (1989) and *The Bridges of Madison County* (1995). Why were families flocking to Dyersville and tourist buses stopping at Winterset? In our view these two sentimental Hollywood films offered a magical Iowa rural landscape that promised reconciliation, love, and the illusion of returning to a simpler past.

Believing that the Iowa film tradition itself would throw light on the tourism, we recalled the few Iowa-related films that we knew well. There was the colorful Rodgers and Hammerstein musical *State Fair* (1945), which linked Iowa with wholesome farm families and big pigs. Equally charming, *The Music Man* (1962)—composed by genial, Mason City-born Meredith Willson—celebrated early twentieth-century small town life in Iowa. As residents of Sioux City, we knew the film *Crash Landing: The Rescue of Flight 232* (1992) that dramatized the 1989 air disaster and rescue at our city's airport. We also knew of Stephen King's gruesome horror film *Children of the Corn* (1984), filmed in Whiting, Hornick, and Sioux City, though set in Nebraska. This was hardly a list to unlock the secret of the new film-based tourism in Dyersville and Madison County.

Expanding our filmography and talking to individuals and community groups brought to light some intriguing dissonances between

3

sentiment directed toward Iowa film places but not toward Iowans themselves. The history of Iowa films in the twentieth century suggests that while some films presented a depressing or comic view of people's lives in the heartland, the most popular Iowa film image revealed a rural landscape associated with core American values such as patriotism, romance, family and community connections, and love for the land. The continued popularity of the Madison County and Dyersville tourist destinations and the 2001 opening of yet another attraction—Music Man Square in Mason City—suggested that Iowa pastoral nostalgia remained appealing to movie viewers, including Iowans, despite the fact that most of the native Iowans in *Field of Dreams*, *The Bridges of Madison County*, and other pastoral Iowa films were often portrayed as narrow-minded, gossipy, and unimaginative. Meredith Willson, creator of *The Music Man*, from Mason City, expressed his affection for Iowa small town life in one word: "Innocent—that was the adjective for Iowa . . . . I didn't have to make up anything for *The Music Man*. All I had to do was remember."[5] While his memory led him to portray the Paroos warmly, the rest of River City's residents are comically stubborn, gullible, and questionable in their taste.

Although pastoral portrayals of Iowa (if not Iowans) and the tourist sites remained profitable at century's end, we began to wonder about images that were not aligned with the state's educational, cultural, and industrial realities. Agriculture remains a major factor of Iowa's economy, but who would infer from the films that Des Moines is one of the nation's leading centers for insurance and investment products? There is nothing pastoral about that—or about the Casey's-type mini-marts ubiquitous in Iowa's small towns. The grim economic views of Iowa in films such as *What's Eating Gilbert Grape* (1993) or *Miles from Home* (1988) were closer to the reality of life in small towns and increasingly depopulated rural areas. What about the majority of Iowans who live in the state's larger cities and their suburbs? Modern cityscapes were almost non-existent in twentieth-century mainstream movies set in Iowa. In *Sleeping with the Enemy* (1991), Julia Roberts' character, fleeing from her abusive husband on the East Coast, enters Cedar Falls but does not discover a tangle of interconnecting interstate highways leading to nearby streets lined with chain restaurants, malls, businesses, a major university, museums, and libraries. Instead, she sees a peaceful town square with farmers in bib overalls raising an American flag while children joyfully play, a scene that could feature in a Norman Rockwell painting. Late twentieth-century audiences of Iowans found such outdated images laughable but were nonetheless strongly drawn

4

to them emotionally, a reaction that reveals the mythic power of agrarian nostalgia. Iowans' emotional conflict about our movie image created—and continues to create—a quandary for Iowa's leaders in economic development. What image of Iowa should be sold: the pastoral movie images or the reality, towns full of old-fashioned rustics or cities with highly trained workforces?

A more complex question than stereotyping lay in the surprisingly large number of twentieth-century Iowa movies we discovered. Research in well-indexed filmographies revealed that no comparably scaled body of films exists for our neighbors Kansas, Minnesota, Nebraska, Missouri, or South Dakota.[6] This led us to wonder why there are so many films with Iowa characters or settings. Twentieth-century cinematic history suggested several explanations that we explore here:

- Iowa's literary talent has led to the creation of Iowa films.
- Iowa has welcomed Hollywood and independent filmmakers.
- Famous Iowans and Iowa history have inspired filmmakers.
- Iowa as "the heart of the heartland" flexibly allows filmmakers to dramatize rural-urban conflicts, nostalgic stories, real historical events, and comedies and tragedies of family and community.

Iowa's Literary Talent

Numerous films can be traced to talented Iowa natives who used their art to depict some aspect of their Iowa experience. For example, Phil Stong wrote the Depression era bestseller *State Fair* in 1932. Within a year he had a Hollywood invitation to assist with the Fox Studio production of a popular film based on his book.[7] This experience became his ticket to provide scripts for additional Iowa-themed films. *The Stranger's Return* (1933), directed by King Vidor with a Stong screenplay, appeared the same year as its novel and as the *State Fair* film. Stong later wrote screenplays based on his novels *Farmer in the Dell* (1935) and *Career* (1936).

Another notable Iowan's literary star shone in the World War II years: MacKinlay Kantor. His sense of patriotism and kinship with servicemen led him to write the story and the script for the patriotic *Happy Land* (1943), set in "Hartfield, Iowa" (likely Webster City, Kantor's hometown). It was highly regarded by the Office of War Information, which lauded it as "the most effective portrayal of straight America to date."[8] *Happy Land* was likely used to sell war bonds at theaters.[9]

5

Invited to write a screenplay for a drama about the problems of post-war adjustment for veterans, Kantor improbably wrote a novel in blank verse, *Glory for Me* (1945), which evolved into the screenplay for the much Oscared *The Best Years of Our Lives* (1946). Between 1936 and 1966 ten more Hollywood films would be made from Kantor's novels or short stories.[10]

The phenomenon of Iowa literature becoming films continued with William Kinsella, a Canadian whose experience in Iowa led to the novel *Shoeless Joe* (1982), which became the startlingly successful movie *Field of Dreams*. Robert Waller, once a business professor at the University of Northern Iowa, temporarily became America's best known romance writer through his bestselling book *The Bridges of Madison County* (1992). Set in Iowa's Madison County, the book lyrically describes an affair between an Italian-American farm wife and an itinerant photographer. The film starring Clint Eastwood and Meryl Streep inflamed additional ardor in fans, who, for more than a decade later, came to see the magical covered bridges or dance in the kitchen of Francesca's house—that is, until the house burned down. The story was resurrected one more time in a Broadway musical launched in 2014.

Jane Smiley's Pulitzer Prize-winning novel, *A Thousand Acres* (1991), published while she served on the Iowa State University faculty, in 1997 became the identically titled film featuring Hollywood stars. Muscatine's multi-talented and prolific author Max Allan Collins—whose bibliography includes crime fiction, comic books, graphic novels, novelizations, and biographical/critical books—directs films with recognizable Iowa settings or themes and novelized the screenplay of the film *Saving Private Ryan*. Literary connections of this kind are significant and scattered throughout our listings. Found in the filmography, for example, are the names of Bess Streeter Aldrich, Peter Hedges, and Charles Nordhoff.

Iowa's Welcome Mat for Film Production

Oscar Micheaux, a novelist and the earliest known African-American filmmaker, was a turn-of-the-twentieth-century South Dakota homesteader, who turned his dismal experience into a novel called *The Conquest: The Story of a Negro Pioneer* (1913), later rewritten as *The Homesteader* (1917). Moving to Sioux City in 1915 after his homestead failure, he founded the Western Book and Supply Company. We mention his experience here because it illustrates how far Iowa later traveled in becoming hospitable to filmmakers.

When the Lincoln Film Company of Los Angeles offered to film *The Homesteader*, he felt the confidence to found his own Oscar Micheaux Film and Book Company in Sioux City, with a branch office in Chicago. He described his situation to George P. Johnson of the Lincoln Film Company:

> Although Sioux City is mentioned as the office city, that is only because I expect to sell most of the stock to Sioux City people and in that vicinity and do not feel that they would appreciate the office being so far off from where they live. But as soon as the subscribed stock is paid up, incorporation completed, etc., I expect to establish the main office in the business district of Chicago."[11]

Micheaux did just that, finding in Chicago African-American acting talent and other production resources. There he created *Within Our Gates* (1919), the African-American reply to D. W. Griffith's *The Birth of a Nation* (1915), the film that placed the Ku Klux Klan" in such a favorable light. He went on to make some forty-three films, bridging the silent and the sound eras of film.[12]

The Iowa of recent years could have offered significant assistance to an independent filmmaker like Micheaux. The Iowa Film Office (1984-2009) made Iowa a hospitable environment for film and television shoots. In addition to hosting *The Bridges of Madison County* and *Field of Dreams*, the office lent skills in site selection and resource location to film and television projects which numbered by 2012, Governor Branstad stated, "59 major features and several thousand smaller film projects."[13] Films such as *Pennies from Heaven* (1981) and *Twister* (1996) all have their recognizable Iowa scenic moments, even when the fictional actions occur elsewhere.

The most surprising Iowa-hosted film productions are those of the revered Italian director Pupi Avati. Pulled initially to Iowa by the legend of the great Bix Beiderbecke, he made his 1991 film *Bix: An Interpretation of a Legend* here. So pleased was he by Iowa's friendliness to filmmakers that he returned to make other films without Iowa themes, most of which have never been screened here or dubbed in English.

The longest running story of twentieth-century Iowa film production was that of Russell S. Doughten, Jr., who formed Heartland Productions in Des Moines in 1965. In a personal interview, Doughten explained how he became an Iowa filmmaker. He was born in Iowa and lived in several small towns before military service in 1944. After drama studies at Drake University and some years of teaching high school, he attended Yale's graduate school of drama. Then he began to fulfill his religious goals by working as a producer, director, editor, and writer with Good News Productions in Pennsylvania. After creating feature films and an assortment of projects including a children's gospel hour and a Salvation Army recruiting film, Doughten moved on to Hollywood, hoping that he would learn how to make "quality Christian films" there.

Eventually despairing about Hollywood, he returned to Des Moines where he formed Heartland and successor companies that eventually produced dozens of feature-length films. The Iowa Development Commission, to whom Doughten first went for assistance in the mid-1960s, thought he was crazy. They couldn't understand his liking for the clear shooting conditions most of the year and his feeling that Iowa was the right environment for his films. (Later, of course, the Iowa Development Commission accepted Doughten's assessment and established the Iowa Film Office.) Heartland's early films *The Hostage* (1966) and *Fever Heat* (1968) were aimed at theatrical distribution and sought to convey Christian messages indirectly through parables. Doughten's later films were more explicitly Christian. "The only reason to make films is to lift up Christ the savior," Doughten stated, noting that the name of the original company, Heartland, conveyed his aim to achieve conversions "one heart at a time."[14] Subsequently, the films, many in collaboration with another Christian filmmaker Donald W. Thompson, would use various film genres to show resistant characters who eventually respond to the Word of God. The most popular Doughten-Thompson collaboration, *A Thief in the Night* (1972), influenced Jerry Jenkins and Tim Lahaye's best-selling *Left Behind* series of books and films.

Russell Doughten's religiously-centered film business evolved through 35mm and 16mm film, VHS, and now DVD. His audiences are largely church groups and individuals who order the films via print catalogs or Christian film websites. Although his films since the 1960s have rarely been shown theatrically in Iowa, the sheer volume of films produced by Heartland, Mark IV Productions, and Russell Doughten Productions means that his enterprises, with and without Thompson's collaboration, rank him as the most prolific and widely screened Iowa filmmaker.[15] Because the Doughten-Thompson stories focus on salvation, Iowa settings are usually incidental. In Doughten's opinion, "Des Moines works as a universal place." While Iowa culture is not emphasized, there is no attempt to hide the fact that certain scenes are shot in central Iowa. Viewers occasionally catch glimpses of the state capitol, for example, or a character is seen reading the *Des Moines Register*.

Iowa's Historical Events and Famous Iowans

Iowa has experienced significant historical events, and some inspired twentieth-century filmmakers. The Mormons trekked through Iowa to Utah, an experience reprised in the 1940 *Brigham Young—Frontiersman*. The laying of the transcontinental railroad, with its construction of the first railroad bridge across the Mississippi River to Davenport, was the theme of *The Rock Island Trail* (1950). Cecil B. DeMille's epic *Union Pacific* (1939) was filmed partially in Council Bluffs. A Vietnam War casualty led to C. D. B. Bryan's widely read reportage *Friendly Fire* (1976), which became the identically titled movie of 1979 and focused on the anti-war efforts of Gene and Peg Mullen from La Porte City. In rock and roll history, the deaths of Buddy Holly, the Big Bopper, and Ritchie Valens near Clear Lake in 1959 have been retold in Hollywood's *The Buddy Holly Story* (1978) and *La Bamba* (1987) as well as the independent documentary *The Surf Ballroom* (1999). The Weaver family of the Ruby Ridge shootout had roots in Iowa, shown in the CBS docudrama *Siege at Ruby Ridge:* (1996). The United 232 airplane crash in Sioux City generated not only a TV movie, *Crash Landing*, but also George Lindblade's widely distributed documentary training videos for disaster planning.

Other twentieth-century documentaries explore the internationally famous, as in *Dvorak and America* (2000), and the regionally known, as in *Freestyle: The Victories of Dan Gable* (1999). They also explore the less famous when they represent a significant social or economic condition: *Yidl in the Middle* (1999) portrays filmmaker Marlene Booth's years growing up Jewish in Des Moines; *Troublesome Creek* (1995) looks at the farm crisis in the lives of older Iowans, in this case filmmaker Jeanne Jordan's parents.

Iowa as "The Heart of the Heartland" in the Twentieth Century

Because Iowa has a strong tradition of agriculture and rural life, it early took on an identity as the quintessential farm state. In entertainment films throughout the twentieth-century decades, we discovered a nearly uniform picture of Iowa as a collection of small towns and farms that appear to be stuck in a time warp, at least twenty or thirty years— or more—behind the year of any given film's release. Most Hollywood producers, even in the late twentieth century, deliberately drew the curtain on much of the Iowa familiar to residents. They remind us of the presidential caucus journalists who come to Des Moines looking for their photo-op at the local hog farm. The contemporary Iowa that we knew before the year 2000 had factories, city apartments, office buildings, franchise outlets, art museums, botanical gardens, casinos, malls, suburbs, computer technology, the Internet, and major universities. Iowa's population had transitioned to its predominantly urban character back in the 1950s[16], yet Iowa repeatedly got Hollywood's casting call for the archetypal old-fashioned small town or farmscape.

Why did Iowa's rural past remain dominant even in late twentieth century? One answer is that popular films use a limited repertoire of regional images that communicate quickly during a movie's brief screen time. This practice can also be seen in depictions of the South, Texas, New York, and California—a state with far greater and rarely shown agricultural production. Iowa's image was easy to push in the rural direction because so many of its acres were dedicated to corn and soybeans. And since Iowa lacked mountains, deserts, oceans, and major urban attractions, it had few associations in the national mind apart from fields of corn, livestock, pickup trucks, and small towns with mom and pop stores. In addition to the limiting imperatives of popular communication, important literary and philosophical traditions lay behind the rural images locked to Iowa's past.

The theme of contrast between urban and rural places had already surfaced among ancient Greek and Roman writers. The literary genre of pastoral romance and the agrarian ideology of virtue induced by honest work were early markers of city and country differences. Hesiod, Homer, Aristophanes, Virgil, Horace, Longus, and other classical writers launched this durable tradition. Since its earliest years, the United States—with its fast-growing cities like Boston, New York, and Washington—was always ripe for literature that explores contrasts between urban and rural ways of life. Thomas Jefferson's *Notes on the State of Virginia* (1800) expresses his profound distrust of urban culture and his faith in the yeoman culture as the foundation of democracy. Henry David Thoreau's *Walden; or, Life in the Woods* (1854) similarly idealizes the simple life lived close to nature.

In view of these cultural influences, it is not surprising to find some competition during our national history for a designation as the most perfected rural state. In the case of Iowa, a complex mixture of reasons—related to physical geography, farm economics, and Iowa's own regionalist literature—resulted in its "election" during the 1920s and 1930s as the US national farm place, the "heart of the heartland" as so often proudly stated. Cultural geographer James Shortridge's 1989 book *The Middle West: Its Meaning in American Culture*[17] plausibly lays out the chronology and historical factors that made Iowa an archetypally rural state and the nostalgic repository of those agrarian virtues and limitations associated with farms and small towns.

Iowa's cultural identity as the representative heartland state gave rise to pervasive themes in Iowa films centered on the difference between the city and the country. Many twentieth-century Iowa films celebrate rural virtue, sometimes in its small town setting and sometimes when Iowans leave their farms and small towns to confront the world. Other films present a more dark and disturbing view of Iowans and Iowa life. What follows are some thematic categories and examples that allow us to see some kinship relations among the twentieth-century Iowa films in our filmography.

Twentieth-Century Themes

Building the Nation through Agrarian Virtue

This group of films took up the agrarian theme that has been a recurring motif since the time of the ancient Greeks and Romans. Consistent with Jeffersonian pastoral themes from our national and state history, several films emphasize building America through solid character and sacrifice. In this vein are *Cheers for Miss Bishop* (1941), based on a Bess Streeter Aldrich story, which casts golden light on educating immigrants of the prairie; *One Foot in Heaven* (1941), based on Hartzell Spence's biography of his Methodist preacher-father, which extols building churches in the heartland; and *State Fair* (1933, 1945), which celebrates feeding the world through animal and crop production. These films reflect the sentiment that the sacrificial life in smaller communities offers the best foundation for building the nation's vital institutions.

Defending the Nation

Where does a nation turn to find a source of martial virtue? The films of war and character celebrate heartland sacrifices to the cause of World War II. From the war years are *Happy Land* (1943), *The Best Years of our Lives*, *The Sullivans* (1944), *They Were Expendable* (1945), *Johnny Comes Flying Home* (1946), and *High Barbaree* (1947). Reviving this tradition of Iowa sacrifice were the 1990s films *The Tuskegee Airmen* (1995), *Saving Private Ryan,* and *The Straight Story* (1999). Each of these films affirms the idea that "Iowa character" is exemplary in the nation's physical or military challenges.

11

Magic Pastoralism

Another group of films compels us to see Iowa's landscape as a source of psychological magic: conflicts are healed, safety is found, romance is discovered, and people re-establish their sense of values. In *The Music Man,* a charming con man from elsewhere changes a bickering community into a happy place. Though the band's training is a scam, the community's transformation is real. More recent versions of rural magic are seen in *Field of Dreams, Sleeping with the Enemy* (1991), *The Bridges of Madison County,* and *Michael* (1997). In such tales, Iowa natives themselves seem unable to make miracles happen, requiring, instead, mediation by a more skilled, insightful outsider. Iowa's leading film tourism sites tapped into this notion of magic places, separated from contemporary urban stresses. When the magic is present, families can reaffirm their bonds, and lovers can liberate themselves from whatever prevents them from indulging passions that give them joy and deepen their commitment to one another. The documentary *Dreamfield* (1998), narrated by James Earl Jones, provides testimonials to this phenomenon from tourists who were transformed by their visits to the *Field of Dreams* baseball field in Dyersville.

Puncturing Iowa Pastoralism and Moralism

No pastoral icon is ever safe from mockery. Several twentieth-century films poke fun at "Iowa traits." Exaggerated Iowa moralism is the target of Billy Wilder's film *A Foreign Affair* (1948), in which a prudish Iowa congresswoman attempts to reform the occupation zone morals of GI's and their girlfriends in post-WWII Berlin. *Cold Turkey* (1971) pictures a small town of petty hypocrites who accept bribes to stop smoking. *The Last Supper* (1995) satirizes Iowa's image as conservative and law-abiding by showing graduate students calmly murdering dinner guests whose political views are repugnant to their liberal hosts. The campy suspense thrillers *Mommy* (1995) and *Mommy's Day* (1997), created by Max Allan Collins, poke fun at archetypal 1950s TV moms like *The Donna Reed Show's* star Donna Reed from Denison, Iowa. The killer Mommy looks and dresses like Reed's Donna Stone character but perpetrates multiple murders in the heartland. In *Mommy's Day,* Paul Petersen, who lived in Cherokee as a child and played the son in *The Donna Reed Show,* plays against type as an unscrupulous journalist. All of these films have taken a measure of the myth of rural virtue and deflated it with comic wit.

Like the larger world of literature, film often expresses urban skepticism about the material crudity and moral restrictions of life in the provinces and does so in a melodramatic as opposed to comic vein. Several films bemoan the intolerance in Iowa's small town culture. They invoke the spirit of Sinclair Lewis's novel *Main Street* (1920) and its indictment of Gopher Prairie's pinched thinking. *The Strange Woman* (1918) and *That French Lady* (1924) offered early silent film rejections of Iowa moralism. Like this pair, many successor films focus on the small town penchant to bring offending women back into line. In *The Tarnished Angels* (1957), the adventurous bad girl must leave an Iowa to which she is finally forced to return after developing too many complications in her life. *Terms of Endearment* (1983) gives us an Iowa that is emotionally and sexually repressed compared to Texas and New York. The plot of *The Bridges of Madison County* exposes the censorious watchfulness of an Iowa small town.

Iowans Who Travel

One constant in history has been the migration from town to city. The traveler theme captures one of the most popular of all stories—an Iowan seeking fortune in a more urban setting. As Margy laments in her *State Fair* song "It Might as Well Be Spring," "I keep wishing I was somewhere else." The plucky Iowans who leave encounter threats but often survive because of their integrity and quiet cleverness. In *Stardust* (1921) an Iowa girl succeeds at opera in New York after nearly dying there. *Midnight Daddies* (1930) shows us vacationing Iowans who are almost swindled out of their money but are saved by the wife's wily insight into the scam. *Farmer in the Dell* displays a farm family making it in Hollywood when Pa becomes a film star. This sympathetic vision of escaping Iowans persists into the last two decades of the twentieth century with, for example, *Out of Bounds* (1986), *Married to It* (1993), and *What's Eating Gilbert Grape* (1993).

But Iowans can't all make it in the outside world. More frequently it is women who are rebuffed in their quests for something more than Iowa offers. *The Major and the Minor* (1942) shows us a young woman trying to make it in New York business but surrendering after she has been pawed too many times by clients. *Ice Castles* (1978) tells the story of a young ice skater who aims at a professional career but crashes physically and psychologically because she can't deal with the pressure. *Lunatics: A Love Story* (1991) portrays a young woman from Iowa who becomes demented from the stress of coping with abusive men and gangs in urban California. The Homer Simpson character in *The*

Day of the Locust (1975) finds that his Iowa "niceness" makes him a victim in a deadly Hollywood. The alienated teenage rappers from Iowa in *Whiteboys* (1999) discover violence, not a spiritual home, in Chicago's Cabrini Green, and they flee back to the safety of the Iowa cornfields. The message of these films seems to be that life outside Iowa is more challenging and far less nurturing.

Some of these traveling Iowans are buffoons, giving us the laughable version of the escape story, one in which the Iowan's rural naiveté is comically converted into the means of survival. *Flying Deuces* (1936), *Bud Abbott and Lou Costello in Hollywood* (1945), *What's Up, Doc?* (1972), *Fraternity Vacation* (1985), and *Joe's Apartment* (1996) all compliment Iowans in this backhanded way. The Iowan characters' ignorance, unworldliness, enthusiasm, and unfashionable principles lead them to success.

Iowa as a Place to Work

Literature sometimes addresses the realities of work, and film occasionally joins in. A few twentieth-century productions offer rare glimpses of factory and urban work in Iowa. These films are *Pajama Game* (1957), based on a novel by Iowa native Richard Bissell; *Take This Job and Shove It* (1981); and Michael Moore's look at Iowa's downsized workers, benefits, and opportunities in *The Big One* (1998), a documentary. All three films show the realities of hard work and low pay, though the first two, comedies, transplant Iowa pastoral virtues to the city. Given the importance of a healthy yeomanry to the Jeffersonian mythos, the economic condition and morale of farms and towns is a concern. Several films such as *Country* (1984) and *Miles from Home* tell of the agony of hard work, disappointing commodity prices, and farm foreclosures during the 1980s farm debt crisis.

Agrarian Realist Visions of Iowa

Some films offer a tragic view of agricultural life. *A Thousand Acres*, based on Jane Smiley's novel, emphasizes sexual predation, environmental pollution, and death as realities in the contemporary Iowa farm community. *What's Eating Gilbert Grape* (1993), which used West Des Moines native Peter Hedges' novel as its text, shows us the economic and psychological burdens borne by young Gilbert, his family, and his dying small town community. *Alkali, Iowa* is a short film, part of *Boys Life 2* (1998), that reveals the reality of rural gay culture and the violent anger directed against it. As a group, these films call up the spirit of Hamlin Garland. In his Preface to *Main-Travelled Roads* the Iowa born

14

novelist writes that the farm road "has a dull little town at one end and a home of toil at the other" and that along such roads "the poor and weary predominate."[18]

Popularity in the Twentieth Century

When one looks at these themes, a filmography raises important issues of popularity. Which images of Iowa sold best to critics and to large film audiences? Based upon box-office receipts and tourism, *Field of Dreams* and *The Bridges of Madison County* won hands down over the grim *A Thousand Acres,* which lost money miserably. Each of these three films is based on a text written by a long-term Iowa resident. Both Iowans and non-Iowans, critics and audiences alike, seem ed to despise *A Thousand Acres.* This is surprising because the movie had big-name stars and was based on a book honored with a Pulitzer Prize. Reviews and interviews suggest that audiences did not want to see an Iowa farmer portrayed as a greedy capitalist, an incest perpetrator, and an environmental polluter—nor the miserable consequences for those affected. Although Iowa, like every other state, had, and has, many social problems, twentieth-century audiences preferred an Iowa that is a haven from the miseries of modern life. James Shortridge has discussed the twentieth-century theme of a national "need for pastoral values"[19], which frequently expresses itself through nostalgia as a response to the deficiencies of urban life, frustrations with war, and concerns about degradation of environment. Late in the century, it also seemed that audiences wanted to escape feeling overwhelmed by technology. Agrarian tragedy runs counter to this emotional need for the myth of a calming pastoral life.

An interesting feature of in-state responses to *Field of Dreams* and *The Bridges of Madison County* is that audiences seemed to ignore the decidedly negative portrayal of native Iowans in the films, images squarely in the demeaning tradition of Sinclair Lewis's *Main Street.* Instead, the state's audiences seemed to revel in the films' romantic fantasies, leading them to accept Shoeless Joe's quip that Iowa is indeed like heaven.

Cultural histories of the 1980s and 1990s such as Susan Faludi's *Stiffed* (1991) provide insight into America's end-of-the-twentieth-century obsession with an America that never was and its loathing of what it fears it has become. At times of great economic stress during the late twentieth century, some Iowa leaders seemed increasingly aware that we were trapped by the nation's, and our own, preoccupations with nostalgia, a powerful emotional response to the alienation and despair many felt then. David Ostendorf, the Director of PrairieFire Rural Action, put it harshly during the 1980s farm debt crisis: "The sheen is off Iowa; the virtue is gone . . . . Iowa's identity is no longer tied to the land and its people, or to the small towns it still claims when it has to. It tries to maintain the fading image of the old rural Iowa, with its implicit values of neighborliness and trust, but the mythical message doesn't play well these days."[20]

When we returned to update the Iowa filmography in 2013, we wondered what themes we would find in the movies of the 2000s—especially if, as Ostendorf surmised, the agrarian myth of Iowa had played out and the fate of *A Thousand Acres* suggested that there was no audience for dramas about Iowa's social problems. Would films continue to show Iowa in a time capsule? Would Iowans in film endlessly replicate stoical war heroes, mothering Donna Reeds, or good-hearted, naive Radar O'Reillys? Twenty-first century cinematic developments in Iowa surprised us and marked a major turning point in Iowa film history.

Mapping the Twenty-First Century Iowa Film Landscape

The new millennium brought huge changes in Iowa film production. Increasingly finding its profits in high action/low dialogue action movies appealing to overseas markets, not in Iowa movies, Hollywood almost completely stopped making films set in Iowa or featuring Iowans. With assistance from the Iowa Film Office and the Iowa Motion Pictures Association, and, for a short period, attractive tax incentives, independent filmmakers compensated for Hollywood's neglect. With lower cost, high quality digital filmmaking equipment more widely available, independent filmmakers, many of them native Iowans, began to follow Russell Doughten's footsteps by creating films that reflected their own interests and regional experiences.

Like Doughten, many of these filmmakers functioned as their own scriptwriters. Widespread DVD distribution followed by online streaming and downloading possibilities, the rise of film festivals across Iowa, and the expansion of Internet Movie Database and Amazon.com to include even the lowest budget, amateur movies—all these marketing and distribution developments led independent filmmakers to feel their films could find a significant, if not national or international, audience. As a result, the pace of Iowa film creation has increased dramatically. From 1918 through 2000 our filmography lists 251 Iowa films; in the twelve years from 2001 through 2013, 159 films appeared. A few of the post-millennium films continued down well-worn paths, depicting pastoral images of Iowa or creating plotlines featuring traveling Iowans, but we also saw satiric treatment or commentary on these traditional storylines. Characterizing the new group of films was experimentation with film genres and an unsparing realism.

Some Higher-Profile Films Since 2001

The few Iowa films made or distributed by Hollywood companies were economic disappointments. *I Spy* (2003) and *Team America: World Police* (2004), which spoof the comic traveling Iowan and the patriotic Iowa hero traditions in films, lost at the box office. Columbia Pictures produced and distributed *I Spy,* based loosely on the TV show starring Robert Culp and Bill Cosby. Bumbling spy Alex Scott resents being upstaged by Carlos, a James Bond-like spy with high-tech gadgets, flamboyant heroism, and seductive charm with women. "The guy is from Iowa," Alex laments, incredulously.

Team America was created by the *South Park* gang and reflects its outrageous, anti-PC sensibilities. The starring marionette is Gary Johnson, an academic star from the University of Iowa drama program who wowed Broadway with his sensitive acting in an AIDS musical and who has the requisite Iowa patriotism. He is drafted by the red-white-and-blue Team America to help save the world from lonely terrorist Kim Jong Il and left-wing Hollywood liberals. Gary triumphs, but his Iowa niceness and patriotism are satirized in extended scenes where he spews gallons of vomit and has obscene marionette sex with his blonde girlfriend. Neither film had financial success. Four other films that had some national distribution, each with at least one bankable star—*Burlesque* (2010), *Butter* (2011), *Cedar Rapids* (2011), and *At Any Price* (2012)—earned poorly.[20]

Two television broadcasts drew on already established Iowa film connections with only moderate success. In 2003 Walt Disney and Touchstone produced a new TV version of *The Music Man* with Kristin Chenoweth as Marian the Librarian and Matthew Broderick as Harold Hill. William Shatner, whose career-defining film role has been *Star Trek's* Captain James T. Kirk, produced for Spike TV a four-part reality TV series, *Invasion Iowa* (2005), in which he ostensibly brought a

17

science fiction movie to Riverside, Iowa, for shooting. Previously, Gene Roddenberry identified Iowa as Kirk's home state in the book *The Making of Star Trek* (1977) and in 1985 gave Riverside his permission to advertise itself as Kirk's future birthplace. *Star Trek IV* (1986) identified Iowa as Kirk's birthplace, a cinematic tradition confirmed in the documentary *Trekkies* (1997), the *Star Trek* parody *Galaxy Quest* (1999), and the profitable 2009 Hollywood film *Star Trek,* which showed young Kirk growing up in Riverside. Shatner's pretend filming of an outrageously awful science fiction movie in Riverside, using local talent as part of the cast and crew, was perhaps an attempt to pay tribute to open-hearted Iowans. More likely, it was an attempt to ridicule the gullibility and small town ways of the citizens of Kirk's Iowa hometown, while, at the same time, satirizing the eccentricity and self-absorption of Hollywood folks—including Shatner himself. Both the *Music Man* remake and *Invasion Iowa*, seen by more viewers than most of the post-millennium films put together, do not represent a new direction for Hollywood's portrayals of Iowa but, rather, exploitation of long-established cinematic traditions. Neither television broadcast was popular enough to justify making further use of Iowa film traditions.

Survivals of Pre-2000 Cinematic Trends

Although they are not trends in twenty-first century Iowa filmmaking as a whole, we did see some continuation of the pastoral Iowa, traveling Iowan, and *Star Trek*/Kirk traditions, as well as reflective commentary on these traditions. The Iowa with old-fashioned, wholesome ideals appears mainly in Christian and children's films such as Jamey Durham's *Prairie Pirates* (2007) and *Winning Favor* (2012), both set in Orange City, and Dan Nannen's *A Cop's Christmas* (2003). These films combine family and community comedy or drama with explicit Christian messages. The children's film *Sam Steele and the Junior Detective Agency* (2009), inspired by 1940s private eye movies, while not explicitly Christian, presents a comically wholesome view of family life in suburban Des Moines. In *Smitty* (2012), Ben, a thirteen-year-old boy from Chicago, has gotten in trouble with the law and is ordered by the court to spend a summer on his taciturn grandfather's Iowa farm. The grandfather (Peter Fonda) turns out to have better tough love parenting skills than his estranged daughter, a single mom. The grandfather and his elderly friend Smitty (Louis Gossett, Jr.) teach Ben about the value of hard work, responsibility, and love of a good dog. By the summer's end, Ben has learned good Iowa values and matures as he is faced with the death of Smitty and the near-death of his dog. The family finds reconciliation and love in Iowa.

The adult comedy romance *Sister Patchouli* (2008), produced by My Town Pictures, presents contemporary Fairfield, Iowa, home of Maharishi International University, in a relatively pastoral way, though the people in this small farming town do have problems that they confide to Sister Patchouli, who struggles herself between her love of the town and her perception that her family sees her as a failure. While the film affirms pastoral values, it shows, in a memorable scene, bicoastal scorn of Iowa small towns. An LA plastic surgeon, Jake, has decided to become a farmer in the Fairfield area. Jake brings his African-American actor friend Ray to see Fairfield. Ray is flabbergasted that Jake would even consider giving up his practice to settle in Iowa, where the cows use the land as a litter box and the locals can't tell the difference between Shakespeare and Larry the Cable Guy. Fairfield wins Jake's heart and even charms the skeptical Ray, who is stunned when locals at a Fairfield café start quoting Shakespeare. Although these remnants of the pastoral tradition remain in evidence among the newer Iowa films, passtorialism is no longer a predominant theme.

The earlier traveling Iowan films contrasted rural and urban characters and settings and often portrayed Iowans as beyond their element, either failing in new surroundings or improbably succeeding due to their unfashionable "Iowa" traits. Since 2001, the number of traveling Iowans has also decreased dramatically. Besides *Team America* and *I Spy*, the only other films in this category have been *Burlesque*, *Hollywood Dreams* (2006), and *Promised Land*, described earlier. *Burlesque,* a performing vehicle for Cher and Christina Aguilera, is the more traditional treatment. Ali (Aguilera) leaves her job at a rundown bar in a no-hope Iowa small town to try for stardom in Hollywood as a singer. In the burlesque lounge run by Tess (Cher), Ali is called "Iowa" by a scornful rival, to whom Ali replies that "she knows a cow when she sees one" and retains her Iowa sense of fair play and loyalty. Unlike Homer Simpson in *The Day of the Locust*, a man destroyed by Hollywood, Ali saves the club from financial ruin and, ironically, finds love, success, and family there. *Hollywood Dreams* presents a more untraditional view of the traveling Iowan. Margie Chizek, a movie fan from a large Mason City family, confidently goes to Hollywood to become a star but fluffs her lines and bursts out crying in her first audition. She is proud of Iowa and will tell anyone who will listen about John Wayne, Meredith Willson, Donna Reed, Glenn Miller, George Gallup, and other Iowa celebrities. We learn, however, that Margie is more opportunistic than she first seems, has a lesbian aunt and a cross-dressing brother who committed suicide, and attracts a Hollywood boyfriend who pretends to be gay to get parts. Margie is both proud of and troubled by her Iowa past and is much more complex than the usual traveling Iowan. The contemporary realism that characterizes more recent Iowa films is especially clear in these two films.

Star Trek is another narrative that crossed into the new millennium in a big budget film (the 2009 *Star Trek* and two low budget independent films. We mentioned previously that the big budget films *Star Trek IV* and *Galaxy Quest* kept the Kirk-Iowa connection alive. In *Fanboys* (2009) four zealous *Star Wars* fans from Ohio take a road trip to Lucas Ranch in Marin County, California, to see *Star Wars: The Phantom Menace* (1999) before its release. En route they stop at Riverside and scuffle with equally zealous *Star Trek* fans. Iowa does have its own *Star Wars* fans, as shown in the 2002 documentary film *The Formula*.

While some trends link pre-and post-millennial Iowa films, the more recent films clearly strike out in new directions, with new genres and a new realism, made by a new breed of Iowa filmmakers whose films are reshaping Iowa's film tradition. These filmmakers have been supported by state government, non-profit organizations, local film festivals, more informal networks of filmmakers, and family and friends.

Some New Iowa Filmmakers

Modern American Cinema

Digital video production and distribution have enabled a kind of filmmaking populism that bypasses studio capital costs, publicity departments, and distribution commitments for theatrical showings. The new barebones model requires nothing more than a camera, a group of actors, a website, a Wikipedia or IMDb entry, and a YouTube or Vimeo trailer linked to a streaming site. Sean Gannon, who directed *Something Blue* (2009), made this Director's Statement on his film's website:

> *Something Blue* is an ultra-low-budget movie shot entirely in Polk County, Iowa, where I grew up. A friend with whom I co-founded the Iowa Scriptwriters Alliance helped produce, a theatre professor friend helped cast the movie, two dear friends played supporting roles, high school friends were extras, and my mom catered. We shot on my family's century farm, in my hometown, and in a favorite local restaurant established the month my parents were married.

Everybody involved in the production is an Iowan and/or attended my alma mater, Drake University.[22]

Something Blue offers a realistic portrayal of an engagement process that does not end in a wedding. It showed at several Iowa Festivals, picking up awards at the Cedar Rapids Independent Film Festival, the Landlocked Film Festival in Iowa City, and the Wild Rose Independent Film Festival in Des Moines. Such venues allow filmmakers to get "four wall" public showings outside the competitive venues like Idaho's Sundance, Austin's South by Southwest, or New York's Tribeca Film Festivals. Like Sean Gannon, the current generation of filmmakers is building its reputation and audience through local film festivals and the Internet as well as by participating in the state's supportive creative arts networks.

Blue Box Limited

Some newer generation of filmmakers have learned their craft on low budget films and entered national competitions as a road to success. According to the Blue Box Limited website, Scott Beck and Bryan Woods of Bettendorf met as sixth graders. Beginning with stop-motion movies featuring their *Star Wars* action figures, the pair kept making movies through middle school and high school when they directed feature films on a shoestring using local acting talent and their own (or neighbors') houses and backyards for settings. Their films were also screened at Iowa film festivals. In 2001 they formed a production company, Bluebox Limited Films, that would produce films, commercials, and television content that they wrote, directed, and produced.

While still teenagers, they were shortlisted as two of the top 50 directors (out of 2000 applicants) for Ben Affleck and Matt Damon's Project Greenlight series on Bravo. MTV awarded them, while college students, a feature film development deal. In 2010 they wrote, directed, and produced the short film *Impulse*, starring Chris Masterson from *Malcolm in the Middle*. *Impulse* was screened in international film festivals and acquired by Shorts International for worldwide distribution, where it became the #1 downloaded short film in its first week of release. After studying communications at the University of Iowa, they relocated to Los Angeles and are completing a supernatural thriller, *Nightlight*, produced by Herrick Entertainment and Oscar-nominated producer Michael London, whose films include *Milk* (2008) and *Sideways* (2004). At a lecture at Morningside College, Scott and Bryan discussed their cinematic influences. Their jointly directed *The*

Bride Wore Blood (2006) pays homage to John Ford and to Sergio Leone's "spaghetti westerns." Bryan's fascination with M. Night Shyamalan's *The Sixth Sense* (1999) shaped his film *For Always* (2004). Both used their early feature films, often created for less than $300, to experiment with story-telling techniques, symbolism, and non-realistic elements and to sharpen their skills as screenwriters and filmmakers.

AriesWorks Entertainment

Kimberly Busbee's career trajectory follows a different pattern: she brought years of professional experience back to the Iowa film scene. According to her AriesWork Entertainment website, for twenty plus years she accumulated international experience "with hundreds of plays, musicals, films," and "over 250 commercials, industrials, and TV/radio spots." She "founded and served as Artistic Director for Music/Theatre Artists, an award-winning international touring theatre company, which played New York, Chicago, and Las Vegas" and featured "Janet Jackson, Debbie Reynolds, Redd Foxx, and others." She toured with the USO. Returning to Iowa, she has worked as an actress, educator, casting director, and film director. She owns Aries Works Entertainment and is a co-founder and festival director for the Wild Rose Independent Film Festival in Des Moines, Kimberly has cast several recent Iowa films including *The Crazies* (2010) and *Dead Awake* (2010). She has also written, cast, and directed *Haunting Villisca* (2006) and a current film project, *Garner, Iowa,* is in postproduction. Her husband, John Busbee, is also a multi-talented film professional, and her daughter directed *Molly's Girl* (2012). Kimberly has her fingers in the arts and filmmaking scene throughout Iowa, not only doing her own work but collaborating with and encouraging other filmmakers.

My Town Pictures

A unique model of filmmaking has been developed by Scott Thompson's My Town Pictures. Thompson offers to write a community-based feature film with a 7-9 day shooting schedule. Casting is achieved through open auditions in the community. Iowa productions include *After Life* (completed in 2013), filmed in Lake Mills, Buffalo Center, and Forest City, and *A Place for Heroes*, filmed in Traer and Clutier and scheduled for a 2014 debut. An experienced screenplay writer, Thompson writes in various genres and includes local details.

Fourth Wall Films

Among the Iowa documentary filmmakers, a passion for persuasion and telling true stories in an artful way motivates Kelly and Tammy Rundle at Fourth Wall Films. Kelly Rundle, from East Moline, Illinois, and his wife Tammy, from Waterloo, Iowa, met at Park University in Kansas City, Missouri. After two decades of professional work in the LA area, they moved their independent production company Fourth Wall Films to the Quad Cities and began producing documentaries about Midwest history, with Kelly directing and Tammy producing and writing. One documentary received an Emmy nomination, and others have won numerous film festival and humanities awards. Besides the three-part documentary on the Ioway tribe (2007, 2013)[23], they have made *Villisca: Living with a Mystery* (2004), *Country School: One Room—One Nation* (2010), and *Movie Star: The Secret Lives of Jean Seberg* (2013), a film about the Marshalltown-born film star and political activist. A not-yet-released film is *River to River: Iowa's Forgotten Highway 6,* on Iowa's segment of the longest transcontinental highway in America.

The Iowa Film Office and Produce Iowa

Since 1984, the Iowa Film Office (IFO) and the Iowa Motion Picture Association (IMPA) have aggressively promoted the making of films in Iowa. Governor Branstad established the Iowa Film Office in 1984, as part of the Iowa Department of Economic Development, appointing Wendol Jarvis as director. In addition to promoting Iowa filmmaking, Jarvis helped producers of Hollywood and independent films, TV programs, and commercials find settings and local film production services. In 1992 the non-profit Iowa Motion Pictures Association (IMPA) began as a group of film, video, and multimedia professionals creating moving images in the heartland. Its goals included education, outreach, and promoting collaboration. In 2002, Jarvis resigned from the Iowa Film Office, after working with 59 made-in-Iowa films including *Field of Dreams*. When a one-year director left, IFO director Tom Wheeler took over in 2004. In 2007 Iowa offered to filmmakers generous tax incentives, the highest in the nation. This helps explain, in part, the increase in film production in the past decade.

The tax incentives program had a short life, however. In 2009, amid allegations of mismanagement, Tom Wheeler and five staff members were fired, the tax incentives were abolished, and the Iowa Film Office closed, but litigation continued through 2012.[24] In 2013 a new state media production office called Produce Iowa was created and housed in the Iowa Department of Cultural Affairs. A new director, Liz Gilman, was hired to support Iowa filmmaking in the Wendol Jarvis tradition, with no tax incentives. Ms. Gilman brings to the job her years of high-profile experience as a media entrepreneur and as owner of Gilman Media, based in West Des Moines. Except for the 2009-13 hiatus, as can be seen, the state of Iowa has offered support to both experienced and up-and-coming filmmakers and will continue to do so for the foresee-able future.

The Pattern for New Iowa Filmmakers

From this selection, we can see that all of these filmmakers have their own personal stories and preferred subject matter, genres, and techniques. Their ability to produce and to screen films depends upon new technology and distribution methods, support from the state, net-working, and the existence of local, national, and international film fes-tivals. Unlike the older film tradition, few of these new films are based on literary works. This sampling suggests that the newer films are scripted by the director/producer, by someone known to the director/producer, or by historians or other experts who are willing to advise on documentary films.

New Genres in Iowa Films

Psychological Drama

Perhaps reacting against the tendency of twentieth-century films to depict Iowans stereotypically rather than as complex human beings, recent films have moved into the genre of psychological drama. They show Iowans as not merely complicated but in some cases as absolutely twisted. Perhaps reacting to Iowa cornfields represented either as a boring pragmatic reality or as Heaven on earth, other filmmakers have moved Iowa films into the horror genres.

The psychological genre in post-2000 films explores dysfunctional family situations and resulting pressures, the capability of a seem-ingly normal and rational human beings to become violent in certain situations, mental disorders, and the impact of laws and social norms on those who are different or victims of violence and abuse. *Molly's Girl*, filmed in Iowa, shows how parental idealization of one daugh-ter while abusing another harms both, leading to isolation, depression, anger, and creating false faces for the world. *The Experiment* (2010), set in the Anamosa prison surrounded by cornfields, was inspired by the

24

famous Stanford psychological experiment that locked paid volunteers in a prison setting, assigning some to be prisoners and some guards. In this film the two main characters, one a rational pacifist and the other a conforming Momma's boy now grown up (played by Adrian Brody and Forrest Whittaker, respectively), both become violent within the prison setting. Along the same lines, in *Ash* (2010) a good father, husband, and former cop secretly holds captive a serial homosexual rapist and then makes sure someone else kills him. In conversations between the two, we see that the good father's own history of being sexual abused, which he thought he had repressed, is driving his violent response to the perpetrator, a man who begs to be killed because he cannot control criminal impulses arising from his own personal history.

Peacock (2010) shows us a disordered identity: a mild-mannered small town bank employee by day transitions into his own fictitious wife at other times. The bleak film *Rain* (2001), directed by Katherine Lindberg and produced by Martin Scorsese, reveals the increasing despair and violence of a farm wife with severe mental health problems. The documentary *The Grey Area* (2012) films conversations with women incarcerated in the Mitchellville Prison, some of whom were repeatedly sexually abused and violently treated on the outside or were imprisoned for drug crimes carried out by men with whom they lived. The legal system and parole system seem ill-equipped to handle these cases. Exposing these women to feminism, however, seems to help restore their psychological equilibrium.

Scott Beck's *University Heights* (2004) links four psychologically powerful storylines on the University of Iowa campus: a philosophy professor laments his dead wife and his former drug dealing; a young man in a dorm feels peers pressuring him toward drinking, smoking pot, and viewing his nice girlfriend as a sexual conquest; a closeted gay teacher is tormented to the point of suicide by his sexual identity and his own homophobia; an insecure boy is too much influenced by his friend's poisonous racism and homophobia (the friend most likely a voice in his own head). The tortuous threads culminate in a classroom murder—echoing the U of Iowa graduate student Gang Lu's killing of four professors and an administrator in 1991.[25] These portrayals of psychologically troubled people violate twentieth-century Iowa stereotypes and show that Iowans can be complicated and confused, if not mentally ill, like people everywhere.

Horror

Prior to 2001, we saw a few horror films played mostly for laughs: *Mommy, Mommy's Day, Zadar! Cow from Hell* (1989), and *Ed and His Dead Mother* (1992). The Doughten-Thompson *Thief in the Night* Christian tetralogy had horrors aplenty, but they were part of the films' portrayal of the Book of Revelation. There were only three conventional horror films. The 1971 film *What's the Matter with Helen?* revealed a seemingly normal Iowa mother, possibly with lesbian leanings, as a serial murderer of her husband, friend, a lawyer, and her own rabbits. *The Funhouse* (1981) presented horror film-loving teens trapped at a carnival. In *Robert A. Heinlein's The Puppet Masters* (1994) alien parasites took over the brains of Iowans.

Post-2001, horror films have proved a popular genre for filmmakers. The Iowa farmscape is now full of slashers, lunatic killers, and zombies. In *Through the Night* (2007) escapees of a mental hospital terrorize people trapped in a farmhouse, killing those who, according to horror conventions, deserve death. In *Husk* (2011) young people on a farm near Roland are attacked by zombies. In *Dropping Evil* (2012), a boy named Nancy, given LSD as a joke, goes on a killing rampage in a wooded area of rural Iowa. The most outrageous horror film, *2001 Maniacs: Field of Screams* (2010), explicitly counters the *Field of Dreams* image of Iowa as Heaven. In this off-the-scale violent-bad taste-offend everyone film, zombies from the South, still bitter about the Lost Cause, come to Iowa to revenge themselves on some damn Yankees. In fact, they meet up not with local Iowans but with a Hollywood crew heading east to make a film. *Legend Has It* (2008) is a meta-horror film with a writer trapped in a bad horror script. He tries to write his way out of danger while at the same time commenting on the genre's clichés. There are other horror films shot in Iowa but set in nearby states.

Interestingly, several horror films have dealt with "real life" supernatural and horror legends in Iowa, the most famous of which is the Villisca house, where unsolved 1912 axe murders took place and which is reputedly haunted by the eight victims. A particularly silly film, *Haunted Iowa* (2011), features the Calhoun County Paranormal Investigating Team, a group of college-age students who investigate the Villisca House, the Dubuque Opera House, a theatre in Cherokee, and a school in Farrar—all said to be haunted. Most of the film consists of heavy breathing, weird noises, and "Oh, my God!" and "What was that?" comments. More serious treatments of the Villisca story are the

Rundles' documentary *Villisca: Living with a Mystery* and the fictional *Haunting Villisca* (2006), directed by James Serpento.

Science Fiction and Fantasy

These genres were almost non-existent prior to 2001. In *The Crazies* (2010), set in Ogden Marsh, Iowa, near Cedar Rapids, bacteria contaminate the water supply and turn the citizens into violent psychopaths, while the government covers up and attempts to contain the incident. In *Black Web* (2012) a young man who grew up along the Mississippi River in Dubuque receives his own obituary and attempts to change the future. *Diary of a Superhero* (2009) is a save-the-world narrative with spaceships, cyborgs, and time travel. The fantasy *Dead Awake* (2010) shows a young man, who works in a funeral home, obsessing over a fatal taxi accident. Throughout the film, as past and present confusingly merge and separate, we are not sure who is dead and who is alive.

The horror and science fiction films make use of Iowa settings in interesting ways—a farmhouse full of zombies, the haunted Villisca house, a *Doctor Who*/TARDIS-type time travel station in an Iowa City porn shop—but the characters are not necessarily marked as Iowans by any particular traits. These films move away from nostalgic myths about Iowa to scary fantasies squarely set in Iowa. The psychological dramas and the horror films certainly evoke a dark vision and question that Iowa is a safe, innocent place.

New Directions for Iowa Films

Realism

The independent filmmakers who know Iowa as lived by real people present them in their complexity and diversity. These films are moving Iowa on screen into the mainstream of modern American life with its joys, challenges, frustrations, and sometimes overwhelming personal and social devastation. We see this realistic trend in fictional comedies and dramas, documentaries that shine light on horrific social problems, political films reflecting Iowa's status as first primary state, and exposés of agriculture in the age of mega-corporate control. The new filmmakers also explore Iowa's increasing cultural diversity and showcase in documentary films Iowa's real history, historical figures, geography and traditions, and colorful eccentrics.

Social Issues

Several films, ranging from comic to dramatic, present everyday Iowa. Becky Smith's *16 to Life* (2009) shows a day in the life of workers at a McGregor ice cream stand on the Mississippi River. The characters are funny, individualized, and very real. Kate, for example, spends her 16th birthday reading a book about the Chinese Cultural Revolution— while hoping for her first kiss. Joe Clarke's *The Wedge* (2012) follows an Iowa City pizza delivery guy during a single day. Scott Thompson's *Fortnight* (2010) tells the story of Edme, a culturally pretentious suburban wife who invites two world travelers for a visit and feels dismayed when they seem to be uncouth, quirky frauds. *Butter* (2011) uses the African-American character Destiny to give us a glimpse of children neglected in and abused by the foster parent system before she finds "Iowa nice" parents. In Mas Gardner's *Boone Style* (2005), we see "your typical semi-dysfunctional Midwestern family reunion," taking place in Des Moines, through the eyes of 8-year-old Ruby. Men preside over the barbeque while grandmas make Jell-O and desserts. The children chase each other. The young adults discuss their lives and choices. Mom tries to organize everything while she hides her anguish over her husband's silences.

Sean Gannon's *Something Blue* shows us the details of wedding plans complicated by the bride's dysfunctional family whom the groom refuses to challenge, distressing his future bride. More anguish appears in Jeff Lipsky's *Twelve Thirty* (2011), in which an agoraphobic mom, her two daughters, and her bi-sexual ex-husband begin to work on their communication problems after a formerly virginal young architect has sex with both daughters and Mom in one week. All these characters live in contemporary Iowa, not a time capsule. They use cell phones, wear Iowa Hawkeye sweatshirts, drive past recognizable landmarks, and have the problems, hopes, and dreams of ordinary people. Furthermore, they are sometimes not white and not heterosexual, reflecting the diversity of real Iowans.

Many recent Iowa fictional films are shockingly bleak as they expose social ills that exist here, as elsewhere, and they offer no easy answers. Trouble in assorted River Cities goes far beyond a tempting new pool table, and a new boys' band will not make the trouble go away. These documentaries and films in the social realism genre expose a host of social evils that affect real people who, in some cases, are both victims and victimizers. These social evils include:

Methamphetamine addiction: *Crank* (2005), *Iowa* (2005),
   Janie Jones (2010), *Indelible* (2007)

Prostitution: *The Poker House* (2008)

Sexual abuse and domestic violence, verbal abuse:
   The Grey Area (2012), *Indelible* (2007), *Something Blue* (2009)

Untreated, severe mental health problems: *Rain* (2001),
   Peacock (2010), *University Heights* (2004)

Criminal activity of all kinds, including murder: *Fell* (2010),
   Lucky (2011), *Rain* (2001)

Prison experiences and parole system problems:
   The Experiment (2010), *The Grey Area* (2012)

Custody disputes, abandonment: *Ticket Out* (2011), *Butter* (2011)

Bullying: *Bully* (2012), *Arnolds Park* (2007)

Racism: *University Heights* (2004), *AbUSed: The Postville Raid* (2010)

Homophobia : *Molly's Girl* (2012), *University Heights* (2004)

One example of such films, and not the most gruesome, is Lori Petty's autobiographical *The Poker House*, in which three young girls live in a drug-dealing household full of addicts, including their mom who turns tricks. Mom is a drug addict who defends her pimp when he rapes her oldest daughter—a smart girl and a local basketball star who has learned survival skills and taught them to her sisters. These films are not in the horror genre, but they show horrible conditions in which some Iowans live their lives. Petty, who graduated from North High School in Sioux City, has stated that the film is her "account of her life as a teenager in Council Bluffs."[26] The causes of such social issues are manifold, and the films vary in the extent to which they simply show the problems or attempt to get at the underlying causes. There are very few happy endings, though in several films, such as *The Poker House*, young women with few resources show remarkable resilience.

Caucuses

A reality in the lives of all Iowans is the presidential caucus, a once-every-four-years event preceded by nearly two years of candidate visits, heated debates, acrimonious community meetings in cafes and living rooms, relentless advertising, persistent telephone calls, and endless rallies in school gyms, parks, or auditoriums. While these first-in-the-nation caucuses help the Iowa economy, they strain residents.

Iowa's role in the presidential election process has led to several films in the past decade. Michael Moore's *Slacker Uprising* (2007) tells of his get out the vote tour, including an ISU stop in Ames, aimed at getting young Americans to unseat George W. Bush. *By the People: The Election of Barack Obama* (2009) presents an admiring view of his 2008 Iowa campaign. In contrast, we have *The Hope and the Change* (2012), a propaganda film aiming to unseat Barack Obama in 2012 by showing people who wildly supported him in 2008 but by 2012 think he is the worst president. *Janeane from Des Moines* (2012) is a part documentary/part staged film that features Janeane, a home health care aide with Tea Party politics, whose fictitious identity is accepted by news organizations and the Republican candidates she corners to share her faux story and her pretend views.

Farming, Food Safety and Nutrition

While there are still family farm operations, we have come a long way from *State Fair* with Pa's tender loving care of his prize pig, Blue Boy, and Ma's pickles and brandy-soaked mincemeat. We live in an age of corporate agriculture, genetically modified seeds, hog confinement lots, processed food, and attempts to revive the past through organic farming. Farm areas and the small towns that serve them suffer from dwindling population and the resultant loss of schools and businesses. Walmarts and franchised gas station/mini-marts have become the go-to shopping places for people who don't have time or money to drive longer distances to city malls. Furthermore, some methods of food production are deleterious to Americans' health. All these issues appear in recent Iowa documentaries distributed through theatrical release, public television, DVDs, and online streaming.

One of the higher-profile documentaries is *King Corn* (2007) in which two Bostonians with family roots in Greene, Iowa, return for a season to plant one acre of corn and trace its path through growing, cattle feeding, and corn syrup processing, the latter an essential in Americans' high fat, high sugar diet. *King Corn* shows that well-intentioned farm subsidies and a need for cheap food have led us to our current epidemic of obesity and diabetes. *Food, Inc.* (2009) focuses on cruelty to factory-raised animals and the bacterial bombs brewed and released by major food processing corporations. The revealing title of the documentary *Fat, Sick and Nearly Dead* (2010) suggests the personal costs of eating bad food, in this case for Phil Staples, a 430-pound truck driver from Sheldon who gradually regains his health and will to live when he gives up processed food and begins a nutritional juice diet.

American Meat (2013) shows us what Blue Boy's life would be like today in a hog confinement operation such as the one run by Dave Struthers of Collins. Besides the indifference to animal suffering, corporate-controlled businesses like Dave's dictate production for maximum profit. Because these businesses have such high overhead costs and use so much fossil fuel in transporting hogs, grass-feeding is presented as an alternative that can be efficient, profitable, and better for people's health. The fictional film *At Any Price* (2012) is a tragedy about a farm family that has lost its moral compass in the contemporary world of agri-business. Big landowner and seed salesman Henry Whipple alienates his resentful father, his sons, and his neighbors in his quest to succeed.

Racism

Spike Lee's film *Bamboozled* (2000) has a scene in which a young Iowa scriptwriter in New York reluctantly admits his only knowledge of "black people from Africa" comes from *The Jeffersons* (1975-1985), a TV show. The myth of Iowa has long been that the state is full of white people who have no experience with cultural diversity. Yet some original Iowans were Ioways, an Indian tribe whose sad history of relocation and cultural genocide is told in a three-part documentary, *Lost Nation: The Ioway*, (2007, 2013), directed by Kelly Rundle. Iowa has never been "all white," as we were reminded in the earlier Iowa films *Cora Unashamed* (2000) and *The Tuskegee Airmen*. Historically and still today, Iowa, like other states and the US as a whole, has had episodes in which it showed cultural ignorance, overt and subtle prejudice and hostility, along with racism in public policy and local customs. But Iowa also has people committed to social justice, in the past and now. The documentary *Gospel without Borders* (2011) highlights Des Moines' multicultural Trinity United Methodist Church that has been transformed physically and spiritually by its committed ministry to immigrants. As we have seen earlier, people of color are finding their way into fictional films, sometimes in non-stereotypical roles (for example, Ray in *Sister Patchouli* and Destiny in *Butter*). The fictional film *Sugar* (2009) tells the story of a talented young baseball pitcher from the Dominican Republic who finds himself on a minor league team in Iowa, living with a farm family and not understanding the language, food, dating customs, and Protestant church services. The cultural shock and the pressure on him are nearly overwhelming, but his family in the Dominican Republic depends upon his financial success in America.

31

Immigrants

Several documentaries tell similar stories about immigrants who have come to Iowa hoping to find better living conditions and jobs that will support themselves and families. Sudden recruitment of large numbers of immigrants into small Iowa meatpacking towns such as Perry, Storm Lake, Marshalltown, and Postville has brought challenges for both communities and the newcomers. *A Little Salsa on the Prairie* (2007) tells how Perry's population increased from 47 Latinos in 1990 to 1837 in 2000. Most were recruited from Mexico and Central America by IBP and its successor, Tyson. This rapid population change required transformations of schools, businesses, city government, and interpersonal relationships. The community responded with some heartening results. Immigrants to Perry experienced some of the same challenges Sugar faced—as well as, in some cases, undocumented status, separated families, and harsh working conditions.

AbUSed: The Postville Raid (2010) exposes the working conditions in Postville's Agriprocessors, Inc., kosher meatpacking plant. The film presents evidence that the company permitted sexual harassment, knowingly hired undocumented workers, violated child labor laws and health and safety standards, paid below Iowa's minimum wage standard (or no wages for forced overtime), and sometimes prohibited bathroom breaks during 12-hour shifts. When the federal Immigration and Customs (ICE) officers raided the plant with helicopters, buses, and vans in 2008, 389 workers were denied their legal rights in the rush to prosecute them. This scandal made Postville a rallying cry for those hoping to reform the meatpacking industry, immigration laws, and ICE's tactics.

Another documentary, *Train to Nowhere* (2010), presents a nightmarish story of eleven immigrants who suffocated in a locked train car that was finally noticed in Denison—months after their deaths. The documentary focuses on family efforts to find them. These films have given rare voice to the stories of the state's newer immigrants, stories that need to be heard for better cultural understanding and for the sake of justice.

The Documentary Trend

The exploration of Iowa's immigrants illustrates a larger movement to use documentary as a genre for clarifying Iowa's present and past. There has been a surge of documentary films since 2001. Funded through a variety of sources, including Humanities Iowa, these films, often found their way onto Iowa Public Television (IPTV). They trace Iowa's historical events, survey the cultural geography, and tell the stories of Iowa's leaders.

Iowa has a rich history. The three-part *Lost Nation: The Ioway* documentary shows Iowa's earliest history when the Ioway tribe—as well as the Sauk, the Fox, and other tribes—lived on the land that became the state. *Forgotten Journey* (2001) tells the harrowing story of the first group that survived an 1844 trek from Council Bluffs over the Rockies and the Donner Pass in the Sierras to Sutter's Fort in California. All survived, thanks to exceptional leadership and the trust that allowed them to separate when needed and come back for each other later. *Country School: One Room—One Nation* presents photos of and historical narrative about Iowa's 13,000 one-room schools. In the 1930s, despite Prohibition, farmers in south Carroll County began cooking whiskey to survive economically during the Great Depression, even creating their own innovative technology they couldn't patent. Templeton Rye, named after the tiny town of Templeton in Carroll County, was Al Capone's favorite whiskey. Kristian Day's *Capone's Whiskey: The Story of Templeton Rye* (2011) recounts this history through photos, narrative, and interviews. The history of Sioux City's famous Fourth Street—one end hosting fancy stores and the other end bars, brothels, and restaurants frequented by farmers who had brought their animals to the stockyard and by Chicago gangsters hiding out from the law—is told in George Lindblade's *High Times on Lower Fourth* (2010).

The People in the Pictures (2002) and *Picture Perfect: Iowa in the 1940s* (2009) present photographs from the 1930s and 1940s that represent a social history of rural Iowa. *Iowa's World War II Stories* (2006) presents interviews with more than 20 of the 276,000 Iowa men and women who served in the war. *More Than a Game: 6-on-6 Basketball* (2013) pays tribute to a century of high school girls' basketball in Iowa, celebrates the players' athleticism, and commends the local communities and the state for supporting its young women. *The Radio Homemakers: Up a Country Lane* (2010) provides a social history of Iowa rural life since the 1920s, focusing on farm wives and the radio programs broadcast to serve their changing needs. *The Farm Crisis* (2013) recounts the various factors that led to the painful results of the farm debt crisis of the late 1970s and 1980s, which caused numerous foreclosures, family stresses, failure of small town businesses, and even suicide. Since 1973, a big part of recent Iowa history has been the *Register*'s Annual Great Bike Ride across Iowa (RAGBRAI), which attracts riders every summer from around the world. They ride from the Missouri River to the Mississippi

River, taking different routes each year. *A Million Spokes* (2010) follows the 2009 ride from Council Bluffs to Burlington, capturing Iowa landscape and interviewing riders.

The weather has clouded Iowa life throughout its history. *Epic Surge: Eastern Iowa's Unstoppable Flood of 2008* (2008), produced by KCRG TV of Cedar Rapids, chronicles the once-in-500-years event that devastated Cedar Rapids, Iowa City, and other towns. *New York Says Thank You* (2011) tells how NYC firefighters and others came to Little Sioux to help the community build a chapel at the Boy Scout camp there where a deadly tornado had killed four boys. By helping disaster victims in various states, New York City yearly says "thank you" to the rest of the nation for its help and support after 9/11.

Recent documentaries have also educated Iowans about landscape and architecture. The lush cinematography in *America's Lost Landscape: The Tallgrass Prairie* (2005) shows Iowans the costs of totally destroying their natural prairies. Inspired by Iowa native Aldo Leopold's *Sand County Almanac*, conservationists have preserved the prairie at the Neal Smith Wildlife Refuge near Prairie City and in western Iowa's Loess Hills region. The 2004 documentary *A Century of Iowa Architecture* gives viewers an architectural tour of Iowa's 50 most significant buildings designed by Frank Lloyd Wright, Louis Sullivan, I. M. Pei, and others. *A Ride along the Lincoln Highway* (2008) is a cultural history of this transcontinental highway. The film highlights the Lincoln Café in Mt. Vernon and a Lincoln statue along Highway 30, erected by a Scranton man.

Looking back at the twentieth century we see that the last decade's films highlight the earlier penchant for reducing the Iowa landscape to four easily recognized icons, which are especially prominent when journalists and documentarians come around for our presidential caucuses: a hilly gravel road, a windmill, a cornfield, and an American flag. In their positive uses these recurrent images link Iowa to service and sacrifice—feeding the world, serving the community, protecting the family, and defending the nation. Flowing from this imagery are the most important Iowa archetypes in the movies: the stoical farmer, the dedicated prairie professional, the dedicated soldier, the good mother raising the next generation, and the loyal rural child who dreams of life elsewhere but values Iowa roots. None of these archetypal figures is stylish or intellectual, but each is hard-working, pragmatic, intuitively wise, and principled. They all have a highly developed sense of responsibility. Think of Ma and Pa Frakes, the five Sullivan brothers volunteering for the Navy to serve in World War II, Marian Paroo and her stewardship of the Madison Public Library, Jewell Ivy in *Country* fighting fiercely to keep family and farm intact, Miss Bishop sacrificing love and travel to teach immigrants at a prairie college, or Gilbert Grape struggling to support his mother and siblings after his father committed suicide.

Iowa documentaries, which have flourished since 2001, paint a picture of real Iowans who actually fit the Iowa archetypes of sacrifice and service, yet are much more than that. It is almost uncanny how the film biographies of real Iowans consistently reveal, beyond these agrarian archetypal traits, imagination, intelligence and learning, courage, creativity, a powerful way with words or images, an entrepreneurial spirit, an understanding of national and international issues, and an ability to collaborate with others while holding tight to convictions, a vision of the future, and, above all, leadership and passion. Iowa has grown not only corn but nationally and internationally admired leaders throughout its history.

One such leader is Ann Landers (Eppie Friedman Lederer) of Sioux City, an interview with whom is recorded in *Dear Ann Landers* (2013). Her widely-syndicated advice column dispensed researched advice to ordinary people with problems. Ann also took courageous political stands—for example, against the Vietnam War—while speaking early and openly about divorce, homosexuality, and women's liberation. Ann Landers' column, as did her twin sister Abigail Van Buren's column, had a huge influence in America. The 1999 TV film *Take My Advice: The Ann and Abby Story* and the 1999 A&E biography *Ann Landers: America's Confidante* also celebrate the achievements of these Iowa women.

Another outstanding Iowa woman, celebrated in the *Iowa's Radio Homemakers* documentary, is Evelyn Birkby of rural southwest Iowa, who has written a weekly homemaker column since the early 1950s and shared her life, viewpoints, and recipes on a syndicated radio program. Throughout her many decades as a newspaper and radio journalist, Evelyn has spoken to and for farm wives—understanding their isolation, praising their partnership in farm operations, passing on valuable information, and recognizing their important role in creating community in rural Iowa.

Iowa produced a musical genius in Arthur Russell, cellist, singer, and composer, featured in the documentary *Wild Combination* (2008). Growing up in Oskaloosa, he spent his adult life in San Francisco in the 1960s and later in disco-era Manhattan, where he was part of the avantgarde music and arts scenes. A reserved perfectionist, innovator, and well-read loner, Russell constantly mixed sounds and styles in his music and encouraged other artists to innovate. A friend of Allen Ginsberg , Russell was also gay. Russell's Iowa family never quite understood his music but supported and loved him and his long-time partner, Tom Lee. Another influential Iowa artist was Paul Engle, portrayed in *City of Literature* (2012), the founder of the famous Iowa Writers' Workshop, which has produced 40 Pulitzer Prize-winning writers.

Two multiple Pulitzer Prize-winning political cartoonists from Iowa, Paul Conrad and Jay "Ding" Darling, courageously used their artistic skills and wide reading to influence millions of readers to think critically about American democracy, politics, and social justice. Paul Conrad from Cedar Rapids began his cartooning career on *The Daily Iowan* at the University of Iowa and moved on to the *Denver Post* and later to the *Los Angeles Times*. For 50 years, as the documentary *Paul Conrad: Drawing Fire* (2006) narrates, his fierce drawings and outspoken commentary challenged the policies of eleven US presidents. His favorite targets were Nixon, Reagan, and George W. Bush. An outspoken supporter of free speech and social justice, Conrad never stopped, even when he received death threats. Like Conrad, Jay Darling began work on an Iowa paper, the *Sioux City Journal,* before taking up a long career at the *Des Moines Register.* Like Conrad, Darling's political commentary influenced public attitudes. As *America's Darling: The Story of Jay N. "Ding" Darling* (2012) reveals, Darling motivated people in Washington and across the country to support wilderness preservation. His achievements include the establishment of the US Fish and Wildlife Commission, the Duck Stamp (which funds preservation), the establishment of programs at land-grant universities to train environmental scientists, and a natural wildlife refuge in Florida. Ding Darling also worked for FDR and traveled to Russia at Stalin's invitation.

Notable Henry Wallace is presented in *Henry Wallace: An Uncommon Man* (2011). He was an environmentalist, statesman, internationalist, and intellectual. From rural Adair County, Wallace was mentored by George Washington Carver at Iowa State. He founded Pioneer Hi-Bred, which increased crop yields, tackled challenging rural problems under FDR during the Depression as U.S. Secretary of Agriculture, and innovated new programs such as food stamps, school lunches, and rural electrification. As FDR's Vice President, he supervised industrial mobilization for WWII. Wallace didn't smoke or drink and disliked political games, alienating the Washington establishment and eventually failing to be reselected for the vice presidency. Wallace was a progressive who supported the environment, civil rights, women's rights, international cooperation and peace; he criticized segregation, the defense industry, and the Cold War. Wallace went on to edit *The New Republic* for a brief time. Though a cosmopolitan intellectual, Wallace was known for his ability to connect with plain people who lived close to the land in countries around the world. Another documentary with international resonance is *A Promise Called Iowa* (2007) that reminds us about a lost generation of bipartisan cooperation on immigration when the state's Republicans, led by Governor Robert Ray, and Democrats permitted substantial Southeast Asia migration in the 1970s and 1980s.

These influential Iowans display the work and service ethic central to the Iowa mythic archetypes as well as their share of "Iowa stubborn." But they also have immense creativity and a passion for using their considerable intelligence and visionary leadership to serve the public. They have the confidence to stand for their beliefs, even when they go against mainstream thinking. These Iowa documentaries have a huge potential to be used in Iowa public school and higher education settings to teach a new generation about Iowa's history and heroes.

Conclusion

The 21st-century Iowa films we have collected surprised us with their quantity as well as the new genres and new directions they represent. We have found ourselves inspired by how much we have learned from them. Even when they are mostly entertaining, they suggest to us much that we would like to understand. When we considered emerging filmmaking technology and distribution methods and Iowa's support and incentives for filmmaking in the state during the past decade, the increased pace of production by filmmakers who are closer to Iowa realities became understandable. We have also seen the fulfillment of David Ostendorf's 1980s prophecy that the pastoral myth of Iowa would not play forever.

Between the fall of the Berlin Wall (1989) and 9/11, the nostalgic view of Iowa appeared to be durable. American movie audiences then looked backward, consuming a surprising number of films based on classical literature by Jane Austen, William Shakespeare, Edith Wharton, and Charles Dickens. American producers offered films with nostalgic themes such as *Field of Dreams* and *The Bridges of Madison County*. Iowa's image as an old-fashioned rural state appealed to late twentieth-century viewers who weren't sure they liked the technological transformations and corporate-driven media influences in their lives.

It is natural that a new century and a new millennium would lead people to look forward and to accept these transformations as the realities on which the future would be played out. The economic calamities of the post-9/11 period, coming on the heels of the 1980s farm crisis seemed to carry a strong message to "get real!" Thus the Iowa films after 2001 have explored new genres such as horror that slashed and trashed the old mythology of safe, virtuous rural Iowa safety and have shown, instead, contemporary Iowans, contemporary social problems in Iowa as elsewhere, and contemporary Iowa life. The documentaries do look backward, but to tell the stories of the real Iowa, not Hollywood's Iowa, and in the process, they redefine our state, its residents, its varied landscape, and its heroes. Iowans on screen seem to be emerging from the cocoon of a national perception that did not sync with who we really are, leaving us with a split sense of identity. Like the Villisca house, we have too long been haunted by a past that has defined our present. While Iowans may lose the moral high ground when portrayed as crack addicts, abuse victims, and employees of greedy agribusinesses—or simply as ordinary Americans, we have a history of progressive Iowa leadership and significant accomplishment, based on reality and not on myth. That can inspire young Iowans, urban and rural, to follow their visions to improve the nation, state, and the world—and to make more films.

Endnotes*

[1] Eddy, Lisa. "Going Hollywood." *Iowa Living Magazines.* Iowa Living Magazines, 24 Oct. 2012. Web. 13 May 2014. The fuller story of those events, along with vintage film reviews from *The New York Times* and *Variety,* can be found in Appendix B.

[2] de Wit, Cary. "Flyover Country." *The American Midwest: An Interpretive Encyclopedia.* Ed. Andrew R. L. Cayton, Richard Sisson, and Chris Zacher. Bloomington: U of Indiana P, 2006. 66. Print.

[3] Savane jeans. Advertisement. *Texas Monthly Magazine* Oct. 1998: n. pag. Print.

[4] Ross, Harold. Qtd. in Daly, Christopher B. *Covering America: A Narrative History of a Nation's Journalism.* Amherst: U of Massachusetts P, 2012. Print.

[5] Willson, Meredith. Qtd. in "The Theatre: New Musical in Manhattan." *Time.com.* Time, Inc., 30 Dec. 1957. Web. 25 May 2014.

[6] "Maps of Movies Filmed in Kansas." *Washburn University Center for Kansas Studies.* Washburn University, 2014. Web. 25 May 2014. This website's categories—Set in

---

* We have modified the style of our Endnotes slightly to meet the requirements of other publication formats. Throughout the book we have dropped some diacritical markings from foreign languages

Kansas, Shot in Kansas, Kansas Literature in the Movies—resemble ones that we have used.

[7] Stong, Phil. "Writer in Hollywood." *The Saturday Review of Literature* 10 Apr. 1937: 3-4, 14. Unz.org., n.d. Web. 25 May 2014. Canby, Henry Seidel. "A Novel for the Movies." *The Saturday Review of Literature* 18 Jan. 1936: 36. Unz.org, n.d. Web. 25 May 2014.

[8] Qtd. in Koppes, Clayton R., and Gregory D. Black. *Hollywood Goes to War: How Politics, Profits and Propaganda Shaped World War II Movies*. New York: Free Press, 1987. 162. Print.

[9] For a description of film-related bond sales, see Chapter 3 of Samuel, Lawrence R. *Pledging Allegiance: American Identity and the Bond Drive of World War II.* Washington: Smithsonian Institution Press, 1997: 45-73. Print.

[10] Additional Kantor films were *The Voice of Bugle Ann* (1936), *Mountain Music* (1937), *The Man from Dakota* (1940), *Gentle Annie* (1944), *The Romance of Rosy Ridge* (1947), *Deadly is the Female* (1949), *Hannah Lee* (1953), and *Follow Me, Boys* (1966).

[11] Micheaux, Oscar. Letter to George P. Johnson. Qtd. in Bowser, Pearl, and Louise Spence. *Writing Himself into History: Oscar Micheaux, His Silent Films, and His Audiences*. New Brunswick, NJ: Rutgers UP, 2001. 9-10. Print.

[12] See the filmography in Green, Ronald J. *Straight Lick: The Cinema of Oscar Micheaux*. Bloomington: U of Indiana P, 2000. Print.

[13] Boshart, Rod. "Iowa looks to Reboot its Film Industry." *QCTimes.com*. Quad City Times, 12 Aug. 2012. Web. 25 Mar. 2014. Governor Branstad is quoted as saying that IFO assisted "59 major features and several thousand smaller film projects." This number reflects the years of the Wendol Jarvis direction from 1984-2002, during which state tax credits were not offered as financial incentives to filmmakers.

[14] This quotation and other details come from Doughten, Russell S., Jr. Personal interview by Marty S. Knepper. 11 Oct. 2002. Doughten died 19 Aug. 2013. In a 29 June 2014 email to John Lawrence, Kimberly Busbee called Doughten "the godfather of independent film in Iowa." She reports that he regularly attended the Wild Rose festival and mentored many of Iowa's indie filmmakers.

[15] Balmer, Randall. *Mine Eyes Have Seen the Glory*. New York: Oxford UP, 1993. Print. Balmer estimates viewings of *A Thief in the Night* in the tens of millions (30). At the time of Balmer's book, Doughten estimated 4 million conversions as a result of screening the film in churches followed by altar calls to be saved (62). In 2003, Doughten estimated in a personal interview with Marty S. Knepper an audience of 300 million for the 16 millimeter format alone with 6 million conversions. Additional viewers have seen *Thief* in VHS and DVD.

[16] Sage, Leland. *The History of Iowa*. Ames: Iowa State UP, 1974. Print. This source cites 1956 as the year in which urban population exceeded rural (314). See also Schwieder, Dorothy. *Iowa: The Middle Land*. Ames: Iowa State UP, 1996. Print. Schwieder elaborates on the shift toward urbanization and the industrialization of Iowa's economy (288-95).

[17] Shortridge, James. M. *The Middle West: Its Meaning in American Culture*. Lawrence: UP of Kansas, 1989. Print.

[18] Garland, Hamlin. "Preface." *Main-Travelled Roads*. New York: Macmillan, 1891. Print.

[19] Shortridge, James. M. *The Middle West: Its Meaning in American Culture*. Lawrence: UP of Kansas, 1989. 67. Print. See also the entire chapter, "A Need for Pastoral Values" (67-74).

[20] Ostendorf, David. "Iowa's Rural Crisis of the 1980s." *Family Reunion: Essays on Iowa*, Ed. Thomas J. Morain. Ames: Iowa State UP, 1995. 68. Print.

[21] *Burlesque*, with a star-saturated budget estimated at $55 million, grossed theatrically $39,440,655—promising for the long term perhaps, but hardly a blockbuster; *Cedar Rapids* opened on a mere 15 screens and grossed $6,857,503 in theatrical release (no estimated budget available); *Butter* managed to open on 90 screens and collapsed after a single week with grosses of $70,931, suggesting a real treasure for investors seeking to buy tax losses; *At Any Price* opened on four screens on 28 April 2012 with $16,095 and had earned $379,791 through 28 July.

[22] Gannon, Sean. "Director's Statement." Somethingbluefilm.com, n.d. Web. 25. May 2014.

[23] "The Filmmakers." *Lost Nation: The Ioway*. Iowaymovie.com, n.d. Web. 25 May 2014.

[24] Rood, Lee. "Criminal Charges filed in Film Credit Tax Scandal." *DesMoinesRegister.com*. Des Moines Register, 8 Feb. 2010. Web. 25 May 2014. Boshart, Rod. "Former Iowa Film Office Head Gets Deferred Judgment, Probation." *The Gazette* [Cedar Rapids]. The Gazette, 18 Oct. 2011. Web. 25 May 2014. For the scale of subsidy see Boshart, Rod. "Iowa's Payouts Spike with Film Credit Deals." *The Gazette* [Cedar Rapids]. The Gazette, 29 July 2012. Web. 25 May 2014. Boshart characterizes the incentives as follows: "a 25 percent tax credit for production expenditures in Iowa, and a 25 percent tax credit for investors for projects that spent at least $100,000 in Iowa."

[25] Marriot, Michael. "Iowa Gunman Was Torn by Academic Challenge." *NYTimes.com*. New York Times, 4 Nov. 1991. Web. 25. May 2014.

[26] Petty, Lori. Qtd. in Miller, Bruce M. "Former Sioux Cityan Lori Petty Gives Right Direction." *SiouxCityJournal.com*. Sioux City Journal, 24 July 2009. Web. 25 May 2014.

Chapter 1: Preview List of Iowa Films

In both this Preview List and the Guide to Iowa Films, we classify films into six categories, which indicate their place within Iowa film history. The previews in this chapter chronologically list the films with dates, titles, categories, and brief summaries. The Guide to Iowa Films (Chapter 2) provides more detailed information about directors, actors, production companies, and review citations, as well as longer descriptions of the films, with emphasis on their Iowa connections.

Many independent films have been shot in Iowa without reaching film festivals or any other kind of distribution, often a tribute to the hospitality, grants, and technical assistance of the Iowa Film Office (now Produce Iowa) and the local communities that assist producers. We have been able to see and to describe quite a few of these undistributed films, thanks to producers who gave or lent them to us, but, like much older films, they might be quite difficult to obtain. A few films have been shot by foreign companies, who later distribute their films in other languages; such films rarely migrate back to American screens. One significant exception is *Bix: The Interpretation of a Legend* (1991), by Italian filmmaker Pupi Avati, who has shot several films in Iowa. (All films that we have acquired are at the Sioux City Public Museum.)

Six Categories of Iowa Films

I. **Iowa Settings, Fictional Films.** These are fictional stories set at least partially in Iowa.

II. **Iowa Settings, Historical Films.** These include historic episodes in Iowa, ranging from the Mormon crossing in *Brigham Young—Frontiersman* to the tragic 1989 air disaster at Sioux City portrayed by *Crash Landing: The Rescue of Flight 232*.

III. **Traveling Iowans.** These feature at least one fictional Iowan as a significant character in a location outside the state.

IV. Iowa Documentaries. These films, nearly all at a minimum of 60 minutes in length, present some aspect of Iowa in a factually informative style.

V. Made in Iowa. These films are recognizably Iowa in physical setting, but their fictional stories place them elsewhere or give them a generic, "anywhere" setting. The fact that they are shot in Iowa often fades into the false recollection that they are "about" Iowa—particularly when communities remember the experience of filming. An example is *Children of the Corn* (1984), filmed in Whiting, Hornick, and Sioux City, but set in Nebraska.

VI. Films That Mention Iowa. Numerous films briefly mention Iowa or Iowans to evoke some stereotype of place or character. While such films lack Iowa focus, their references become part of Iowa's cultural identity as safe, nice, naive, or dim. For example, in *Made for Each Other* (1939), a character quips, "Hollywood is the place where people from Iowa mistake each other for stars." The First Husband in *Kisses for My President* (1964) welcomes a lisping Campfire Girl from "Thioux Thity." The "mention" films are described only in this listing, not in the Guide.

The Complete Preview List

1918   *The Strange Woman,* **I.** Parisian Inez exposes the hypocrisy of an Iowa town but settles down there

1919   *Bill Henry,* **III.** Iowa lady claims farm in Alabama, foils schemers, and sells property with oil on it

1919   *Crooked Straight,* **III.** Iowa boy is tricked into life of crime in big city but goes straight finally

1921   *Get-Rich-Quick Wallingford,* **I.** Men aim to con small Iowa town but end up marrying locals

1921   *Stardust,* **III.** Iowa girl with musical talent succeeds in opera, despite forced marriage to rich brute

1921   *The Wonderful Thing,* **I.** American hog farmer's daughter marries Englishman; scenes in Centerville

1922   *Watch Your Step,* **I.** Elmer, who thinks he has killed a cop while speeding, hides in Iowa

1923   *The Covered Wagon,* **VI.** In pioneer epic Jim Bridger brings goods from Council Bluffs to Rockies

1924   *That French Lady,* **I.** Remake of *The Strange Woman* (1918)

1925   *Night Life of New York,* **III.** Father plots to keep Iowa son from settling in NYC; scheme succeeds

1925   *A Slave of Fashion,* **III.** Iowa girl assumes identity of NYC woman whose purse she has taken

1927   *A Harp in Hock,* **VI.** A boy who fights a bully in NYC is sent to a foster family in Iowa

1927   *With Sitting Bull at the Spirit Lake Massacre,* **I.** Indians abduct two young women and attack frontier settlement

1929   *Midnight Daddies,* **III.** Iowa vacationers in big city nearly get duped by greedy ex-Iowan cousin

1930   *High Society Blues,* **III.** Rich Scarsdale families feud: native Iowans vs. native New Yorkers

1933   *As Husbands Go,* **III.** A pair of women from Dubuque meet men in Paris who visit them in Iowa

1933   *Design for Living,* **VI.** George paints a rotund woman from Des Moines, Iowa, in Nice, France

1933   *State Fair,* **I.** In Depression comedy based on Phil Stong novel, the Frake family goes to the fair

1933   *The Stranger's Return,* **I.** Phil Stong tale on adultery and squabbling over who gets the farm

1934   *Men of the Night,* **III.** Unsuccessful in Hollywood as an actress, Iowa girl gets involved with police

1935   *Times Square Lady,* **III.** Iowa heiress shows New Yorkers she is no patsy, marries converted swindler

1935   *Village Tale,* **I.** A depressing small town story about gossip and hostility, based on a Phil Stong book

1936   *Farmer in the Dell,* **III.** Satire on Iowans in Hollywood, based on a Phil Stong book

1937   *The Law Commands,* **II.** Conflict about land resulting from 1862 Homestead Act

1937   *We Have Our Moments,* **III.** Bride-to-be balks at Sioux City honeymoon, flees to Monte Carlo

1938   *Keep Smiling,* **III.** Secretary to out-of-work film director is pressured by fiancé to return to Iowa

1938   *Penitentiary,* **V.** An innocent convict learns about "the criminal code" in a drama shot at Anamosa

1939   *Career,* **I.** Small town Iowa drama about failing bank and father's and son's romances

1939   *The Flying Deuces,* **III.** Dumped by heartthrob, Ollie, from Des Moines, joins the Foreign Legion with Stan

1939   *King of the Underworld,* **VI.** Crime boss's henchman mistakes Napoleon's Waterloo for Waterloo, Iowa

1939   *Made for Each Other,* **VI.** Hollywood is called "place where people from Iowa mistake each other for stars"

1939   *Union Pacific,* **II.** DeMille movie about bringing transcontinental railroad to Council Bluffs

1940   *Brigham Young—Frontiersman,* **II.** Mormon trek through Iowa after Joseph Smith's murder

1940   *Lillian Russell,* **VI.** Biopic about turn-of-the-century singer who was born in Iowa

1941   *Cheers for Miss Bishop,* **I.** Tribute to unmarried teacher; adapted from Aldrich story

1941   *High Sierra,* **VI.** Ex-con Roy Earle tells a cautionary tale of a robbery in Iowa: a talkative man got killed

1941   *Let's Go Collegiate,* **III.** Alum sports fans from Des Moines hold a cop hostage so Rawley can win at rowing

1941   *Melody Lane,* **III.** Singing group from Yuba City, Iowa, goes to NYC to sing for ads

1941   *Navy Blues,* **III.** Shy sailor Homer Matthews is from an Applington farm with corn and more than 1000 pigs

1941   *One Foot in Heaven,* **II.** Based on Hartzell Spence memoir about his minister father

1942   *Don't Get Personal,* **III.** Iowan inherits pickle fortune and foils scheming company execs

1942   *The Major and the Minor,* **III.** In a comedy, Iowa woman poses as a child to get home from NYC

1942   *Orchestra Wives,* **I.** Marriage of swing band member reaches crisis during Iowa City gig

1943   *Gung Ho,* **VI.** The "Good Old Dubuque" steamroller helps the WWII Marine invasion of Makim Island succeed

1943   *Happy Land,* **I.** Small town father grieves over death of son in WWII

1943   *The Hard Way,* **VI.** Katie, with her "stage sister," joins a vaudeville act, playing Des Moines and all over

1944   *Buffalo Bill,* **VI.** Buffalo Bill and Sgt. Chips take train from Council Bluffs to head east

1944   *Double Exposure,* **III.** Native Iowa journalists, Pat and Ben, are manipulated by NYC editor

1944   *Double Indemnity,* **VI.** Cynical Walter Neff observes that "native" Californians are all from Iowa

1944   *Hollywood Canteen,* **VI.** The Andrews Sisters sing about Des Moines; Slim's girl is from Altoona (perhaps IA?)

1944   *The Sullivans,* **II.** Five Irish Catholic brothers from Waterloo die together in WWII

1945   *Blonde from Brooklyn,* **III.** Vet from Dubuque wants to sing and dance, but lands in radio

1945   *Bud Abbott and Lou Costello in Hollywood,* **III.** Abbot and Costello become agents to aspiring singer from Des Moines

1945   *Keep Your Powder Dry,* **I.** WACs at Camp Fort Des Moines fight and bond

1945 *State Fair,* **I.** Pa and Ma Frake win prizes and the kids find romance at the fair in this musical

1945 *They Were Expendable,* **III.** Iowan nurse Sandy and Rusty Ryan, USN, have a WWII romance in S. Pacific

1945 *You Came Along,* **I.** Air Force buddies and Ivy Hotchkiss visit Des Moines and elsewhere to sell war bonds

1946 *The Best Years of Our Lives,* **I.** WWII vets return to "Boone City" to find things changed

1946 *Johnny Comes Flying Home,* **I.** Vets return to Iowa, but end up in business with pal from California

1946 *The Postman Always Rings Twice,* **III.** Cora, from Iowa, and drifter Frank murder her husband

1946 *Sioux City Sue,* **VI.** Gene Autry croons popular song about "Sioux City Sue" from Ioway

1947 *Angel and the Badman,* **VI.** John Wayne's Quirt Evans remarks on Sioux City's wild reputation

1947 *High Barbaree,* **I.** Story of romantic pair from an Iowa small town in Pacific theater of WWII

1947 *It Happened on Fifth Avenue,* **VI.** Rich girl claims to have 13 sibs and a drunken father in Dubuque

1948 *A Foreign Affair,* **III.** Primly moralistic congresswoman from Iowa visits post-WWII Germany

1948 *Sealed Verdict,* **III.** Iowa grandparents want to raise child of their murdered soldier son and a German woman

1949 *Hideout,* **I.** Gang leader steals diamond necklace and disguises himself as solid citizen of Hilltop, Iowa

1949 *The Seven Little Foys,* **I.** Eddie Foy performs in Dubuque, unaware his wife is dying, leaving him with 7 kids

1950 *The Mormon Battalion,* **IV.** Historical episode in which Mormons were recruited to fight in Northern Mexico

1950 *The Rock Island Trail,* **II.** Reed Loomis fights to build the first railroad bridge over the Mississippi into Iowa

1951   *Detective Story,* **VI.** NYC policeman rethinks his rigid moral code; Des Moines mentioned

1951   *Go for Broke!* **III.** Story of a U.S. Nisei 442nd Regimental Combat Team, including former Iowa egg farmer

1951   *The Home Economics Story,* **IV.** Four girls at ISU pursue home economics in college and later in careers

1951   *You're in the Navy Now,* **VI.** Harkness mentions recruiting in Iowa, an unlikely place for sailors

1954   *Go, Man, Go!* **I.** Dubuque man helps promote Harlem Globetrotters

1955   *Mister Roberts,* **VI.** WWII cargo ship crew fights boredom; one recalls selling booze to U of Iowa students.

1955   *Why Study Home Economics?* **V.** A HS counselor tells 1950s girls why they should pursue home economics

1956   *Our Miss Brooks,* **III.** Connie struggles to land bashful biology teacher Boynton, who has IA connections

1957   *The Pajama Game,* **I.** Workers in an Iowa pajama factory demand a 7½ cent raise; a musical

1957   *Small Town, USA,* **IV.** A documentary about life in the rural small town of Anamosa, Iowa

1957   *The Spirit of St. Louis,* **VI.** Air exec says flying NY-Paris is not like "dropping off a mailbag in Keokuk"

1958   *The Tarnished Angels,* **III.** A teenage girl flees Iowa to follow a stunt pilot in a carnival

1960   *The Apartment,* **VI.** Baxter's date for *The Music Man* loves a heartless Harold Hill type and stands him up

1960   *Elmer Gantry,* **VI.** Gantry hops a train to win over Sister Sharon after her revival in "West Iowa"

1962   *The Music Man,* **I.** Meredith Willson's musical about con man's stay in and transformation of "River City"

1963   *All of Me,* **III.** Aspiring model from Iowa is attacked and exploited in NYC; visits nudist camp

1964   *Kisses for My President,* **VI.** The First Husband welcomes a lisping Campfire Girl from "Thioux Thity"

1966   *The Fat Spy,* **IV.** In beach musical cosmetics boss has Iowa farms speed up pig fat production for beauty creams

1966   *The Hostage,* **I.** A boy is trapped in a moving van driven by violent men; filmed in Des Moines area

1967   *Bonnie and Clyde,* **II.** Bank robbers are ambushed in a shootout at Dexter, Iowa

1967   *In Cold Blood,* **VI.** A man can give Dick and Perry a lift to Iowa; the two men steal a car from an Iowa barn

1967   *The Last American Hobo,* **IV.** Documentary on hobo life, including a hobo convention in Britt

1968   *Fever Heat,* **I.** Romance between stock car driver and Iowa widow who become business partners

1969   *Gaily, Gaily,* **V.** Shot partly in Dubuque, this comedy takes naive Ben from Galena, Illinois, to Chicago

1969   *The Rain People,* **VI.** Brain-damaged football player travels and sees Nebraska sign pointing to Sioux City

1969   *The Trouble with Girls,* **I.** Elvis manages 1927 Chautauqua troupe visiting Iowa

1970   *Sidelong Glances of a Pigeon Kicker,* **VI.** NYC taxi driver flees stressful city for Des Moines

1971   *Cold Turkey,* **I.** Comedy about Iowa town that takes a bribe to stop smoking

1971   *What's the Matter with Helen?,* **III.** In this horror pic, two Iowa mothers of murderers flee to Hollywood

1972   *A Thief in the Night,* **I.** A Christian "Rapture" movie set in central Iowa

1972   *What's Up, Doc?* **III.** Comedy about ISU musicologist and wife in California

1973   *Dillinger,* **II.** FBI Agent Purvis narrates the Dillinger saga, including a bank robbery with deaths in Mason City

1975   *The Day of the Locust,* **III.** Iowan Homer Simpson finds Hollywood disturbing and deadly

1975   *Hearts of the West,* **III.** A naive writer of westerns from Iowa goes to Hollywood

1975   *Huckleberry Finn,* **V.** TV version starring Ron Howard was filmed along the Mississippi River

1976   *The Bad News Bears,* **VI.** Hollywood girl has sold maps to the stars' homes to "half of Iowa"

1977   *All the King's Horses,* **V.** A troubled couple near divorce finally commits to a Christian marriage

1977   *The Goodbye Girl,* **VI.** Elliott Garfield cynically says Ames, Iowa, is where to make it as an actor

1977   *One in a Million: The Ron LeFlore Story,* **I.** East Detroit kid moves from prison to Detroit Tigers via Clinton, IA

1977   *Ride the Wind,* **I.** Two gangs of kids compete in building and racing homemade planes

1977   *Sammy,* **I.** A handicapped boy's disappearance unites a Des Moines family and leads them to Christ

1977   *Telefon,* **VI.** When double agent Barbara crosses from Canada to the USA, she claims to be from Sioux City

1978   *The Buddy Holly Story,* **II.** Film climaxes with Buddy's final concert in Clear Lake

1978   *F.I.S.T.,* **V.** Filmed in Dubuque, this movie presents a portrait of a Jimmy Hoffa-like labor leader

1978   *Nite Song,* **I.** Two teens—one black, one white—struggle to rid their neighborhood of drug pushers

1979   *A Distant Thunder,* **I.** Further Tribulations of Iowans "left behind" in Rapture of *Thief* (1972)

1979   *Friendly Fire,* **II.** Drama about Mullens' fight with Pentagon to discover truth after son dies in Vietnam

1979   *Hardcore,* **VI.** Midwest Christian youth go to decadent LA where one girl is lured into porno industry

1979   *Ice Castles,* **I.** An Iowa skater finds success, is blinded, and learns to skate again

1980   *Dribble,* **I.** Des Moines women's basketball team plays to survive in this comedy

1980   *Heaven's Heroes,* **I.** A war hero and Christian family man risks his life as a Des Moines cop in this true story

1980   *Image of the Beast,* **I.** Continuing struggle (*Thief,* 1972; *Distant,* 1979) of wavering believers to resist the Mark

1980   *Whitcomb's War,* **I.** In "Hurrah, Iowa," a minister, David, brings light to businessman Phil Esteem

1981   *Bill,* **II.** The story of a mentally retarded man who becomes part of U of Iowa community

1981   *Bix: Ain't None of Them Play like Him Yet,* **IV.** On jazz great Bix Beiderbecke of Davenport

1981   *For Ladies Only,* **III.** U of Iowa theater grad becomes a male stripper in NYC

1981   *The Funhouse,* **I.** Teens spend night at carnie funhouse in horror film with Iowa setting

1981   *Home Safe,* **V.** Filmed in Des Moines area, a family learns the meaning of Bible teachings on discipline

1981   *Pennies from Heaven,* **V.** Musical about a sheet music salesman; filmed in Dubuque

1981   *Take This Job and Shove It,* **I.** Local boy returns to run Dubuque brewery

1982   *Airplane II: The Sequel,* **VI.** Man with bomb mentions sex institute in Des Moines

1982   *Face in the Mirror,* **I.** Friends and family of a suicidal teen experience guilt and turn to Christ

1983   *Bill: On His Own,* **II.** More life events for Bill, mentally retarded kiosk operator at U of I

1983   *The Healing,* **I.** A despairing, drunken doctor finds a new life on Des Moines' Center Street

1983   *Heat and Dust,* **III.** Iowan in this James Ivory drama is out of place in India

1983   *The Prodigal Planet,* **I.** The end of post-Rapture Tribulation for Iowans begun in *Thief* (1972)

1983   *Terms of Endearment,* **I.** Married woman from Texas has affair with Iowa banker

1983   *Who Will Love My Children?* **II.** Dying Iowa mom strives to find loving homes for her 10 kids

1984   *Children of the Corn,* **V.** Stephen King story of crazed, murderous teens who emerge from cornfields

1984   *Country,* **I.** Drama about farm crisis focuses on the Ivy family's struggles

1984   *Mass Appeal,* **VI.** Two priests are threatened with possible posts in Iowa, as if Siberia

1984   *The Shepherd,* **I.** Two Vietnam vets, now Iowa Air Guard pilots, conquer their pride, resentment

1984   *Starman,* **V.** Film about an alien come to earth; shot in Cedar Rapids area

1984   *This Is Spinal Tap,* **VI.** The world's loudest rock band has sunk so low Des Moines won't have them

1985   *Fraternity Vacation,* **III.** Nerdy Iowa boy wins gorgeous woman in Palm Springs

1986   *Out of Bounds,* **III.** Naive Iowa boy is pursued by drug dealers and cops in LA

1986   *Star Trek IV,* **III.** Captain Kirk, identified as Iowan, travels with Spock to California to find whales

1986   *Wisdom,* **I.** John and Karen raid banks to burn mortgages in Iowa and elsewhere

1987   *La Bamba,* **II.** Rock and roll singer Ritchie Valens dies in Clear Lake Charter Service plane

1987   *Brother Enemy,* **V.** After teens demolish a puppeteer's studio, they are sentenced to help him

1987   *Life Flight,* **I.** Des Moines Life Flight crew members rescue citizens and search for God's will

1987   *The Secret Government: The Constitution in Crisis,* **VI.** PBS feature on Iran-Contra interviews Jim Leach

1988   *Fort Figueroa,* **III.** TV pilot about Iowans who have lost the farm becoming LA apartment owners

1988   *Married to the Mob,* **VI.** An FBI agent poses in Miami as a tourist from Dubuque

1988   *Miles from Home,* **I.** Angry brothers protest the loss of their family's farm

1989   *Field of Dreams,* **I.** Fantasy of reconciliation and second chances through baseball on an Iowa farm

1989   *Harry Hopkins . . . At FDR's Side,* **IV.** Sioux City man served as presidential aide and international envoy

1989   *Your Mother Wears Combat Boots,* **III.** Davenport mom sneaks into airborne training to keep son from jumping

1989   *Zadar! Cow from Hell,* **I.** Duck's Breath's satire on Hollywood films about Iowa

1990   *The Civil War,* **IV.** This acclaimed Ken Burns' documentary notes that 13,001 Iowa men died in the Civil War

1990   *Luther the Geek,* **V.** Chicken-themed horror movie is set in Illinois but filmed partially in Iowa

1990   *Quick Change,* **III.** Man in convertible with Iowa plates holds up unlucky bank robbers in Brooklyn

1991   *Bix: An Interpretation of a Legend,* **I.** Bix's playing and drinking disappoint his Davenport family

1991   *Indian Runner,* **V.** A failed farmer and a Vietnam vet, brothers, struggle in this family tragedy

1991   *Lunatics: A Love Story,* **III.** Michigan man and Iowa woman despair in LA

1991   *Sleeping with the Enemy,* **I.** Abused wife fakes death and takes refuge in Cedar Falls

1991   *Soapdish,* **III.** Girl from Des Moines becomes "America's Sweetheart" on a soap

1991   *Where the Night Begins,* **I.** Irving returns to Davenport to right wrongs of his father in this melodrama

1992   *The Bodyguard,* **VI.** An Iowa Rapids chaplain refers to God the protector as Frank Farmer scans the crowd

1992   *Crash Landing: The Rescue of Flight 232,* **II.** Story of plane crash and rescue response in Sioux City

1992   *Ed and His Dead Mother,* **I.** Shy guy from Manning is plagued by murderous dead mom

1992   *Incident at Oglala,* **IV.** Film argues Peltier is a victim of government injustice; includes Cedar Rapids trial

1992   *In the Best Interest of the Children,* **II.** TV docudrama about neglectful Estherville mom

1992   *Noises Off,* **I.** Inept theater company begins road tour in Des Moines

1992   *Taking Back My Life: The Nancy Ziegenmeyer Story,* **II.** True story of rape of Grinnell woman

1992   *Whispers in the Dark,* **I.** A Manhattan psychiatrist gets involved with a charter pilot from Keokuk

1993   *Dave,* **VI.** Iowa Senator Tom Harkin has a cameo in this political comedy about a US President

1993   *Married to It,* **III.** Comedy about young ISU graduates who are establishing careers in NYC

1993   *The Program,* **VI.** Collegiate football film features a crucial game against the Iowa Hawkeyes

1993   *Shimmer,* **I.** Teens in Iowa youth detention facility speak code to help them envision better places

1993   *What's Eating Gilbert Grape,* **I.** Gilbert, from Endora, Iowa, struggles with family, economic burdens

1993   *Whose Child Is This?* **II.** Story of the Iowa versus Michigan custody battle for baby Jessica DeBoer

1993   *The Woman Who Loved Elvis*, **I.** Deserted wife from Ottumwa has Elvis shrine on her porch

1994   *An American Love*, **I.** An Italian professor comes to U of Iowa and is torn between a journalist and his wife

1994   *Dumb and Dumber*, **I.** Candidates for "dumbest guys in world" take road trip to Aspen, through Iowa

1994   *Robert A. Heinlein's The Puppet Masters*, **I.** Aliens invading Iowa take over the brains of natives

1994   *The Room Next Door* (Italian title: *La stanza accanto*), **I.** Martin returns to scene of triple murder he witnessed in Iowa

1994   *Sioux City*, **I.** Native American doctor returns to Siouxland to investigate his past

1994   *The Stand*, **I.** Plague survivors prepare for a battle between good and evil; two survivors are Iowans

1994   *Wyatt Earp*, **II.** Saga of Earp begins in Pella, where he spent early years

1995   *The Bridges of Madison County*, **I.** Romance of Iowa farm wife and traveling photographer

1995   *The Last Supper*, **I.** Liberal graduate students kill conservative guests in this satire

1995   *Mommy*, **I.** Muscatine mother devoted to daughter becomes crazed serial killer

1995   *A Mother's Gift*, **I.** Iowa teacher gives up opera in NYC to follow husband into Nebraska after Civil War

1995   *Omaha*, **V.** Partly shot near Council Bluffs, the comedy refers to Harkin, ISU, and Iowa kickboxers

1995   *Operation Dumbo Drop*, **III.** Disney comedy about a Green Beret caper in Vietnam War

1995   *Tommy Boy*, **VI.** Sweet, dumb Tommy travels Midwest to save family auto parts business

1995   *Troublesome Creek: A Midwestern*, **IV.** Documentary about family nearly losing their farm near Atlantic

1995   *The Tuskegee Airmen,* **II.** Iowa pilot succeeds in Army Air Corps during WWII

1996   *Citizen Ruth,* **V.** Abortion groups battle over Ruth's baby in this movie filmed in Council Bluffs

1996   *Donna Reed,* **IV.** A&E Biography shows Denison's Donna as professional and peace activist, not just mom

1996   *Harvest of Fire,* **I.** Urban FBI agent investigates hate crimes in Amish community; her life changes

1996   *Iowa: An American Portrait,* **IV.** Sesquicentennial documentary about Iowa

1996   *Joe's Apartment,* **III.** Comedy about naive Iowan who shares NYC apartment with roaches

1996   *Kingpin,* **III.** Iowa man from Ocelot becomes big time bowler in Reno and saves an Amish town

1996   *Michael,* **I.** Angel transforms lives of cynical tabloid journalists doing a story in Iowa

1996   *Mystery Science Theatre 3000: The Movie,* **VI.** "I'll gas up [the spaceship] in Des Moines."

1996   *Siege at Ruby Ridge,* **II.** An Iowa family is attacked by the FBI in their Idaho cabin

1996   *Twister,* **V.** Film shot in Iowa about an Oklahoma tornado

1997   *Boys Life 2* ("Alkali, Iowa" segment made in 1995), **I.** A young farmer discovers his father was gay

1997   *I'll Be Home for Christmas,* **I.** Tale of a small town that gets a doctor through romance

1997   *The Man Who Knew Too Little,* **III.** Des Moines Blockbuster employee plays spy in London

1997   *Mommy's Day (Mommy II),* **I.** Murderous Muscatine mother is improbably rehabilitated

1997   *Murder at 1600,* **III.** Female Secret Service agent from Iowa helps solve White House murder

1997   *Orgazmo,* **VI.** Mormon missionary gets pulled into LA porn industry; accused of being an Iowan

1997   *A Thousand Acres,* **I.** Based on Jane Smiley's Iowa version of the *King Lear* tragedy

1997   *Titanic,* **III.** An aged but still spunky Rose, from Cedar Rapids, tells her story about the sea disaster

1997   *Touch,* **I.** An ex-priest/celebrity with healing powers escapes from LA to Iowa at film's end

1998   *The Big One,* **IV.** Michael Moore's tour of downsized businesses brings him to Iowa

1998   *Le cerveau en emoi,* **IV.** French documentary presents brain/mind explorations of U of Iowa's Damasio team

1998   *A Civil Action,* **VI.** This environmental litigation drama refers to "the Farmers Bank of Iowa"

1998   *Crimes of Passion: Nobody Lives Forever,* **V.** TV cop movie filmed in Davenport and Kalona

1998   *Dreamfield,* **IV.** Documents fan culture/pop religion surrounding *Field of Dreams*

1998   *Mercury Rising,* **VI.** Woman gives up a sales trip to safe Des Moines to help protect hunted autistic boy

1998   *Overnight Delivery,* **I.** Boy-girl road trip from Minnesota to Memphis has stops in Iowa

1998   *Saving Private Ryan,* **III.** WWII mission to find a private from Iowa after his three brothers die

1998   *Streetcars of Omaha and Council Bluffs,* **IV.** History of streetcars in the two cities, 1947-55.

1998   *The Truman Show,* **VI.** In the script of Truman's life, his father is from Des Moines

1998   *Yidl in the Middle,* **IV.** Documentary on growing up Jewish in Iowa in the 1950s and 1960s

1999   *Alert 3: The Crash of UA 232,* **IV.** The video documents the plane crash and rescue

1999   *Alert 3: Lessons Learned from the Crash of UA 232,* **IV.** Sioux City area's emergency responses to crash

1999   *Ann Landers: America's Confidante,* **IV.** Sioux City figures in early life of advice columnist Ann Landers

1999   *Bleeding Iowa,* **I.** A felon, Iowa Jackson, returns home to find Iowa in bloody distress

1999   *Donna Reed: Intimate Portrait,* **IV.** Biography of Denison film actress, TV star, and anti-war activist

1999   *Election,* **V.** Satire on an ambitious senior's drive to be student council president; filmed partly in Carter Lake

1999   *Freestyle: The Victories of Dan Gable,* **IV.** Documentary about Iowa's legendary wrestler and coach

1999   *Galaxy Quest,* **VI.** In this *Star Trek* spoof, Commander Taggert gets Iowa beef because he was born in Iowa

1999   *It's Yesterday Once More!* **IV.** History of state of Iowa through focus on Mason City's growth

1999   *The Straight Story,* **II.** Story of Alvin Straight, who rides mower from Laurens to Wisconsin

1999   *The Surf Ballroom,* **IV.** Documentary about ballroom in Clear Lake, site of Buddy Holly's last concert

1999   *Take My Advice: The Ann and Abby Story,* **I.** Eppie and Popo grow up in Sioux City and reconcile there

1999   *Trekkies,* **IV.** A documentary with footage of Kirk's "birthplace" and memorial statue in Riverside

1999   *Whiteboys,* **I.** White boys, hip-hop fans, disdain Iowa until their deadly trip to Chicago's Cabrini Green

2000   *Bamboozled,* **III.** A writer of the "new millennium minstrel show" is from Iowa

2000   *Cora Unashamed,* **I.** PBS drama about black maid Cora and white family in 1930s small town Iowa

2000   *Dvorak and America,* **IV.** Documentary about Spillville's influence on composer Antonin Dvorak

57

2000 *Happy Accidents,* **III.** Sam, claiming to be from "future Dubuque," charms Ruby

2000 *Running Mates,* **III.** Katie from Cedar Rapids is the youngest delegate to the Democratic convention

2000 *Silverwings,* **V.** *Star Trek* fantasy with Renaissance era setting amid Des Moines landmarks

2000 *Thirty Year Cold Turkey Reunion,* **IV.** Short documentary of return of *Cold Turkey* stars to Iowa

2000 *The True Story of the Fighting Sullivans,* **IV.** Documentary on the Sullivan brothers in WWII

2001 *Forgotten Journey,* **IV.** 1844 Stephens-Townsend-Murphy group left Council Bluffs and made it to California

2001 *Hybrid,* **IV.** Documentary about idiosyncratic centenarian who pioneered corn hybridization

2001 *Rain,* **I.** This arty melodrama set in Iowa County is perhaps the bleakest of all Iowa films

2001 *Real Time: The Siege at Lucas Street Market,* **I.** Punks hold up Davenport convenience store and take hostages

2002 *About Schmidt,* **VI.** Schmidt, retired, is replaced by a young business graduate from Drake

2002 *The Formula,* **IV.** Docudrama about the experience of making a *Star Wars* fan film in Cedar Rapids

2002 *I Spy,* **III.** James Bond-like spy Carlos is, surprisingly, from Iowa

2002 *Mr. Deeds,* **I.** A NYC television reporter pretends to be from Winchestertonfieldville, Iowa

2002 *The People in the Pictures,* **IV.** Amateur photographer documents farm life during Depression years

2002 *Picture Perfect: Iowa in the 1940s,* **IV.** Amateur photographer makes snapshots of people of Ridgeway

2002 *The Road to Perdition,* **V.** Midwest gangster-hit man has son who sees him commit a murder

2002 *Tully,* **V.** A Nebraska farmer and his two sons learn about love and sacrifice; filmed partly in Iowa

2003 *A Cop's Christmas,* **I.** *Andy Griffith* parody has Iowa humor, Christian evangelism, and realism (a meth lab)

2003 *Crank: Made in America,* **IV.** HBO documentary on three Iowa families whose lives are destroyed by meth

2003 *Cutter,* **I.** Farcical competition for lawn mowing contract at a large mall in Des Moines

2003 *Discovering Dominga,* **IV.** Algona friends/family help Denese Becker research her family's deaths in Guatemala

2003 *Legally Blonde 2: Red, White, and Blue,* **VI.** Minority whip in Congress is from Iowa; his wife just left him

2003 *Lost/Found,* **I.** A writer without hope meets a stranger who helps him give hope to others

2003 *The Music Man,* **I.** Disney remake that preserves the look of early 20th-century Mason City

2003 *Puttin' on the Glitz: The Restoration of the Sioux City Orpheum Theatre,* **IV.** Funding, craftsmanship triumph

2004 *A Century of Iowa Architecture,* **IV.** Survey of fifty most architecturally significant buildings in Iowa

2004 *Death to Mental Slaves,* **V.** Filmed in Cedar Rapids, this CD and DVD combo highlights black metal bands

2004 *For Always,* **I.** A young man, with no parents or girlfriend, follows a puzzle to confront a murderer and himself

2004 *Her Summer,* **I.** Two Iowa friends explore a crime case's artifacts; a rookie cop finds his brothers murdered

2004 *Lights, Camera, Kill!* **I.** Horror begins with a stolen snuff film; the killer gets indiscriminate revenge

2004 *The Talent Given Us,* **I.** The dysfunctional Wagners drive through Iowa en route to LA to see their son/brother

2004 *Team America: World Police,* **III.** Actor Gary Johnston, U of Iowa alum, saves world in Trey Parker satire

2004   *University Heights*, **I**. Four Iowa City men struggle with their identities and ethics in interwoven storylines

2005   *America's Lost Landscape: The Tallgrass Prairie*, **IV**. Promotes prairie restoration in Iowa and other states

2005   *Bad Girls from Valley High*, **VI**. Spoiled teen princesses prematurely age in a comedy that mentions Des Moines

2005   *The Bag Man*, **I**. A screwball horror film with a wimpy, abused video clerk who becomes a serial killer

2005   *Bonnie and Clyde: The Story of Love and Death*, **IV**. Includes a scene of Bonnie and Clyde in Dexter

2005   *Caveman: V. T. Hamlin and Alley Oop*, **IV**. Comic strip creator Hamlin grew up in Perry

2005   *Boone Style*, **I**. We see a typical dysfunctional Des Moines extended family through the eyes of 8-year-old Ruby

2005   *Eliot Ness: An Untouchable Life*, **V**. One-man show on crime-stopper Eliot Ness, staged in Des Moines

2005   *Invasion Iowa*, **I**. Bill Shatner comes to Kirk's hometown, Riverside, to shoot a movie, really a reality TV series

2005   *Iowa*, **I**. Violent, depressing love and methamphetamine story set in Centerville, Iowa

2005   *Villisca: Living with a Mystery*, **IV**. Documentary on 1912 axe murders in Villisca and the aftermath

2006   *The Bride Wore Blood*, **I**. A Sergio Leone-style mystery/suspense movie with lots of narrative twists and turns

2006   *Going to Tromadance*, **IV**. Prescribed Films' self-documented journey from Ottumwa to Park City, UT, festival

2006   *Paul Conrad: Drawing Fire*, **IV**. Passionate political cartoonist Paul Conrad has roots in Iowa

2006   *Farmlands*, **I**. Moralistic serial killer stalks teenagers on a hot night in the Sioux City area

2006   *Haunting Villisca*, **II**. Community where notorious axe murders occurred restages trial and looks for ghosts

2006   *Iowa's World War II Stories,* **IV.** Iowans who served and still survive relate their experiences

2007   *Arnolds Park,* **I.** Mystery set in Arnolds Park with formerly bullied fat boy set up for a murder

2007   *Bill's Big Pumpkins,* **IV.** Bill Foss of Buffalo, MN, brings a giant pumpkin to the Anamosa Pumpkinfest

2007   *The Final Season,* **I.** True story of Norway Tigers' miraculous 20th state baseball championship

2007   *Hall Pass,* **I.** Johnson County foster child encounters sexual predators at home and at school

2007   *The Hideout. [Il nascondiglio],* **I.** A thriller about an Italian woman who opens a restaurant in Davenport

2007   *Hollywood Dreams,* **III.** Quirky actress from Mason City aims for Hollywood stardom, despite troubled past

2007   *Indelible,* **I.** Brutal film about "failed fatherhood, loss, and redemptive powers of love"; filmed in Des Moines

2007   *King Corn,* **IV.** A documentary on economic and health aspects of corn production is set in Greene, Iowa

2007   *King of Kong,* **IV.** Documentary about Donkey Kong championship set in Fairfield

2007   *A Little Salsa on the Prairie,* **IV.** Demographics change in Perry as Latinos take jobs in meat-packing

2007   *Lost Nation: The Ioway,* **IV.** Documentary on the small Ioway tribe and the loss of its lands and culture

2007   *Michael Clayton,* **VI.** Brief Council Bluffs scene in thriller about deadly law firm and chemical company client

2007   *The Prairie Pirates,* **I.** This family comedy filmed in Orange City shows four children seeking pirate treasure

2007   *A Promise Called Iowa,* **IV.** Iowa's welcoming SE Asian refugees aided in post-Vietnam War healing

2007   *Sigma Die!* **V.** Slasher film/mystery filmed partly in Dubuque features sorority girls gone wild

2007   *Slacker Uprising,* **VI.** Michael Moore's 2004 get out the vote tour makes a stop at ISU in Ames

2007   *The Thickness of Delirium,* **V.** A depressed man travels across country to confront the day he left Utah years ago

2007   *Through the Night,* **I.** Farmhouse horror-slasher film featuring escaped mental patients

2008   *Being Lincoln: Men with Hats,* **IV.** America's Lincoln presenters gather in Mt. Pleasant to discuss their craft

2008   *Beneath the Mississippi,* **I.** Documentary filmmaker explores dangerous stretch of river, discovering terror, death

2008   *The Coverup,* **II.** Docudramatic interpretation of a man's death at Marshalltown while in police custody

2008   *Epic Surge: Eastern Iowa's Unstoppable Flood of 2008,* **IV.** KCRG covers the 500-year flood devastation

2008   *Expelled: No Intelligence Allowed,* **IV.** Stein interviews ISU prof denied tenure for espousing intelligent design

2008   *Freakin' Records Freakin' Movie,* **IV.** A concert DVD featuring three musical groups performing in Ottumwa

2008   *A Friend Indeed: The Bill Sackter Story,* **IV.** Biography of a loving Iowa City man with retardation

2008   *Legend Has It,* **I.** Low budget horror film self-consciously explores teen horror film plot formulas

2008   *The Poker House,* **I.** Agnes and her sisters live in a Council Bluffs house with prostitution, gambling, drugs

2008   *Ready, Set, Bag!* **IV.** A New Hampton woman and 22 others compete for title of Best Bagger in America

2008   *A Ride along the Lincoln Highway,* **IV.** IA highlights: Lincoln Café in Mt. Vernon, a Scranton Lincoln statue

2008   *Sister Patchouli,* **I.** "Patch" accepts her vocation, caring for Fairfield neighbors, despite her disapproving mom

2008   *Spring Break Massacre,* **V.** This slasher movie with mystery elements was filmed partly in Dubuque

2008   *Wild Combination: A Portrait of Arthur Russell*, **IV**. Documentary on Oskaloosa-reared, avant-garde cellist, composer, singer

2009   *By the People: The Election of Barack Obama*, **IV**. Admiring portrayal of 2008 Iowa campaign

2009   *Children of the Corn*, **V**. Same director remakes 1984 film, this time with Stephen King's hand in the writing

2009   *Diary of a Superhero*, **I**. In Iowa-made sci-fi fantasy, characters struggle for Book of Bizarre and to save earth

2009   *Fanboys*, **I**. *Star Wars* fans on a road trip skirmish with Trekkies in Riverside and strip at a gay biker bar in Iowa

2009   *Food, Inc.*, **IV**. A critical look at factory-produced meat; includes views of Iowa State food scientists

2009   *Landslide: A Portrait of Herbert Hoover*, **IV**. Born in Iowa, Hoover became humanitarian and US President

2009   *Megafault*, **V**. This improbable earthquake disaster movie was filmed in Davenport

2009   *Peace Patch*, **I**. Boone neighbors feud over how to mow lawns and then mediate their differences

2009   *Sam Steele and the Junior Detective Agency*, **I**. 40s-style PI Sam and friend Emma solve art thefts in D.M. area

2009   *Something Blue*, **I**. Documentary-style film shows the angst of moving from engagement toward matrimony

2009   *Star Trek*, **I**. A young James T. Kirk, from Riverside, Iowa, adventures his way into captaining the *Enterprise*

2009   *Sugar*, **I**. A young baseball pitcher from the Dominican Republic experiences culture shock in Bridgetown, Iowa

2010   *16 to Life*, **I**. A day in the life and loves of workers at an ice cream stand along the Mississippi in McGregor

2010   *2001 Maniacs: Field of Screams*, **I**. Dixie revenge fantasy with lots of gory killings and un-PC humor

2010   *AbUSed: The Postville Raid*, **IV**. Agriprocessors, Inc., and ICE abuse rights of immigrant workers

2010   *Ash,* **I.** An ex-cop and family man deals with personal nightmares of abuse while holding an abuser captive

2010   *Burlesque,* **III.** Singing waitress leaves distressed Iowa background to find family in a west coast bar setting

2010   *Brent Houzenga: Hybrid Pioneer,* **IV.** Artist/musician transforms Des Moines art, music scene

2010   *Country School: One Room, One Nation,* **IV.** Images and narratives of upper Midwest schools, some restored

2010   *The Crazies,* **I.** Toxic chemicals turn Ogden Marsh residents into violent psychopaths

2010   *Dead Awake,* **I.** Mysterious, fatal taxi accident haunts funeral parlor employee in fantasy filmed in Des Moines

2010   *Dog Jack,* **V.** Slave Jed and dog Jack escape and join a Union regiment; filmed partly in Mt. Pleasant

2010   *Driver's Ed Mutiny,* **V.** Three troubled teens hijack their driver's ed car to drive from Chicago to LA

2010   *The Experiment,* **I.** A psychological experiment gets sadistic and bloody in a facility surrounded by corn

2010   *Fat, Sick and Nearly Dead,* **IV.** Phil from Sheldon and Siong from Waterloo get healthy via juice fasts

2010   *Fell,* **I.** In horror film set in a Des Moines apartment, a man kills his girlfriend and keeps her in his bathtub

2010   *Fortnight,* **I.** Edme wants culture she feels Iowa lacks; houseguests change her views of Iowa and her marriage

2010   *Ghost Player,* **IV.** The Ghost Players from *Field of Dreams* keep the magic alive at home and abroad

2010   *Go-Bama: Between Hope and Dreams,* **IV.** A Sudanese-German man films the Obama 2008 campaign

2010   *High Times on Lower 4th,* **IV.** Sioux City's 4th St. had ritzy shopping—and bars, brothels, and gambling

2010   *Iowa's Radio Homemakers: Up a Country Lane,* **IV.** These shows created community for Iowa rural women

2010   *Janie Jones,* **I.** Abandoned by her mom, Janie tours with and redeems her has-been rock musician father

2010   *Kung Fu Graffiti,* **I.** Misbehaving Shanghai teen is sent to an Iowa ex-marine in a kung fu genre sendup

2010   *Louis Sullivan: The Struggle for American Architecture,* **VI.** Includes images of Grinnell's "jewel box" bank

2010   *A Million Spokes,* **IV.** The documentary follows individuals and teams participating in 2009 RAGBRAI

2010   *Peacock,* **V.** A train crash exposes double identity of Nebraskan John/Emma; filmed in Lorimer, Iowa

2010   *Roll Out, Cowboy,* **IV.** Saddened, populist singer tours Midwest to stir sentiment for income equity

2010   *Train to Nowhere: Inside an Immigrant Death Investigation,* **IV.** 11 dead migrants found in Denison train car

2010   *Winnebago Man,* **IV.** Outtakes of Jack Rebney's industrial video go viral, earning him fame as angriest man

2011   *Bully,* **IV.** An anti-bullying documentary features Sioux City East Middle School bullying victim Alex Libby

2011   *Butter,* **I.** Butter sculptors underhandedly compete in Iowa City and at the Iowa State Fair

2011   *Capone's Whiskey: The Story of Templeton Rye,* **IV.** Carroll County ran stills to survive the Depression

2011   *Cedar Rapids,* **I.** Naive Wisconsin insurance agent grows up at a convention in Cedar Rapids

2011   *Chasing Hollywood,* **IV.** Mockumentary about young Des Moines actors who audition in Chicago

2011   *Farmageddon,* **VI.** Government raids organic farmers; includes Vermont sheep transported to/killed in Iowa

2011   *Fertile Ground,* **V.** Horror film in which urban refugees move into a haunted home with family history

2011   *Gospel without Borders,* **IV.** Christian take on immigration focuses on Des Moines' Trinity United Methodist Church

2011   *Green Fire: Aldo Leopold and a Land Ethic for Our Time,* **IV.** Profile of an environmentally influential Iowan

2011   *Haunted Iowa,* **I.** Iowa college students document their encounter with ghosts at Villisca and other sites

2011   *Henry Wallace: An Uncommon Man,* **IV.** Documentary on Iowa intellectual, scientist, visionary, statesman, VP

2011   *Husk,* **I.** Slasher film in which young people face off against scarecrow monsters in a cornfield

2011   *Lucky,* **I.** The Iowa lottery-winning "Council Bluffs Killer" plays mind games with his scared, greedy wife

2011   *New York Says Thank You,* **IV.** NYC helps Little Sioux rebuild a chapel where four Boy Scouts died in a tornado

2011   *Sick of Larry,* **I.** Psycho-thriller: widow takes in student renters, then seems to die suspiciously

2011   *Ticket Out,* **I.** Mother, her abused son, and his sister flee with protector through Iowa to Canada

2011   *Twelve Thirty,* **I.** Iowa City family drama: agoraphobic mom, bisexual ex, two troubled daughters

2012   *America's Darling: The Story of Jay N. "Ding" Darling,* **IV.** On the Iowa cartoonist and conservationist

2012   *At Any Price,* **I.** A Churdan farmer/genetic seed salesman and his son learn the price of slippery ethics

2012   *Black Web,* **I.** Easton Denning returns to Dubuque to try to prevent his predicted death

2012   *City of Literature,* **IV.** Story of how Iowa City became one of UNESCO's three designated Cities of Literature

2012   *Dropping Evil,* **I.** A teen camping trip monitored by a mysterious corporation turns violent

2012   *Finding John Smith,* **I.** TV journalists seek in Iowa the father of a 12-year-old Iraqi war refugee

2012   *The Grey Area,* **IV.** Stories of women in Mitchellville prison receive feminist analysis

2012   *The Hope and the Change,* **IV.** Anti-Obama campaign propaganda featuring Dems disillusioned with Obama

2012   *Janeane from Des Moines,* **IV.** Fake Tea Party activist draws out Republican candidates in 2012 caucus period

2012   *The Matchmaker,* **IV.** Two Iowa City filmmakers seek love at the Lisdoonvarna matchmaking festival in Ireland

2012   *Molly's Girl,* **V.** Dramedy about lying, abuse, gay marriage politics, and loving the face in the mirror

2012   *Promised Land,* **III.** Natural gas salesman from Eldridge markets fracking until he sees the light

2012   *Smitty,* **I.** Chicago boy learns life lessons from his grandfather and a devoted dog one summer in rural Iowa

2012   *The Wedge,* **I.** July 4th comedy about Iowa City pizza delivery guy with the worst (and ultimately best) luck ever

2012   *Winning Favor,* **I.** Four boys from Orange City become state champions and good men on two different teams

2013   *American Meat,* **IV.** Iowa farmers discuss problems with industrialized farming—and organic alternatives

2013   *Bonnie and Clyde,* **I.** Retelling of the robbery and murder rampages; includes shootout in Dexter

2013   *Dear Ann Landers,* **IV.** A 1970s interview by David Susskind of Sioux City native Eppie Lederer (Ann Landers)

2013   *Caucus,* **IV.** Focused on Tea Party favorites, a detached tracking of 2012's Republican candidates

2013   *The Farm Crisis,* **IV.** Retrospective on collapse of Iowa's farm economy during the late 1970s through 1980s

2013   *The Formula,* **I.** Two engineering students develop a math formula to make themselves irresistible to women

2013   *Great Plains: America's Lingering Wild,* **IV.** Exploration of wildlife ecology visits Broken Kettle Preserve

2013   *Lost Nation: The Ioway 2 and 3,* **IV.** The continued history of the Iowa tribe in IA, WI, NE, KS, and OK

2013   *Married and Counting,* **IV.** 25-year gay partners celebrate with marriages in 7 locations, including Iowa

2013   *More Than a Game: 6-on-6 Basketball in Iowa,* **IV.** History of this popular Iowa girls' sport

2013   *Movie Star: The Secret Lives of Jean Seberg,* **IV.** Marshalltown star's life and early death after civil rights activism

2013   *Spinning Plates,* **IV.** Three restaurants profiled, one of them Breitbach's Country Dining of Balltown

Chapter 2: A Guide to Iowa Films

In this list, a "popular film" refers to a feature-length film made for movie theaters, television, direct to DVD, or Internet streaming. The literary sources, many by Iowa authors, are listed, as are Academy Award wins and nominations. Dates of films are tricky since they can have a differing completion date, copyright date, preview date (for example, at a film festival), initial theatrical release date, video release date, TV debut date, and sometimes even re-release date. We list the initial release date to the general public, generally relying on reviews in the *New York Times* and *Variety* and on scholarly databases such as the *American Film Institute Catalog* and IMDb (International Movie Database). We use here categories we introduced for Chapter 1, Previews:

I.   **Iowa Settings, Fictional Films**
II.   **Iowa Settings, Historical Films**
III. **Traveling Iowan Films**
IV.   **Iowa Documentaries**
V.   **Films Made in Iowa**
VI.   **Films with References to Iowa**

Despite the fact that most films of the 1920s and 1930s eluded our viewing, reliable historical materials allowed us to convey some sense of their narratives. We list all Iowa films for which we found accurate plot descriptions: our summaries of unseen films we derive primarily from the *American Film Institute Catalog of Feature Films (1893-1975)*, supplemented by film reviews from the *New York Times* and *Variety*. When we have not personally viewed a film, we add the notation NS ("not screened"), thus acknowledging that we rely on the descriptions of others—often being very surprised if we finally get to screen the film ourselves. Readers should know that we have not based plot descriptions for unseen films on the literary texts from which they were derived. Films seldom offer faithful adaptations.

Each section of this filmography is organized chronologically. For films of the sound era, the running time in minutes is listed. However, it should be noted that sources report different running times, depending upon the evolution from first screening at a festival to a final version delivered to video/DVD markets. Silent films must be characterized by reels, since movie projectors ran at different speeds.

For the entries that follow, the abbreviation "AFI" means that the film has an entry with a detailed plot description in the multi-volume *American Film Institute Catalog*, and "AFIs" ("s" for "short") means that AFI provides basic production information without any kind of narrative. We also list reviews from the *New York Times* (abbreviated *NYT*) and *Variety* (abbreviated *V*). The reviews from these three sources rarely offer the most insightful comments, particularly from the standpoint of regional portrayal, but they provide accurate filmographic information back to the beginnings of the film industry.

I. Iowa Settings, Fictional Films

The Strange Woman. Dir. Edward J. Le Saint. Fox Films, 1918. 6 reels, silent. Principals: Miss Billy Arnst, Ada Beecher, Gladys Brockwell, Charles Clary, Margaret Cullington, Harry Depp, Lucy Donahue, Louis Fitzroy, Gerard Grasby, William Hutchinson, Ruby Lafayette, Eunice Moore, G. Raymond Nye, Grace Wood. Literary source: William J. Hurlbut's play by the same name (1913) and the identically-named novelization of the play by Sidney McCall (New York: Dodd, Mead, 1914). [The film begins in Paris where the Louisiana native Inez de Pierrefond is recovering from a forced and brutal marriage. As a result, she writes a book called *Free Love*, which argues against marriage as a legal contract, an idea shocking even for Paris. Then she meets John Hemingway from a town named Delphi, Iowa, and he is initially repulsed by her views but becomes enthralled. After she goes as Hemingway's companion to his home in Delphi, the village gossips learn of her book and call a meeting to spread the news of her decadence. Inez turns the tables by denouncing their hypocrisy, reconciling with her future mother-in-law, and consenting to marry John after all. The review in *Variety* misidentifies Ohio as the location of Delphi. Hurlbut's play is emphatically set in Iowa and *Moving Picture World* (2 Oct. 1918, 272) identifies Iowa, several times, but changes the town name to "Delhi." NS. AFI. *V* 27 Dec. 1918, 174.

Get-Rich-Quick-Wallingford. [Alternate title: *Wallingford.*] Dir. Franz Borzage. Cosmopolitan Productions-Paramount Pictures, 1921. 7 reels, silent. Principals: Diana Allen, Mac Barnes, William Carr, Patterson Dial, Billy Dove, Sam Hardy, William T. Hayes, Horace James,

Eugene Keith, Doris Kenyon, Norman Kerry, Edgar Nelson, William Robyns. Literary source: George Randolph Chester and George M. Cohan, *Get-Rich-Quick-Wallingford* (Indianapolis: Bobbs-Merrill, 1908). [Based on the novel and George M. Cohan's play of the same name performed in New York (1910), this story begins with "Blackie" Daw (Norman Kerry) arriving in Blacksburg, Iowa, to carry off an investor scam with the assistance of a supposedly wealthy capitalist, J. Rufus Wallingford (Sam Hardy). They pretend to set up a legitimate business, fleece the local investors, and are about to skip town. Through a remarkable turn of events, their business actually turns out to be profitable. So they marry local Blacksburg women, and all ends happily.] NS. AFI. *NYT* 9 Dec. 1921, 20; *V* 9 Dec. 1921.

The Wonderful Thing. Dir. Herbert Brenon. Norma Talmadge Film Corp., 1921. 7 reels/84 min. Principals: Robert Agnew, Mabel Bert, Fanny Burke, Ethel Fleming, Harrison Ford, Norma Talmadge, Howard Truesdale. [This silent film (with elaborate subtitles) is based on Lillian Trimble Bradley's identically named play. Lively, good-hearted Jacqueline Boggs (Talmadge), daughter of a rich hog rancher from Centerville, Iowa, has been educated by nuns in France and speaks American slang with broken English to her hosts in England, the Mannerbys, a family who are "long on ancestors, short on cash." When Lady Mannerby has a stock market disaster and son Laurie forges his mother's name on a check to a blackmailer, brother Don marries naive Jacqueline for her money. Don falls in love with "Jac" during their honeymoon and can't bear to ask her for financial help after all. The Mannerby women mostly snub Jac at first until her generosity of spirit wins them over: she anonymously helps one sister fund an artistic career, gives another a makeover so she can reunite with a lost love, and sends the family drunk, Laurie, to her recovered alcoholic father in Centerville, to fight demon alcohol and help with the hogs. When the blackmailer tells Jac that Don married her for her money, her heart is broken, but she will not dissolve the God-sanctioned marriage. At this point, the film moves to Centerville, where we see the square, the train station, and the Boggs' hog operation, which is so successful that it advertises in England. Now a recovered alcoholic, Laurie tells Father Boggs how Don took the blame for his mother's stock losses and married Jacqueline to save Laurie from jail and save the family honor. It turns out dad's brother did the same for him. "Though he knew nothing of psychoanalysis," Jacqueline's father uses reverse psychology on his daughter and Don to bring them together. The film repeatedly makes hog, pig, and ham jokes. Jacqueline and her father are generous, intelligent, and good-hearted Iowans, if not especially sophisticated, in contrast to the insufferable Mannerbys who are transformed by Jacqueline's love and generosity toward them. This first film shot in Iowa is available for viewing at the Appanoose County Historical Museum in Centerville.] AFI. *NYT* 7 Nov. 1921, 20; *V* 11 Nov. 1921.

Watch Your Step. Dir. William Beaudine. Goldwyn Pictures, 1922. 5 reels, silent. Principals: Cordelia Callahan, Raymond Cannon, John Cossar, Joel Day, L. H. King, Alberta Lee, Gus Leonard, Cullen Landis, Patsy Ruth Miller, L. J. O'Conner, Lillian Sylvester, Bert Woodruff. [In this comic-romantic melodrama, a character named Elmer Slocum (Cullen Landis) gets a speeding ticket and does some jail time. Once out, he encounters a doctor with an automobile that has failed during a trip to see a patient. Elmer offers to help out, is pursued by police for speeding, and has an accident—which he believes has caused a policeman's death. To escape from the consequences, he boards a train and makes his way to Iowa, where he gets a job and meets Margaret Andrews, daughter of the town's richest man. A jealous rival and Margaret's father, who hires a detective, want to find damaging information about Slocum. At the last minute, word comes that the policeman is not dead, thus permitting the romantic pair to stay in Iowa together.] NS. AFI.

That French Lady. Dir. Edmund Mortimer. Fox Films, 1924. 6 reels, silent. Principals: Charles Colman, Theodore Von Eltz, Clarence Goodwyn, Shirley Mason. [This is a remake of *The Strange Woman* (1918). Again, the French woman who believes in liberated marriage comes to Iowa and shocks the Iowans. She is reconciled with the community and the reality of a conventional marriage after threatening to expose the hypocrisy that she has found in her new community.] NS. AFI. *V* 8 Oct. 1924.

With Sitting Bull at the Spirit Lake Massacre. Dir. Robert N. Bradbury. Sunset Productions, 1927. Principals: Bob Bradbury, Jr., Jay Morley, Ann Schaefer, Bryant Washburn, Chief Yowlachie. [This silent film, lost for 8 decades, has been remastered and a new musical soundtrack added. The screenplay was based in part on the memoirs of Abbie Gardner Sharp [*History of the Spirit Lake Massacre and Captivity of Miss Abbie Gardner, 1857* (Des Moines: Iowa Print Co., 1885)], one of the last known Indian captives. The film tells the story of pioneers in a settlement near Spirit Lake, Iowa, who are attacked by Sioux Indians led by Sitting Bull. The terrain looks nothing like Iowa, and Sitting Bull was not part of this historical event. The film takes other liberties with historical fact, including erasing the government's failure to honor treaties with the Sioux. In the film, the Mulcains, a gang of opportunists ousted from the settlement, betray the settlement to the Indians, and Sitting Bull uses the Mulcain woman's reputation as a witch to convince his tribe that the Great Spirit has ordered the massacre so that the buffalo will return and power will be restored to the Sioux. Two sisters are taken captive and eventually rescued by their devoted cowboy boyfriends. The new musical score combining Hollywood tunes, hymns, and classical music often adds a contemporary irony to the film. When the Indians raid the settlement, the stylized slaughter is accompanied by beautiful classical music. The Indians' Ghost Dance is accompanied by "All Things Bright and Beautiful." Iowa author MacKinlay Kantor based his 1961 novel *Spirit Lake* on this historical event.] AFI. *V* 3 Aug. 1927.

State Fair. Dir. Henry King. Fox, 1933. 96 min. Principals: Lew Ayres, Frank Craven, Louise Dresser, Norman Foster, Janet Gaynor, Victor Jory, Will Rogers. Literary source: Phil Stong, *State Fair* (New York: Grosset & Dunlap, 1932). Academy Award nominations: Picture, Writing. [This black and white depression-era film takes the farming Frake family to the Iowa State Fair, where Pop Frake (Rogers) wins a grand prize for his pampered pig and Ma (Dresser) scores with pickles and mincemeat. Son Wayne (Foster) and daughter Margy (Gaynor) meet sophisticated partners who provide sexual temptations and a glimpse into the world outside rural Iowa. It is an archetypal quest journey for each family member and they all return with an experience that enlarges their world back on the farm. Because the film contained a scene of passionate intimacy between Margy and her pick up partner Pat (Ayres) at the fair, a re-released version in 1936 was cut to conform more closely to Hollywood's Association of Motion Picture Producers Code (*AFI Catalog*). *State Fair* was remade twice, once as a Rodgers and Hammerstein musical with an Iowa setting (1945) and a final time with a Texas setting (1962). Fox's film negative was destroyed in a 1933 fire (Walter Coppedge, *Henry King's America* (Metuchen, NJ: Scarecrow, 1986, 90). Background shooting for the film took place at the 1932 Iowa State Fair; principal shooting occurred at Corona, California. The film is currently out of commercial circulation, but good copies are available for study through the Will Rogers Archive at Claremore, OK, and at the Museum of Modern Art in New York. Copies are sometimes sold on eBay.] AFI. *NYT* 27 Jan. 1933, 13; *V* 31 Jan. 1933, 12.

The Stranger's Return. Dir. King Vidor. MGM, 1933. 88 min. Principals: Lionel Barrymore, Beulah Bondi, Stuart Erwin, Miram Hopkins, Franchot Tone. Literary source: Phil Stong, *Stranger's Return* (New York: Harcourt Brace, 1933). [Made during the peak of Phil Stong's Hollywood career, this film explores sexual temptation in the small town of Pittsville, a fictional town that was likely the counterpart of his hometown, Pittsburg, near Keosauqua. Louise (Hopkins), an easterner, comes back to visit Grandpa Storr (Barrymore) and is drawn into relationship with married Guy (Tone), and she also finds herself in the midst of a squabble about who gets Grandpa's farm. She ends up with the farm herself, but Guy moves away to avoid destroying his marriage. King Vidor reports that the sets for "Pittsville" were painted to match the look of Grant Wood's paintings.] NS. AFI. *NYT* 28 July 1933, 18; *V* 1 Aug. 1933, 14.

Village Tale. Dir. John Cromwell. RKO, 1935. 80 min. Principals: Arthur Hohl, Kay Johnson, Randolph Scott. Literary source: Phil Stong's *Village Tale* (New York: Harcourt, Brace, 1934). [This film presents a dismal view of Iowa small towns as gossipy and full of hostilities. Janet Stevenson (Johnson) is unhappily married to Elmer Stevenson (Hohl). Elmer's brother Drury convinces him that Janet is having an affair with T. N. "Slaughter" Somerville (Scott), whom Drury hates and Janet innocently likes. Gossip leads to misunderstandings and eventually violence. Slaughter is faced with an ethical decision whether to alibi his enemy, Drury, and chooses to do so. Eventually Elmer is convinced to desert Janet, and she is able to marry the man she has always loved, Slaughter. The film mentions preparations for a religious revival.] NS. AFI. *V* 26 June 1935, 23.

Career. Dir. Leigh Jason. RKO Radio Pictures, 1939. 79 min. World Premiere in Des Moines, 2 July 1939. Literary source: Phil Stong, *Career* (New York: Harcourt, Brace, 1936). Principals: John Archer, Janice Beecher, Hobart Cavanaugh, Charles Drake, Edward Ellis, Leon Errol, Harrison Greene, Raymond Hatton, Samuel S. Hinds, Maurice Murphy. [In this drama set in small town Iowa, the leading citizen, known for many good deeds, is called upon to save a failing, depression-afflicted bank. He is confronted by an angry mob when he initially declines to make a large deposit. A subplot involves the thwarted marriage aspirations of both the virtuous father, who had lost his hoped-for bride to the incompetent banker, and his son, whose belle also chooses another.] NS. AFI. *NYT* 28 July 1939, 14; *V* 12 July 1939, 12.

Cheers for Miss Bishop. Dir. Tay Garnett. Richard A. Rowland Productions, 1941. 94 min. Principals: Martha Scott, William Gargan, Pierre Watkin, Mary Anderson, Donald Douglas, Sidney Blackmer. Literary source: Bess Streeter Aldrich, *Miss Bishop* (New York: Appleton-Century, 1933). [This is a testament to a spirited, idealistic "old maid" who sacrificially devotes her life to college teaching. Although the film does not identify the state, Midwestern College, surrounded by a corn-field, is Iowa State Teachers College, now UNI. Like the hero of *It's a Wonderful Life*, Ella Bishop (Scott) yearns for romance and travel but spends her adult life, from the mid-1880s to the late 1930s, serving her community. A fervent believer in the American Dream, Miss Bishop helps her immigrant students toward greatness, while struggling to feel her limited life has been worthwhile. The film portrays the growth of the Midwest from prairie homesteads to settled, prosperous communities. Teaching students is compared to growing corn. The location for the filming was the University of Nebraska in Lincoln, which was the city chosen for the world premiere. *Miss Bishop* was the number 8 best-selling novel in 1933 (Bowkers Annual Booksellers List).] AFI. *NYT* 14 Mar. 1941, 17; *V* 15 Jan. 1941, 14.

One Foot in Heaven. Dir. Irving Rapper. Warner Bros., 1941. 108 min. Principals: Hobart Bosworth, Jerome Cowan, Mary Field, Frederic March, Grant Mitchell, Moroni Olsen. Literary source: Hartzell Spence, *One Foot in Heaven: The Life of a Practical Parson* (New York: McGraw-Hill, 1940). Academy Award nomination: Best Picture. [This film is about a minister, William Spence (March), a man of strict Methodist discipline, oratorical skill, and devotion to his parishes. He spends his career in Iowa and Colorado during the early 20th century. The screenplay is based on a book written by the minister's son. In an especially interesting episode contributing to the social history embedded in the film, a ten-year-old in the family attends a film. Since this is contrary to church discipline at the time, the minister decides to investigate the forbidden attraction and discovers that William S. Hart's western, *The Silent Partner*, is rather engaging.] AFI. *NYT* 14 Nov. 1941, 28; *V* 1 Oct. 1941, 9.

Orchestra Wives. Dir. Archie Mayo. Twentieth-Century Fox, 1942. 97 min. Principals: Lyn Bari, Jackie Gleason, Glenn Miller, George Montgomery, Cesar Romero, Ann Rutherford. [Gene Morrison (Miller) leads a marriage-stressed band that has spent too much time on the road. Young fan Connie Ward (Rutherford) comes to a concert and impulsively marries trumpet player George Abbot (Montgomery) and takes off on the road tour. The catty older wives decide to wreck the marriage. While much of the band and all of the wives are staying in Des Moines, the connivers set up Abbot to be discovered in an apparent infidelity by his young wife. Connie travels to Iowa City and discovers him in the same hotel room with his old flame, the torch singer. The band disintegrates in Iowa as a result of the domestic furor that erupts. This film doesn't really present Iowa culture but merely uses it as the place where the fatigue of constant travel overwhelms judgment. In the end, all is properly understood, the band reassembles in New York, and the young lovers reconcile.] AFI. *NYT* 24 Sept. 1942, 23; *V* 12 Aug. 1942, 8.

Happy Land. Dir. Irving Pichel. Twentieth Century Fox, 1943. 75 min. Principals: Don Ameche, Harry Carey, Frances Dee, Ann Rutherford, Cara Williams. Literary source: MacKinlay Kantor, *Happy Land* (New York: Coward-McCann, 1943). [The father in the film, Lew Marsh (Ameche), a pharmacist in Hartfield, Iowa, grieves over the battle death of his son in World War II. Although it did not appear in the "Why We Fight" format, the film justifies the son's sacrifice through the preservation of "the happy land's" way of life. The idyllic reconstruction of the boy's Iowa life features an affectionate dog, "playing Indians" in a cornfield, young love, and lots of ice cream cones. He is also shown as instinctively generous and caring. In 1956 the 20th Century Fox Hour broadcast a television adaptation titled *In Times Like These.* Additional details about this film are provided in Appendix C.] AFI. *NYT* 9 Dec. 1943, 33; *V* 10 Nov. 1943, 34.

Keep Your Powder Dry. [Alternate title: *Women in Uniform*]. Dir. Edward Buzzell. Metro-Goldwyn-Mayer, 1945. 93 min. Principals: Laraine Day, Agnes Moorhead, Susan Peters, Lana Turner. [Three women enlist in the Women's Army Corps (WAC) and are posted to the Fort Des Moines camp for basic training, later moving on to motor pool training in Fort Oglethorpe and then officer training. Valerie Parks (Turner) is an indulged rich girl who joins the WACs to get an inheritance from her grandfather; she becomes a dedicated, successful

WAC. Leigh Rand (Day) is an ambitious, hard-nosed Army brat jealous of Parks' background and determined to sabotage her training. Ann Darrison (Peters) is the peacemaker between her volatile chums and married to a soldier fighting overseas. Agnes Moorhead has a cameo as a wise, humane WAC officer. This film includes background shooting at the WAC training center in Des Moines. A former vaudevillian turned WAC makes an off-hand remark suggesting Des Moines is not the most exciting posting.] AFI. *NYT* 12 Mar. 1945, C22; *V* 21 Feb. 1945, 8.

State Fair. Dir. Walter Lang. Twentieth Century-Fox, 1945. 100 min. Principals: Dana Andrews, Fay Bainter, Vivian Blaine, Jeanne Crain, Dick Haymes, Donald Meek, Charles Winninger. Literary source: Phil Stong, *State Fair* (New York: Grosset & Dunlap, 1932). Academy Award: Song ("It Might As Well Be Spring"); Nomination: Scoring of a Musical Picture. [This Technicolor Richard Rodgers/Oscar Hammerstein musical version of the adventures of the fair-going Frake family presents a sunnier view of life than the 1930s Depression film. The score includes the song "All I Owe Ioway." The principal romantic plot retains the suave news reporter (Andrews) who rescues Margy (Crain) from the farm, where she suffers terminal boredom from too much exposure to pigs and a boorish fiancé. This film has a happy romantic ending lacking in the 1933 version. Rather than resigning to life on the farm, Margy accepts a marriage proposal from Pat with the expectation of moving to Chicago. Ma (Bainter) and Pa (Winninger) could pass for aging grandparents in this version, and the trip is less of a quest journey for them. Yet both Ma and Pa do bring home their prizes for pickles, mincemeat, and pigs. The *AFI Catalog* indicates that shooting took place "on location at Russell Ranch, King Farm and Sherwood Forest, CA." Unlike the 1933 film, the movie musical has remained in video circulation, and its theatrical version is still performed by community theaters.] AFI. *NYT* 31 Aug. 1945, 14; *V* 22 Aug. 1945, 20.

You Came Along. Dir. John Farrow. Paramount, 1945. 103 min. Principals: Robert Cummings, Don Defore (from Cedar Rapids), Charles Drake, and Lizabeth Scott. [This comic romance with tears follows ladies' man Major Bob Collins (Cummings) and his inseparable Air Force buddies "Shakespeare" (DeFore), a teacher from small town Nebraska, and "Handsome" (Drake), a former boxer, on a war bond tour of the United States, coordinated by beautiful blonde Ivy Hotchkiss (Scott), whom they assumed was a man, I. V. Hotchkiss. At first, she has her hands full corralling these three musketeers, more interested in drinking and women than showing up for war bond rallies. By the Des Moines stop, Shakespeare concedes the competition for Ivy to Bob, and the couple gets married in San Bernardino at an air force chapel, even though Ivy knows Bob's secret: he is terminally ill with only a short time to live. The sassy playboy becomes a loving husband for his last few months, eventually flying off to London (actually Walter Reed Hospital) to die. Bob and Ivy keep their knowledge of Bob's illness secret from each other during their short marriage. Bob's buddies prove touchingly loyal comrades to the couple, banter hiding their deep love and loyalty. The new husband of Ivy's sister's leaves for overseas duty shortly after their wedding. Both sisters weigh the cost of marrying men who may soon die—a common WWII theme in the movies. The Des Moines scene has no iconic Iowa images.] AFI. *NYT* 5 July 1945, 7; *V* 4 July 1945, 8.

The Best Years of Our Lives. Dir. William Wyler. Goldwyn Productions, 1946. 172 min. Principals: Dana Andrews, Hoagy Carmichael, Gladys George, Myrna Loy, Frederick March, Virginia Mayo, Harold Russell, Teresa Wright. Academy Awards: Picture, Actor, Supporting Actor, Film Editing, Screenplay, Musical Score, Director, Special Award (Harold Russell). Literary source: MacKinlay Kantor, *Glory for Me* (New York: Coward-McCann, 1945). [Based on the Iowa writer's novel in blank verse, this film portrays three servicemen returning to fictional Boone City after World War II. Infantryman Al Stephenson (March) rejoins his loving family and gets a promotion at the Cornbelt Loan and Trust. He drinks too much and struggles with the bank executives over loans to vets. Hotshot flyboy Capt. Fred Derry (Andrews), despite his medals, finds his wife unfaithful and work hard to find. Seaman Homer Parrish (Russell) has a loyal family and girlfriend but is ashamed of the hooks that replace his missing hands. The characters represent three social classes, as well as three military branches. The film does not specify Iowa, working instead for a generic midsize city look, but clues in the book strongly suggest Boone City is Des Moines—and a symbol of the national experiences of returning vets. Kantor had worked as an opinion columnist for the *Des Moines Tribune* in 1930-1931 and in his novel used Des Moines' streets, bridges, schools, and other details as he gave substance to his vision of the place for the veterans' homecoming. James I. Deutsch has dispelled the notion that Boone City was actually Cincinnati—as suggested by some studio publicity at the time—coming down firmly for Des Moines ["*The Best Years of Our Lives* and the Cincinnati Story," *Historical Journal of Film, Radio and Television* 26: 2 (June 2006) 215-25]. *Best Years* swept the Academy Awards for 1946. In 1989 the National Film Registry of the Library of Congress added it to its list of "culturally, historically, or aesthetically significant films." In addition, AFI assigned it a rank of 37 on its 2005 list of "America's Greatest Movies." The film had its premiere in New York City.] AFI. *NYT* 22 Nov. 1946, 27; *V* 27 Nov. 1946, 14.

Johnny Comes Flying Home. Dir. Benjamin Stoloff. Twentieth Century-Fox Film, 1946. 65 min. Principals: Richard Crane, Faye Marlowe, Henry Morgan, Charles Russell, Martha Stewart. [Three Army pilots, Johnny Martin (Crane), Miles Carey (Russell), and Joe Patillo (Morgan) receive medical discharge. Johnny is diagnosed with nervous exhaustion and instructed not to fly again for at least a year. Johnny returns with Miles to their hometown of Grantville, Iowa. Finding the work in Iowa tedious, the three return to the adventure of flying in an air freight business they start in California.] NS. AFI. *V* 20 Mar. 1946, 8.

High Barbaree. Dir. Jack Conway. Metro-Goldwyn-Mayer, 1947. 91 min. Principals: June Allyson, Van Johnson, Cameron Mitchell, Thomas Mitchell. Literary source: Charles Nordhoff and James Norman Hall, *High Barbaree* (Boston: Little, Brown, 1945). [This drama is set in WWII's Pacific front. Navy pilot Alec Brooke (Johnson) and Navy nurse Nancy Fraser (Allyson), both from Westview, Iowa, accidentally meet in Hawaii and plan to marry after the war is over. Alec and Lieutenant Moore (Mitchell) are shot down and drift at sea for days before rescue. Much of the story is told as a flashback about idyllic life in Iowa while the pilots wait for rescue. Both Nancy and Alec are portrayed as dutiful Iowans with the character required for American victory.] NS. AFI. *NYT* 6 June 1947, 27; *V* 12 Mar. 1947, 12.

Hideout. [Alternate title: *Gentleman for a Day*]. Dir. Philip Ford. Republic Pictures, 1949. 61 min. Principals: Adrian Booth, Lloyd Bridges, Ray Collins, Sheila Ryan. Literary source: William Porter, "Hideout," *The Saturday Evening Post*, serialized 15 Dec. 1945-5 Jan. 1946. [In Chicago, gang leader Arthur Burdette (Collins) supervises the theft of a diamond necklace. Sending his operatives to New York—and then betraying them—Burdette takes his loot to Hilltop, Iowa, where he assumes the identity of Philip J. Fogarty, retired oil man and alumnus of Gideon College. He employs a local gem expert, Gabriel Wottor (Halton), to cut down the diamonds and then murders him. Burdette

79

is arrested just at the moment he is receiving his honorary doctorate from Gideon College. The film contrasts the red-headed femme fatale Hannah (Booth) from Chicago (one of the gang) with Edie (Ryan), a local gal with a formidable mamma. Edie takes over from Hannah as the local city attorney's secretary and then love interest. There is a mention of Cedar Rapids but few specifically Iowa details.] AFI. *V* 30 Mar. 1949, 13.

Go, Man, Go! Dir. James Wong Howe. Sirod Productions, 1954. 83 min. Principals: Pat Breslin, Dane Clark, Sidney Poitier, Edmon Ryan. [This is a biographical picture about Abe Saperstein (Clark) and his formation of the all-black Harlem Globetrotters basketball team. He finds a supporter in Zack Leader (Ryan) of Dubuque, Iowa, where the team stops during its tour.] NS. AFI. *NYT* 10 Mar. 1954, 29; *V* 20 Jan. 1954, 18.

The Pajama Game. Dir. George Abbott and Stanley Donen. Warner Bros., 1957. Principals: Doris Day, Ralph Dunn, Eddie Foy, Jr., Franklin Fox, Carol Haney, John Raitt, Reta Shaw, Jack Straw. Literary source: Richard P. Bissell, *7½ Cents* (Boston: Little, Brown, 1953). [Based on Bissell's experiences working at the family pajama factory in Dubuque, the film musical, like the 1954 stage play, delighted audiences with cleverly staged and memorable songs ("Hey There," "Steam Heat," "Small Talk") and choreography by Bob Fosse. Although the setting is identified in reviews as Cedar Rapids, only "Iowa Central" on a train car definitely points to an Iowa setting. However, the plot has some typical features of an Iowa film: an outsider-insider romance between Sid Sorokin (Raitt), the new factory superintendent from Chicago, and Babe Williams (Day), head of the Grievance Committee, a self-possessed, tomboyish blonde played by Doris Day; the picnic scene along the river; and the Williams house with flowered wallpaper, old-fashioned fixtures, and porch with swing. Unlike Iowa films that feature corn, pigs, and small towns, *The Pajama Game* captures the ambiance of Iowa's river cities with their factories and wilder lifestyles, as in the dusky café known through the song "Hernando's Hideaway."] *NYT* 30 Aug. 1957, 12; *V* 7 Aug. 1957, 6.

The Music Man. Dir. Morton Da Costa. Warner Brothers, 1962. 151 min. Premiere in Mason City, 19 June 1962. Principals: Paul Ford, Hermione Gingold, Buddy Hackett, Ronny Howard, Shirley Jones, Robert Preston. Literary source: Meredith Willson and Franklin Lacey, *The Music Man* (New York: Putnam's, 1957). Academy Award: Music

Score; Nominations: Picture, Artistic Direction, Costume Design, Film Editing. [Meredith Willson's musical tribute to his hometown, Mason City, gently satirizes the provincialism of Iowa at the time when the Model T Ford and the Wells Fargo wagon are beginning to break down the isolation of Iowa small towns. The song "Iowa Stubborn" with its framed Grant Wood scene, characterizes Iowans as stiff-necked but kindly. Salesman Harold Hill (Preston), the sophisticated, manipulative outsider, transforms River City into a place of camaraderie, music, and fun, while librarian Marian Paroo (Jones), modeled on Willson's own mother, transforms the unscrupulous con artist into a man who feels duty to others. Before it became a movie, *The Music Man* had been a smash hit success on Broadway, winning 5 Tonys in 1957 and running for 1,375 performances. The film helped in establishing its popularity as a stage show that is steadily performed by community groups, schools, and summer stock companies. In virtue of its premier status within Americana, the National Film Registry of the Library of Congress in 2005 added *The Music Man* to its list of "culturally, historically, or aesthetically significant films."] AFI. *NYT* 24 Aug. 1962, 14; *V* 11 Apr. 1962, 6.

The Hostage. Dir. Russell S. Doughten, Jr. Crown International/ Heartland Productions, 1966. 84 min. Principals: Leland Brown, John Carradine, Davey Cleaves, Ann Doran, Pearl Faessler, Raymond Guth, Jennifer Lea, Nora Marlowe, Mike McCloskey, Dick Spry, Dean Stanton. Literary source: Henry Farrell, *The Hostage* (New York: Avon Books, 1959). [Filmed in Des Moines, this movie tells the story of a boy who gets locked in a moving van driven by murderers. This film has a recognizable Des Moines area setting and had its world premiere there.] NS. AFI.

Fever Heat. Dir. Russell S. Doughten, Jr. Fever Heat Ltd./Heartland Productions, 1968. 109 min. Principals: Nick Adams, Norman Alden, Robert Broyles, Jeannine Riley, Vaughn Taylor, Daxson Thomas. Literary source: Angus Vicker, *Fever Heat* (New York: Dell, 1954). [A stock car driver, Ace Jones (Adams), who has been forbidden to compete, passes through Iowa and needs some repairs for his vehicle. He meets another driver's widow, Sandy Richards (Riley), who runs the repair garage where he stops. Ace decides to stick around and become a business partner, helping out by forcing payments from delinquent race car drivers. Conflict develops over his relationship with the widow, and fatal auto accidents at the Stuart raceway ensue before

Sandy decides to accept Ace permanently. Location scenes were shot at Des Moines, Dexter, Oskaloosa, and Stuart. Henry Gregor Felsen, the Iowa author of *Hot Rod* and other teen auto stories, wrote the novel, as well as the screenplay, under the Angus Vicker pseudonym.] AFI. *V* 15 May 1968, 6.

The Trouble with Girls. Dir. Peter Tewksbury. MGM, 1969. 97 min. Principals: Edward Andrews, John Carradine, Dabney Coleman, Marlyn Mason, Sheree North, Elvis Presley. Literary source: Day Keene and Dwight Babcock, *Chautauqua* (New York: Putnam, 1960). [Chautauqua comes to Bradford Center, Iowa, in 1927, bringing lectures ("Cannibals and Culture"), spiritual uplift by Mr. Morality (Price), and highlights from Shakespeare (Carradine). With calm and showmanship, manager Walter Hale (Elvis) handles the inevitable near-disasters: auditioning the mayor's untalented daughter, labor disputes, and the murder of a philandering pharmacist. The 1920s have brought to Bradford Center the automobile, short skirts, business prosperity, and loosening moral codes. The mayor explains that the town is broadminded: "No Klan feeling here." There are several Catholic families, he remarks, and "even a Hebrew family." A black boy and white girl perform song and dance numbers together without comment. Yet this is a town in which a woman with a bad reputation cannot get a fair trial for killing her attacker. Elvis engineers a dramatic confession at the chautauqua to get her the sympathy she would never get in a courtroom—and then provides her money to get out of town fast. This slight film is part musical comedy, part backstage suspense, and part murder mystery.] AFI. *V* 14 May 1969.

Cold Turkey. Dir. Norman Lear. Tandem-DFI, 1971. 96 min. Principals: Bob and Ray, Dick Van Dyke, Edward Everett Horton, Bob Newhart, Pippa Scott, Tom Poston. Literary source: Mac Hammond, *Cold Turkey* (Chicago: Swallow, 1969). [This TV star-studded film uses many of the familiar icons of the Iowa film as the setting for a satire that deflates the pretensions of small town virtue. Eagle Rock, IA, is presented as a community that, in economic desperation, accepts a 25 million dollar bribe to stop smoking. The attempt makes comic the citizens' vanity, greed, and hypocrisy. The "savior figure," a minister played by Van Dyke, turns out to be a manipulator who's dying to move away to a more sophisticated, urban parish. The film used many local citizens as extras, who showed gusto in ridiculing the foibles of small town Iowans. They enjoyed it so much that they later staged a "Thirty

Year *Cold Turkey* Reunion" with the cast and crew in Greenfield. That event became the subject of a 2000 IPTV documentary film.] AFI. *NYT* 18 Mar. 1971, 46; *NYT* 28 Mar. 1971, II, 1; *V* 13 Feb. 1971, 17.

A Thief in the Night. Dir. Donald W. Thompson. Mark IV Films, 1972. 69 min. Principals (for the series of four films): Duane Coller, Patty Dunning, Colleen Niday, Mike Niday, Maryann Rachford, Thom Rachford, Cathy Wellman, William W. Wellman, Jr. [This film, shot in central Iowa, was the first in the "Mark IV Prophetic Film Series," a group of four films that continues the same plot and characters through seven years of millennial experience. According to this Rapture scenario, the true Christians are taken up to heaven. This is followed by the time of tribulation for sympathetically presented, wavering Christians who struggle with the one-world government, UNITE. Sequels were *A Distant Thunder* (1978, 77 min.), *Image of the Beast* (1980, 78 min.), and *The Prodigal Planet* (1983, 127 min.). Without emphasizing Iowa culture or place names, all films show recognizable Iowa scenes in Carlisle, at the Iowa State Fair, and at Red Rock dam near Pella. *The Prodigal Planet* moves to a post-nuclear attack Omaha and concludes in the mountains near Colorado Springs. Russell S. Doughten, Jr., co-author with Donald Thompson of all four screenplays, himself appears in all films convincingly as the Rev. Matthew Turner, a good man with a millennial chart based on Revelation that helps guide those who resist taking the mark from UNITE.]

Dillinger. Dir. John Milius. American International Productions, 1973. 107 min. Principals: Richard Dreyfuss, Ben Johnson, Steve Kanaly, Cloris Leachman, Warren Oates, Michelle Phillips. [FBI agent Melvin Purvis (Johnson) vows to avenge the deaths of friends and colleagues killed by John Dillinger (Oates) and his cohorts when they escaped custody in Kansas City. The Dillinger gang leaves a trail of robberies and murders for law enforcement to follow. A Mason City bank robbery is the beginning of the end. The local sheriff and his men are prepared and kill or injure several of Dillinger's men, but the shootout leaves Mason City victims in its wake. Dillinger is finally killed in front of the Biograph Theatre in Chicago. The Dillinger gang's bank robbery is part of Mason City history, though the details differ from the movie's rendition.] AFI. *NYT* 2 Aug. 1973, 31; *NYT* 2 Sept. 1973, II, 7; *V* 13 June 1973, 16, 22; *V* 25 July 1973.

One in a Million: the Ron LeFlore Story. [Alternate title: *Man of Passion*]. Dir. William A. Graham. EMI Films/Roger Gimbel Productions, 1977. 100 min. Principals: Paul Benjamin, LeVar Burton, James Luisi, Billy Martin, Zakes Mokae, Larry B. Scott. [Based on the Ron Le Flore and Jim Hawkins book *Breakout: From Prison to the Big Leagues* (New York: Harper and Row, 1978), this TV movie recounts the unlikely success story of an East Detroit street kid, Ron Le Flore (Burton). Ron is arrested for armed robbery, but in prison he eventually changes his attitude and learns to play baseball. A fellow inmate (Luisi) convinces Tigers' coach Billy Martin (played by himself) to give LeFlore a one-day tryout with the Tigers. When Ron is released from prison a few months later, he takes the bus to Clinton, Iowa, to start his career as a professional baseball player. His teammates welcome him to "tall corn country" but warn him that the natives, not all farm people, include some rednecks who will heckle him about his past ("Ron the con"). This comes to pass, but Ron proves himself and moves on to Florida, Indiana, and then to the Tigers franchise, where he succeeds as a player and is chosen to play in the 1976 All-Star game. We see LeFlore's skill as a base stealer in the film, and we also see his ultimately unsuccessful attempts to keep his younger brother off drugs and away from the streets. The movie was filmed in Clinton.]

Ride the Wind. Dir. Russell S. Doughten, Jr. Heartland Productions, 1977. 60 min. Principals: Marty Baldwin, Maribeth Murray, Kent Petersen. [A new family moves next door to a Christian family. Both fathers work, apparently in marketing, at a factory. The sign "Grimes Hardware" on a local store seems to set the film in Grimes, Iowa, northwest of Des Moines. Eric, who has just accepted Christ into his life after foolishly trying to parachute jump from a tree, gets off to a rocky start with the neighbor boy, Alan, and they challenge each other to build and race planes with wheels. Eric and his friends build the plane from materials they beg, borrow, and do odd jobs to purchase. Alan's father, who wants to win at any cost, takes over the plane's building, and leaves his son embarrassed and ashamed among his friends. In fantasy scenes, real planes fly over the Des Moines area. After Alan's plane crashes, due to his own sabotage, he blurts out that he hates his dad, who realizes he has been wrong. Father and son both turn to their Christian neighbors for guidance, and the two gangs of kids reconcile.]

Sammy. Dir. Russell S. Doughten, Jr. Heartland Productions, 1977. 68 min. Principals: Eric Buhr, Bill Cort, Peter Hedges, Carol Locatell,

Tom McDonald. [A family feels the strain of paying bills and caring for sweet, exuberant Sammy (Buhr) whose bad leg does not keep him from bringing home every animal imaginable. His father's worries have turned him from faith in God and estranged him from his wife and children. Older brother Matt (Hedges), pressured by his impatient peers and angry father, finally snaps when caring for Sammy keeps him from an after-school job and an important baseball game. A pastor helps the family accept Christ into their hearts when Sammy disappears, locked with his cat, Moses, in the trunk of an old car in an auto graveyard. Matt's friends are newspaper carriers for the *Des Moines Register and Tribune*.]

Nite Song. Dir. Russell S. Doughten, Jr. Heartland Productions, 1978. 65 min. Tom Hoffman. Vicki Nuzum, Bobby Smith. [Filmed in urban Des Moines, this film focuses on two teens, Joe (Hoffman) and Pete (Smith), who love basketball, Jesus, and their families and neighborhood. The two boys climb out their windows at night to sit on the roof, talk, and look at the city lights. Joe sings a haunting song about heartaches and Jesus' death on the cross as his dad drinks, his mom nurses a black eye, and his sister shoots up. Pushers threaten both boys, and the pastor at the local youth center urges Joe to report them. It takes Joe's murder by the pushers, however, for his sister to seek help, his parents to reconcile, and Pete and his teammates to share their faith and courageously take action to clean up their neighborhood by setting up the pushers for arrest. The film's credits, and recognizable Des Moines footage (e.g., the state capitol building), locate the setting for Iowans.]

Dribble. [Alternate title: *Scoring*]. Dir. Michael de Gaetano. Intermedia Artists, 1979. 90 min. Principals: Freya Crane, Charles Fatone, Joseph Hardin, Peter Maravich, Gregg Perrie, Myra Taylor. [This film, which never achieved theatrical distribution, was inspired by the Iowa Cornets of Des Moines, a women's professional basketball venture from 1978 to 1980. It was financed by George Nissen, the Cornets' owner, as an attempt to popularize the sport. The story features the Vixens, a losing, bankrupt women's basketball team located in Des Moines. They join forces with a broke florist and his enterprising son in an attempt to prevent the team's eviction from their premises. The rural landscape and dreary city—relieved only by a scene at the state capitol building and a glimpse of the fountain at Banker's Trust—reinforce the film's emphasis on Des Moines as a hicksville that dooms its team to underdog status. The movie ends with a game against a surprised army men's team who expected male opponents, not female Vixens. Members of the Iowa Cornets women's basketball team, including Molly Bolin, perform in this quirky comedy. The Iowa Women's Archives at the University of Iowa contains a collection of materials related to the Cornets and the film.]

Ice Castles. Dir. Donald Wrye. International Cinemedia Center, 1979. 110 min. Principals: Robby Benson, Colleen Dewhurst, Lynn-Holly Johnson, Tom Skerritt. Academy Award nomination: Best Song "Theme from *Ice Castles*" ("Through the Eyes of Love"). [Lexie (Johnson) and Nick (Benson), an earnest teenage couple from Waverly, share skating ambitions: she to figure skate competitively and he to play professional ice hockey. Their dreams bring them together at first, then divide them when Lexie succeeds and Nick doesn't in the big world outside Waverly, and finally reunite them when Nick helps an injured Lexie learn to skate without her eyesight. The film combines teen romance, success-despite-handicap, and family conflict formulas in a feel-good tear-jerker. Iowa is presented as a handicap for the characters. While affirming the "Iowa values" of courage, hard work, and family, the film also shows it is too easy never to try, to drop out, or to live in the lonely isolation of a small Iowa town. Waverly residents will not recognize the tiny, desolate place depicted in this film as their college town.] AFIs. *NYT* 23 Feb. 1979, 7; *V* 20 Dec. 1978, 27, 30.

Heaven's Heroes. Dir. Donald W. Thompson. Mark IV Pictures, 1980. 72 min. Principals: James O'Hagen, David Ralphe, Heidi Vaughn. [The film is based on the true story of a Des Moines police officer killed in the line of duty. His wife learns of the shooting as the film opens; she struggles with grief, even though belief in salvation helps sustain her. The movie flashes back to scenes from their marriage and family life. This ordinary hero and his partner discuss the Bible and God's plan for salvation as they answer calls throughout the Des Moines area, culminating with the call that leads to the fatal shooting. Des Moines is clearly not a safe place, but Christian faith can help police officers deal with the stress of their jobs and help friends and family cope with the inevitable deaths that happen without warning.]

Whitcomb's War. Dir. Russell S. Doughten, Jr. Heartland Productions, 1980. 67 min. Principals: Leon Charles, Robert Denison, Bill Morey, Patrick Pankhurst, Garnett Smith. [The video jacket describes this Christian movie, shot in Jefferson, Iowa, as a "warm and witty satire with a serious twist." A young, principled minister, David Whitcomb, comes to a church in fictional Hurrah, Iowa, while three of the devil's minions, in red, occupy the church basement to cause trouble. The town is upset that local businessman and professed atheist, Phil Esteem (obviously "Philistine"), insists his employees work on Sunday. With humor, faith, compassion, Bible knowledge, and expert help, young David teaches his flock to love each other, solves the town's power and light problems, and saves a sheep, Esteem, who has hated God since his father died in an auto accident. Despite the earnest Christian message, the satire of small town life, especially congregational behavior, shows wit and authenticity.]

The Funhouse. [Alternate title: *Carnival of Terror*]. Dir. Tobe Hooper. Universal Pictures, 1981. 96 min. Principals: Elizabeth Berridge, Miles Chapin, Kevin Conway, Wayne Doba, Cooper Huckabee, Sylvia Miles, Largo Woodruff. [References to Cedar Falls and Fairfield set this teen horror film in Iowa. Telling her parents she is going to a movie, Amy Harper (Berridge) goes instead to a carnival with her date, Buzz (Huckabee), and two friends, Richie (Chapin) and Liz (Woodruff). Younger brother Joey follows her. The film is both parody of the teen horror genre and a genuine horror film, as it moves from Joey recreating *Halloween* and *Psycho* in an opening prank directed at his sister to real murder and terror after the couples decide to spend the night in the carnival funhouse. The Harpers are not the Cleavers: they reasonably forbid the carnival due to murders when it played Fairfield, not because they are moral crusaders. The whole family, including mom and dad, are horror fans. The teens laugh and have fun on the carnival rides, smoke some pot, and grope each other. They turn out to be ordinary kids—not the usual virgin, slut, jock, and nerd. This visually interesting creation does not present the usual Iowa filmscape, emphasizing instead its colorful, menacing carnival setting. The director earlier made *The Texas Chainsaw Massacre* films (1974, 1986).] AFIs. *NYT* 14 Mar. 1981, 11; *V* 18 Mar. 1981, 133.

Take This Job and Shove It. Dir. Gus Trikonis. Avco Embassy Pictures, 1981. 100 min. Principals: Eddie Albert, Art Carney, Robert Hays, Barbara Hershey, David Keith, Martin Mull, Tim Thomerson. Source: Song by David Allan Coe, "Take This Job and Shove It" (1977). [With a country-western score throughout, the film narrates the return of successful young preppie Frank Macklin (Hays) to his hometown, working-class Dubuque, Iowa, where he takes charge of a brewery for his corporate boss and is reunited with his good-old-boy high school buddies and his old girlfriend, J. M (Hershey). Torn between urban prosperity with its corporation politics and loyalty to his grim but spontaneous hometown, Macklin chooses Dubuque, where life is full of hard drinking, mud wrestling, rowdy football games, practical jokes, big wheel truck competitions, and lots of good fightin' and good lovin'. The usual Iowascape is here, but the emphasis falls on factory work, not farming.] AFIs. *NYT* 29 Aug. 1981, 17; *V* 6 May 1981, 20.

Face in the Mirror. Dir. Russell S. Doughten, Jr. Heartland Productions, 1988. 65 min. Principals: Michael Mitchell, Marlene Q'Malley, Brian Park, Tom Vanderwell, Scott Weir. [The film opens with outcast Danny DeMarco, suffering from a self- inflicted gunshot wound, being rushed to a Des Moines hospital. Flashbacks show that his violent cry for help culminates a series of cynical and despairing remarks that his family and friends have brushed off. While some express anger at Danny, others realize that they have not acted as Christians. One friend sneaks into intensive care and witnesses to Danny, in a coma, which leads not only to Danny's recovery but also to his giving his life to Christ.]

Terms of Endearment. Dir. James L. Brooks. Paramount, 1983. 130 min. Principals: Jeff Daniels, John Lithgow, Jack Nicholson, Shirley Maclaine, Debra Winger. Literary source: Larry McMurtry, *Terms of Endearment* (New York: Simon and Schuster, 1975). Academy Awards: Picture, Actress, Supporting Actor, Screenplay from Another Medium; Nominations: Actress, Art Director, Sound, Editing, Musical Score. [This movie has scenes set in Houston, Des Moines, Lincoln, and Manhattan. As free-spirited earth mother Emma (Winger) moves from place to place, we see how the settings contrast. Iowa is represented by kindly banker Sam Burns (Lithgow), a friendly, trusting, and sexually frustrated Mr. Rogers. The film works hard at contrasting the frozen culture of Iowa with uninhibited, space age Texas and coldly uncivil Manhattan.] AFIs. *NYT* 23 Nov. 1983, III, 18; *V* 23 Nov. 1983, 14.

Country. Dir. Richard Pearce. Touchstone, 1984. 109 min. Principals: Wilford Brimley, Levi L. Knebel, Jessica Lange, Sam Shepard. Academy Award nomination: Actress. [Gil and Jewel Ivy's family farm is threatened by mortgage foreclosure during the farm crisis of the 1980s. The film presents the harsh realities of farm life—e.g, debt, bad weather, farm accidents, hard times, alcohol, domestic violence—that can unravel the fabric of Iowa families and communities. The ending, in which Gil (Shepard) and Jewel (Lange) renew their partnership after a bitter estrangement, affirms the importance of family but represents only a small victory for struggling farmers.] AFIs. *NYT* 28 Sept. 1984, 20; *NYT* 23 Nov. 1984, III, 13; *V* 26 Sept. 1984, 15.

Wisdom. Dir. Emilio Estevez. Gladden Entertainments, 1986. 109 min. Principals: Veronica Cartwright, Emilio Estevez, Demi Moore, Tom Skerritt, William Allen Young. [This story spins out of a long dream sequence in a bathtub. A youthful John Wisdom (Estevez) dreams of responding to society's economic stresses: farm foreclosures, offshore manufacturing, joblessness, delinquent mortgages. Perpetually out of work because of a graduation night prank that resulted in a felony conviction, the dream-Wisdom decides to "become a criminal for the people." Looking backward to *Bonnie and Clyde* while anticipating *Natural Born Killers* and *Miles from Home*, Wisdom and his girlfriend, Karen (Moore), set off on a spree of raiding banks where they burn mortgages. As they work their way from LA toward the Midwest, they earn the adulation of ordinary people. Their crimes become lethal at the Roseville Market in Black Hawk County, Iowa, when a sheriff becomes suspicious. Karen panics and shoots him. They move on to Minnesota for a spectacular car chase and final shootout in St. Paul. Then the real Wisdom wakes up and shaves.] AFIs. NYT 1 Jan. 1987, 1, 9; *V* 7 Jan. 1987, 21.

The Healing. Dir. Russell S. Doughton, Jr. Heartland Productions, 1987. 71 min. Principals: James Andelin, Erin Blunt, Brian Collins, Jon Lormer, Kirk Martin, J. R. Walker, Jan Zembles-Bean. [A rising young doctor about to enter a lucrative practice ignores his pregnant wife's pleas that they work for Christ, not for material gain. When she dies in an accident, in his guilt and grief Dr. Lucas turns to alcohol. One night, in a bar on Center Street, "the most violent street in the city," John Lucas begins a series of steps that lead him, at first a reluctant Christian, to a medical practice at Bethel Mission. There he heals the bodies, and later the souls as well, of drunken derelicts, welfare children, thieves, and drug addicts. This moving drama is set in Des Moines, where, as a last frame shows, Center Street, with its poverty and violence, is surrounded by the skyscrapers of the downtown.]

Life Flight. Dir. Donald W. Thompson. International Cinema Artists, 1987. 83 min. Principals: Lynda Beattie, Michael Cornelison, Pat Delany, Patty Dunning, Jerry Jackson, Jim McMullan. [Des Moines area and Forrest City rescue squads assisted in making this film about the early days of Iowa Methodist Medical Center's helicopter rescue squad. A Vietnam veteran afraid of flying, a Life Flight nurse fighting the hospital bureaucracy for more professional staff, a born-again Christian turning to the Bible when a friend, a religious skeptic, asks questions he can't answer—all these rescue workers explore the meaning of God's will in their lives. The film creates suspense in its portrayal of accidents and rescue. A little girl, for example, plays with a gun she finds in a shoebox for several scenes before taking aim and shooting her mother. The film portrays Iowa medical and rescue professionals, many of them Christians, working together to help their neighbors. The Christian message is more subtle than in other Thompson/Doughten films, but it is the heart of the storyline.]

Miles from Home. Dir. Gary Sinise. Harvest Films, 1988. 112 min. Principals: Kevin Anderson, Brian Dennehy, Richard Gere, Moira Harris, Helen Hunt, Judith Ivey, John Malkovich, Laurie Metcalf, Penelope Ann Miller. [Though they are sons of an award-winning farmer father (Denehy), two brothers lose the family farm to the local bank. They burn the farm, hit the road, and become outlaw celebrities. Frank (Gere) becomes angry, impulsive, and violent; the despair of Terry (Anderson) is mitigated by his love for the daughter of a Cedar Rapids lawyer. Their spiteful actions are aimed at the system that leaves them helpless against predatory creditors. *Miles* was designated as an Official Selection for the 1988 Cannes Film Festival.] AFIs. *NYT* 16 Sept. 1988, C8; *V* 25 May 1988, 18.

The Shepherd. Dir. Donald W. Thompson. Mark IV Pictures, 1988. 79 min. Principals: Nicholas Ashford Ayers, Robert Ayers, Pepper Martin, Christopher Stone, Dee Wallace. [In this action movie filmed and set in Des Moines, a hotshot pilot, Lyle, after years of bitterness and dangerous risk-taking, becomes a Christian when his best friend dies due to his carelessness. His friend's wife and son struggle to forgive him, while the friend's father, Lyle's commanding officer, grapples with his own resentment of Lyle, based on a misunderstood bombing raid during the Vietnam War. The film portrays an Iowa home in which the family reads the Bible, prays, and tries to live according to the Bible's teachings.]

Field of Dreams. Dir. Phil Alden Robinson. Gordon Company, 1989. 106 min. Principals: Kevin Costner, James Earl Jones, Burt Lancaster, Ray Liotta, Amy Madigan. Literary source: W. P Kinsella, *Shoeless Joe* (New York: Houghton-Mifflin, 1982). Academy Award nominations: Picture, Adapted Screenplay, Musical Score. [Originally from Brooklyn, educated at Berkeley, Ray Kinsella (Costner) finds himself living in debt and doubt with his Iowa-born wife (Madigan) and his daughter on an Iowa farm. Voices from the cornfield instruct Ray to build a baseball field. Shoeless Joe Jackson, writer Terence Mann, Doc Graham, Kinsella's own father, and lines of cars from everywhere eventually come to Ray's "field of dreams." The marriage is strengthened through the magic of a shared visionary faith, and Ray is finally reconciled with his father. The repeated "Is this heaven? No, it's Iowa" exchange between the dead and the living became a popular bumper sticker still seen in Iowa. The site for the film straddled two different farms, which led to long running contention and competition between the respective landowners. The Dyersville site remains one of Iowa's most visited tourist destinations.] AFIs. *NYT* 21 Apr. 1989, C8; *V* 19 Apr. 1989, 24, 26.

Zadar: Cow from Hell. Dir. Robert C. Hughes. Duck's Breath Mystery Theatre, 1989. 87 min. Principals: Bill Allard, Dan Coffey, Merle Kessler, Leon Martell, Jim Turner. ["There's something in the cornfield—an evil that has no name." This deadpan introduction to *Zadar* suggests a mere satire on the 1984 *Children of the Corn.* As this amusing tale develops, we learn that its explicit theme is making films *in* Iowa *about* Iowa. Charlie "Sleepless" Walker is a Hollywood filmmaker with family roots in Howdy, Iowa—population 3,237. *Zadar* becomes an exploitative project for the entire community. The film is filled with Hollywood stereotypes of Iowa, each one deftly undercut. *Zadar,* executed by Duck's Breath Mystery Theatre of Iowa City notoriety, failed commercially and is not currently available for purchase.] *V* 8 Feb. 1989, 28.

Bix: An Interpretation of a Legend. Dir. Pupi Avati. Duea Film-Union, 1991. 100 min. Principals: Mark Collver, Julia Ewing, Emile Levisetti, Romano Orzari, Bryant Weeks. [Filmed in Chicago and Davenport, this fictionalized life of jazz legend Bix Beiderbecke presents the troubled relationship with his loving but conventional Iowa family as explanation for his drinking and early death. Told in non-chronological sequence, the story clearly shows his Midwest roots, including a large white family home and nearby Mississippi River.

91

Mom and Dad want Bix (Weeks) to "settle down" with a steady job and a nice girl; brother and sister regret the effect of his drinking and irresponsible behavior on the family. Though all forgive and take him back repeatedly, they don't listen to the records he sends or hear Paul Whiteman's orchestra play in Davenport. Presented as unimaginative, pious Midwesterners, they cannot understand, nurture, and appreciate a musical genius; they can only worry and feel ashamed. Their disapproval torments Bix. Other common Iowa themes develop in the film. In Chicago, young Bix's friends say they will "teach this Iowa boy what modern women are like." Later, friends remark on how remote and hard to find Davenport is. Bix tells his sister of trouble with a piano composition because in Iowa there is "too much silence."] *V* 13 May 1991, 105.

Sleeping With the Enemy. Dir. Joseph Ruben. Twentieth Century Fox, 1991. 98 min. Principals: Kevin Anderson, Patrick Bergin, Julia Roberts. Literary source: Nancy Price, *Sleeping with the Enemy* (New York: Simon and Schuster, 1987). [Laura (Roberts) flees a jealous, compulsive, violent husband (Bergin) and their expensive Cape Cod summer home and hides out in safe, rustic Cedar Falls, Iowa, where she develops a tender relationship with the drama teacher next door. Her vengeful husband threatens the peace and safety of her Iowa refuge, but with the help of her gentle friend from Iowa, she repels his murderous invasion. This film is loaded with an array of Iowa icons that carry messages of safety and wholesomeness.] AFIs. *NYT* 8 Feb. 1991, C10; *V* 11 Feb. 1991, 110.

Where the Night Begins [Italian title: *Dove comincia la notte*]. Dir. Maurizio Zaccaro. Duea Film/Filmauro, 1991. 94 min. Principals: Tom Gallop, Kim Mai Guest, Don Pearson, Cara Wilder. [This screenplay by Pupi Avati was shot in Davenport where a key scene is set at the Davenport Public Library. The film tells the story of Irving's return to Davenport after the death of his father, whose reputation was ruined when the young woman with whom he had an affair became pregnant and then committed suicide. The sensitive Irving would like to right past wrongs but finds himself haunted by the mysterious past and the mysterious present.] NS

Ed and His Dead Mother. Dir. Jonathan Wacks. Twentieth Century Fox, 1992. 93 min. Principals: Ned Beatty, Steve Buscemi, John Glover, Dawn Hudson, Miriam Margolyes. [Shy hardware store owner Ed

Chilton (Buscemi), of Manning, Iowa, lives with his Uncle Benny (Beatty) in a big white house. Ed, who misses his dead mother, pays a salesman from "The Happy People Corporation" of Webster City to reanimate her. Unfortunately, Mom (Margoyles), who used to bake pies and clean house, now eats bugs (and more) and takes after the locals with a chainsaw, while wearing a dress made from an American flag. She is not happy that the girl next door (not a native) is putting the moves on her son. This bizarre film creates laughs by reversing the expectations of Iowa women: the girl next door is a sexpot; mom is not June Cleaver—she wields a cleaver. Ed thought he wanted a dead-again mother but now has to kill her himself.] *V* 14 June 1993, 57.

Noises Off. Dir. Peter Bogdanovich. Amblin, 1992. 104 min. Principals: Carol Burnett, Michael Caine, Denholm Elliot, Julie Hagerty, Marilu Henner, Mark Linn-Baker, Christopher Reeve, John Ritter, Nicollette Sheridan. Literary source: Michael Frayn, *Noises Off* (New York: Methuen, 1983). [This comedy depicts an inept touring stage company whose British director, played by Michael Caine, is rapidly deteriorating. The "star" is an aging Dotty Otley (Burnett), who has financed the show with her own money. Trying to pull itself up toward a Broadway/New York quality performance, the group begins its road tour at the "Des Moines Theater." Despite a stumbling performance, the Iowa audience applauds and sends the troupe on for debacles in other provincial venues.] AFIs. *NYT* 20 Mar. 1992, 10; *V* 23 Mar. 1992, 106.

Whispers in the Dark. Dir. Christopher Crowe. Martin Bregman Pictures, 1992. 103 min. Principals: Alan Alda, Jill Clayburgh, John Leguizamo, Anthony Heald, Anthony LaPaglia, Annabella Sciorra, Jamey Sheridan, and Deborah Unger. [Filmed partly in Des Moines, this thriller features psychiatrist Ann Hecker (Sciorra), originally from Whitewater, Wisconsin, now practicing in Manhattan. While her clients' sex lives are dangerously kinky (which titillates her), she enjoys her new boyfriend, Doug (Sheridan), a charter pilot from Keokuk, "the gentlest man she has ever known." When she visits Keokuk with Doug, she admires his family home (a big white house with a front porch, naturally) and his affectionate mother who makes the couple sleep in separate bedrooms. Doug compares flying to seeing the face of God, and his Mom shows Amy the church where Doug was baptized and married. While the film contrasts Iowa's wholesomeness with the psychological and sexual dangers, secularism, and violence of the big city, we see that small Midwest towns are not all sweetness and light: Amy's father and Doug's wife both committed suicide, and Doug had an affair during his marriage. The film teases us into thinking Doug may be a twisted killer, but in the end we discover he is what he appears to be, an honest, caring Iowan with whom this former Midwesterner can build a solid and safe, if not exciting, future.] *NYT* 7 Aug. 1992, 17; *V* 3 Aug. 1992, 39.

Shimmer. Dir. John Hanson. American Theatrical Playhouse Films, 1993. 95 min. Principals: Tom Bower, Jake Busey, Marybeth Hurt, Marcus Klemp, Patrick Labrecque, Elijah Shepard. [Based on an unpublished play by John Hanson with identical title, the plot focuses on a teenager John Callahan (Klemp) who has been removed from his own home because of abusive parental behavior. He has spent much of his life in an Iowa youth detention facility, where he is called "Spacy" because of his fantasies. He befriends a new inmate, Gary Finch (Shepard), who was convicted of car theft. Together they create a code language called "shimmer" that helps them envision all the other places they would like to be.] NS. *V* 6 Oct. 1993, 71-72.

What's Eating Gilbert Grape. Dir. Lasse Hallstrom. Paramount, 1993. 117 min. Principals: Darlene Cates, Johnny Depp, Leonardo DiCaprio, Juliette Lewis, Mary Steenburgen. Literary source: Peter Hedges, *What's Eating Gilbert Grape* (New York: Poseidon Press, 1991). Academy Award nomination: Supporting Actor. [This quirky, symbolic film depicts the death of the small Iowa town. It highlights the disappearance of locally controlled retail enterprises through the coming of a franchised burger stand and a grocery store chain. The son of a farmer father who committed suicide, Gilbert (Depp) feels trapped by the burdens of aiding the survival of his family, friends, and corpulent mother in Endora, Iowa. His younger brother Arnie (DiCaprio) is autistic and creates constant problems of care and protection. After burning his house, which becomes a funeral pyre for his immovable mother, Gilbert leaves his futureless town for companionship with Becky (Lewis), a better traveled, more adventurous young woman journeying across the country in an Air Stream trailer with her grandmother.] AFIs. *NYT* 17 Dec. 1993, C3; *V* 13 Dec. 1993, 38.

The Woman Who Loved Elvis. Dir. Bill Bixby. Grossbart/Barnette Productions in Association with Wapello County Productions, 1993. 104 min. Literary source: Laura Kalpakian, *Graced Land* (New York: Grove and Weidenfeld, 1992). Principals: Tom Arnold, Roseanne Barr,

Cynthia Gibb, Joe Guzaldo, Danielle Harris, Sally Kirkland, Kimberly Dal Santo. [Set and filmed in Ottumwa, Roseanne performs the role of Joyce Jackson, a woman with an Elvis shrine on her porch. She would like to get back her alienated husband (Arnold) and also find a job. One issue to resolve is whether a welfare case-worker assigned to her will deny benefits or get her back into the work force. The second is whether her husband will return to her. This film seems to be a kind of homage to popular Elvis religion, since Joyce's good works for others in his name prove that she is a caring person, not just a nut.] *V* 16 Apr. 1993.

An American Love [Italian title: *Un amore americano*]. Dir. Piero Schivazappa. Reteitalia/Duea Film, 1994. 176 min. Principals: Carlo Delle Piane, Brooke Shields. [In this TV film, Carlo Fossalto (Delle Piane), a professor of Italian literature, spends a summer teaching at the University of Iowa, where he is welcomed by Greta (Shields), an amateur journalist and his assistant who will follow him throughout the summer. Carlo's wife is in Italy with their daughter and a sick grandchild, causing Carlo immense conflict when his friendship for Greta turns to a reciprocated love, doomed not to be fulfilled because of his obligations.] NS

Dumb and Dumber. Dir. Peter Farrelly. Katja Motion Pictures, 1994. 110 min. Principals: Jim Carrey, Jeff Daniels, Lauren Holly. [Friends Lloyd (Carrey) and Harry (Daniels) flee the East Coast in a van covered with a doggy-looking brown shag carpet. Following them are thugs who want the briefcase of money the duo plans to return to Mary Swanson in Aspen. This comedy is full of dumb remarks by the guys ("tea and strumpets"), crude, physical farce (Lloyd gives Harry a dose of turbo laxative), and some higher wit (a truck stop named "Dante's Inferno"). In Illinois they pick up a thug posing as a hitchhiker with car troubles, heading for a luncheon in Davenport. They drive him crazy with their bad singing and antics and kill him with rat poison at a truck stop located 30 miles east of the Mississippi. The police report the duo is heading west on I-80 through Iowa, but we see them on a two-lane Iowa road, passing a slow moving tractor. A sign announces they are 43 miles east of Omaha.] AFIs. *NYT* 16 Dec. 1994, B10; *V* 19 Dec. 1994, 72.

Robert A. Heinlein's The Puppet Masters. [Alternate title: *The Puppet Masters*]. Dir. Stuart Orme. Hollywood Pictures, 1994. 108 min. Principals: Richard Belzer, Keith David, Yaphet Kotto, Will Patton, Eric

Thal, Julie Warner. Literary source: Robert A. Heinlein, *The Puppet Masters* (Garden City, NY: Doubleday, 1951). [Strongly resembling *Invasion of the Body Snatchers* (1956, 1978), the principal actions of this sci-fi film are set in fictional Ambrose, Iowa (population 10,001), and at the real Des Moines City Hall. An alien craft lands in Ambrose and releases a vicious super parasite—"slugs that are using us like puppets"—that rapidly converts the entire population into wickedly obedient zombies. The parasites quickly neutralize the Iowa National Guard that comes to confront them. Soon thousands of Des Moines residents march into the hive in the basement of City Hall. The parasites have exceptionally large, powerful brains compared to the dimwitted Iowans who offer a generous launch point for the aliens' plans to take over the earth. After killing dozens of Iowans, slick urban outsiders from Washington finally plan a strategy to kill the parasites before they have conquered the entire Midwest.] AFIs. *NYT* 2 Oct. 1994, 8; *V* 22 Oct. 1994, 68.

The Room Next Door. [Alternate American title: *The Bitter Chamber*; Italian title: *La stanza accanto*]. Dir. Fabrizio Laurenti. Duea Film/ Filmauro, 1994. 94 min. Principals: Mark Benninghoffen, Thomas Patrick, Mary Sellers, Coralina Cataldi Tassoni. [In this mystery written by Laurenti and Pupi Avati, Martin (Benninghoffen) returns from Chicago in 1940 to stay at a hotel in his Iowa hometown. There, fifteen years before, his testimony against a suspect in a triple murder case led to the suspect's death in the electric chair. Now almost everyone in the town is convinced that the convicted man is innocent. Martin has trouble remembering what occurred, and he hears noises in the room next door in his hotel. All this leads Martin to an increasingly melancholy quest to discover the truth.] NS

Sioux City. Dir. Lou Diamond Phillips. Rix-Ubell Productions, 1994. 100 min. Principals: Bill Allen, Apesanahkwat, Lise Cutter, Gary Farmer, Leah Goldman, Lou Diamond Phillips, Salli Richardson, Adam Roarke, Ralph Waite. [This geographically mistitled film has a single scene set in Sioux City, Iowa, at a restaurant. Born on a reservation south of South Sioux City, Nebraska, physician Jessie Goldman (Phillips) was later adopted and raised by an affluent Los Angeles Jewish family. He returns to the Midwest to discover his Native American roots, his mother's murderer, and his true parentage. The film reveals that hidden by the myth of Midwest neighborliness lies the reality of racism that can poison romance and family life.] AFIs. *V* 25 Apr. 1994, 31.

The Stand. Dir. Mick Garris. Greengrass Productions/Laurel Entertainment, 1994. 366 min. Principals: Ruby Dee, Rob Lowe, Molly Ringwald, Bridgit Ryan, Jamey Sheridan, Gary Sinese, Adam Storke, Billy L. Sullivan, Ray Walston. [Literary source: Stephen King, *The Stand* (New York: Doubleday, 1978). This four-part TV film shows an accident at a military facility that unleashes a deadly strain of flu virus that kills nearly everyone in the United States within days. The survivors are haunted by dreams of a 106-year-old, god-fearing African-American woman from Nebraska and/or a threatening dark figure hailing from hell. Those with hearts of gold, even if not professing Christians, travel to Nebraska, and from there to Boulder, Colorado, to make plans for a stand against the forces of evil in an apocalyptic confrontation at Las Vegas. Midway through the film, we have a scene set just outside a destroyed Des Moines in which one of the future hero martyrs, Larry (Storke), sings "The Eve of Destruction" and joins forces with Lucy Swann (Ryan) and a "feral child," Joe (Sullivan), from Iowa City, the three eventually forming a family. A pregnant Lucy and Joe are two of the few left alive at the film's end. In this heavily Christian movie, the forces of good seem to be found in a modest farmhouse in Nebraska, while the forces of evil, represented by rats, are located in the surrounding corn. The Iowa scenes were not shot in Iowa. Stephen King has a cameo role as Teddy, one of the good guys.]

The Bridges of Madison County. Dir. Clint Eastwood. Amblin/ Malposo, 1995. 135 min. Principals: Clint Eastwood, Meryl Streep. Academy Award nominations: Actor, Actress. Literary source: Robert Waller, *The Bridges of Madison County* (New York: Warner, 1992). [This romantic drama portrays the four-day love affair between a worldly *National Geographic* photographer (Eastwood) and an Italian-born Iowa farm wife (Streep). He awakens erotic passions in her that had died on the Iowa farm. Although she feels stifled by rural Iowa culture, Francesca Johnson chooses to end the affair and stay with her family. However, she and Robert Kincaid remain faithful in their memory of one another until death. The posthumously revealed story of their affair at the farmhouse ultimately transforms the lives of Francesca's children. Much of the film was shot at "Francesca's House" near Winterset, which became a significant tourist site until it was damaged by arson in 2003. Waller's book was the *New York Times* Number 1 best seller in 1993 and reportedly sold more than 50 million copies worldwide. A 2014 Broadway musical based on the film and book received 4

Tony nominations and two wins for Best Score and Best Orchestration.] AFIs. *NYT* 2 June 1995, C4; *V* 22 May 1995, 91, 96.

The Last Supper. Dir. Stacy Title. The Vault, Inc., 1995. 92 min. Principals: Cameron Diaz, Ron Eldard, Annabeth Gish, Jonathan Penner, Ron Perlman, Courtney B. Vance. [Set in a town with graduate university programs, this film makes several references that establish an Iowa setting. The five liberal graduate students carry disciples' names: Jude, Marc, Luke, Pete, and Paulie. They invite a belligerent Marine vet from Desert Storm to dinner and end up killing him after exchanging insults and threats. While still recovering from the shock of their first murder, the students invite a series of vocal right-wingers to dinner with the plan to kill them and plant them in their garden—but only if the guests prove resistant to their leftist attitudes. The film is a parable about extremism, freedom, and intolerance. The message seems to be that extremism can happen anywhere, even in Iowa. Though the film accurately presents contemporary Iowa with conservatives and liberals living as neighbors, there is no attempt to show that Iowa culture itself promotes the vicious killings.] AFIs. *NYT* 15 Apr. 1996, C12; *V* 2 Oct. 1995, 42-43.

Mommy. Dir. Max Allan Collins. MAC Productions, 1995. 89 min. Principals: Majel Barrett, Michael Cornelison, Rachel Lemieux, Patty McCormack, Jason Miller, Brinke Stevens. Literary source: Max Allan Collins, "Mommy," in Jeff Gelb, ed., *Fear Itself* (New York: Warner, 1995). [The "Mommy" of the title is Mrs. Sterling (McCormack), a beautiful, stylishly dressed Muscatine woman suspected of murdering her previous husbands for their money. She also murders Mrs. Withers (Barrett), the teacher of her beloved daughter, Jessica Ann (Lemieux), for daring to give an outstanding student award to a Mexican-American child. She murders her boyfriend when he is revealed to be an insurance investigator and nearly strangles her own daughter. The police arrest her and send her to death row. The film has the mood of a campy horror film, achieved in part by inside jokes about that tradition and its stars. The real Muscatine, near the Quad Cities, and the surrounding area provide the setting. Max Allan Collins expanded the original short story into a novel with an identical title (New York: Leisure Books, 1997).]

A Mother's Gift. [Alternate title: *A Lantern in her Hand*]. Dir. Jerry London. RHI Entertainment, 1995. 90 min. Principals: Lucy Deakins, Jeremy London, Nancy McKeon, Adrian Pasdar, Adam Storke. [Based on the 1928 novel *A Lantern in Her Hand* by Iowa/Nebraska writer Bess Streeter Aldrich, this CBS TV film follows the life of Abbie McKenzie Deal (McKeon), an Iowa teacher who relinquishes her dream to study opera in New York City to follow her farmer-husband, Will (Pasdar), to the uninhabited Nebraska frontier after he returns from the Civil War. A rich suitor with plans to be a doctor in a city had persistently courted her during the war, but she marries Will instead, choosing love and a challenging life. The former suitor turns up 10 years later in Nebraska.] NS.

Harvest of Fire. Dir. Arthur Allan Seidelman. Hallmark Hall of Fame, 1996. 111 min. Principals: Tom Aldredge, Lolita Davidovich, Patty Duke, Jean Louisa Kelly, J. A. Preston, James Read, Craig Wasson. [An Amish community in Palmersfield, Iowa, experiences four cases of arson directed at barns. A glamorous and culturally naive FBI agent Sally Russell (Davidovich) is sent to investigate and teams up with the African-American sheriff who guides her initially insensitive and patronizing investigation. She is led first to the family of Annie Beiler (Duke), who experienced the first barn fire during a wedding celebration. The Amish of this film are pious, stiffly protective of their customs, and distrustful of interventions by "the English," their term for outsiders. Through Annie, Agent Russell learns to respect the Amish, while Annie reciprocates by cooperating with an outsider who wants to apprehend the arsonist. The film becomes a dialogue between the values of contemporary urban, national culture and those of the Iowa Amish. Each gives something to the other.] *NYT* 19 Apr. 1996, 20.

Kingpin. Dir. Peter Farrelly and Bobby Farrelly. Rysher Entertainment, 1996. 113 min. Principals: Vanessa Angel, Woody Harrelson, Bill Murray, Randy Quaid. [We first see Roy Munson (Harrelson) in 1969 at his clean, wholesome, attractive hometown, Ocelot, Iowa. Nurtured by his loving dad, Roy is a boy with prospects as a bowler. He later wins the 1979 Iowa Amateur Bowling Championship. When he meets con artist bowler Ernie McCracken (Murray), he ends up losing a hand, his self-respect, and more than a decade spent boozing. This often crude comedy takes Roy on a journey with a naive, hulking Amish man, Ishmael (Quaid), and an attractive young women, Claudia (Angel), who has been around and been knocked around. Eventually Roy wins love, friendship, and self-respect, even though he loses a bowling championship in Reno to the despicable McCracken. Roy and Claudia stop at Ocelot in the 1990s and find the town is now a dump—the once popular P & J Soft Serve is now a broken down shack; Roy's home is abandoned and his father dead. Interestingly, at the end of the movie, Roy donates $500,000 earned as a spokesperson for a condom company to help save Ishmael's Amish community but not to restore his hometown in Iowa.] AFIs. NYT 26 July 1996, 18; *V* 22 July 1996, 49-50.

Michael. Dir. Nora Ephron. Turner Pictures, 1996. 105 min. Principals: Teri Garr, Bob Hoskins, William Hurt, Andie MacDowell, Robert Pastorelli, Jean Stapleton, John Travolta. [With a setting in mythical Stubbs, Iowa, this film merges the romance, the pilgrimage/road formula, and the story of a miracle from on high. The *National Mirror* is a supermarket tabloid that sends an improbably joined quartet of investigators, including a dog, to "the middle of nowhere" for a report on an angel. Landing in rural Iowa's Milk Bottle Motel, advertised by a giant bottle, they discover that its owner, an elderly lady, is living with the charming but rather disheveled fallen Archangel Michael (Travolta). Hurt and MacDowell play the emotionally skittish reporters whose journey across the barren heartland, orchestrated by Michael, will eventually lead them to realize that "love is all you need." Hollywood's Iowascape here is familiar, with rolling hills of corn stubble, churches, flags, small cafes, buckle-busting meals, and dumpy interiors. This rural countryside is a place of faith, miracles, and love; significantly, Michael collapses and sheds his feathers as the group enters Chicago. The region's cultural tastes are represented by the World's Largest Ball of Twine, not invented for this film, but likely located in Darwin, Minnesota, or Cawker, Kansas, whose cities both make the claim. And just a tad across the state line in the film's version of Illinois is The World's Largest Teflon Frying Pan—actually in Maine.] AFIs. *NYT* 24 Dec. 1996, C18; *V* 23 Dec. 1996, 40.

Boy's Life 2. Strand Releasing, 1997. With a 17 min. segment "Alkali, Iowa." Dir. Mark Christopher. Wildwood Productions, 1995. Principals: J. D. Cerna, Marybeth Hurt. ["Alkali, Iowa" is a coming-out story with an Iowa setting. A young farmer, Jack Gudmanson (Cerna), unearths a lunchbox full of male erotica buried in a cornfield. He gradually deduces that his father had assumed a gay identity hidden from Jack and his sister. In painful conversations with Jack's mother and grandfather, they fiercely attempt to "bury the secret." As Jack explores his father's past and begins to acknowledge his own attraction to men, we get glimpses of a rural gay culture, including the familiar seed corn caps and pickups.] AFIs. *NYT* 7 Mar. 1997, 12; *V* 10 Mar. 1997, 79.

I'll Be Home for Christmas. Dir. Jerry London. Jaffe/Braunstein Films, 1997. 100 mins. Principals: Ashley Gorrell, Robert Hays, Ann Jillian, Jack Palance. [This Christmas romance, filmed in Canada, is set in St. Nicholas, Iowa, a town with a sign that advertises "The World's Largest Hay Bale." The town is experiencing a crisis because its aged doctor has died and the hospital is being managed by the local veterinarian, Sarah (Jillian). She also heads the town council, who lament that we are "too remote—we need more people," while one member provincially adds that "people don't know paradise when they see it." The romantic and a medical solution appears when a former resident, Michael (Hays), now a big city doctor, experiences disabling anxiety attacks because of lingering sorrow over the earlier death of his wife. Visiting his father (Palance) in St. Nicholas for Christmas, he reluctantly falls in love with the vet, his high school sweetheart, while his daughter falls in love with the pregnant family pig and her formerly feared grandfather. After more stress in the city as his career fizzles out there, Michael returns to St. Nicholas and rescues the hospital.]

Mommy's Day. Dir. Max Allan Collins. MAC Productions, 1997. 88 min. Principals: Michael Cornelison, Rachel Lemieux, Patty McCormack, Jason Miller, Paul Petersen, Brinke Stevens. [A continuation of *Mommy*, this film begins with an unsuccessful attempt to execute Mrs. Sterling (McCormack) by lethal injection. After an improbable rehabilitation, Mommy attempts to communicate with her daughter, Jessica Ann. A series of additional murders and plot twists follows. Although this film was shot entirely on location in Coralville, Iowa City, Muscatine, and other eastern Iowa locations, explicit references to place in this script are muted. Paul Peterson, who grew up in Iowa and played Donna Reed's son in the television series, appears as an overzealous true crime writer married to Mrs. Sterling's sister, Beth. Max Allan Collins wrote a novel with identical title based on the film (New York: Leisure Books, 1998).]

A Thousand Acres. Dir. Jocelyn Moorhouse. 1997. 104 min. Principals: Kevin Anderson, Keith Carradine, Colin Firth, Pat Hingle, Jennifer Jason-Leigh, Jessica Lange, Michelle Pfeiffer, Jason Robards. Literary source: Jane Smiley, *A Thousand Acres* (New York: Knopf, 1991). [Based on the Pulitzer Prize-winning novel, the film is squarely set in Iowa farm culture, a set of legal and agricultural practices as well as a way of life. When a proud, rich, aging patriarch Larry Cook (Robards) divides his land among his daughters, a tragedy, rooted in greedy farm and family practices of the past, begins its spiral of destruction, paralleled by the tragedy of a neighboring farm patriarch and his two sons. Unlike Shakespeare's *King Lear*, the film focuses on the younger generation as victims and ends without significant achievements of self-knowledge or reconciliation. Rural Iowa is shown as a non-pastoral place of incest and environmental poisons—perhaps the reason for its box office failure.] AFIs. *NYT* 19 Sept. 1997, E12; *V* 15 Sept. 1997, 69.

Touch. Dir. Paul Schrader. Lumiere International, 1997. 96 min. Principals: Tom Arnold, Conchata Ferrell, Bridget Fonda, Janeane Garofalo, Skeet Ulrich, Christopher Walken. Literary source: Elmore Leonard, *Touch* (New York: Arbor House, 1987). [In this film and in *Hardcore*, Schrader depicts Southern California's moral corruption, but here he uses satire. Ulrich plays Juvenal, an ex-priest with stigmata who may or may not have healing powers but becomes a celebrity thanks to the media machinations of Bill Hill (Walken). Tom Arnold plays a zealous crusader who leads a group called OUTRAGE, determined to restore traditional Roman Catholicism, including Latin masses. The film presents Juvenal and girlfriend Lynn Marie Faulkner (Fonda) ambiguously. Does she love him, or is she using him? Is he a sincere healer/do-gooder with doubts about organized religion, or is he part of a media deception? Regardless, the two flee LA at film's end, and we see them crossing over from Nebraska ("The Good Life") into Iowa. Earlier, Juvenal had suggested they go to "Denver, Detroit, or Des Moines." Sick of the celebrity/money/media culture of California, they yearn for a saner place.] AFIs. *NYT* 14 Feb. 1997, B5; *V* 10, Feb. 1997, 63.

Overnight Delivery. Dir. Jason Bloom. Motion Picture Corporation of America, 1998. 88 min. Principals: Larry Drake, Paul Rudd, Christine Taylor, Reese Witherspoon. [Minnesota college student Wyatt Trips (Rudd), egged on by a college student/stripper Ivy (Witherspoon) he meets during a drinking bout, sends an insulting overnight mail letter to his longtime girlfriend, Kimberly, whom he thinks has been unfaithful to him. When Kim tells him he is mistaken, he and Ivy take a road trip to Memphis to stop the overnight delivery. The couple, and the delivery truck driver, have a series of farcical mishaps during the trip, but all arrive at the University of Memphis in time. Though filmed entirely in Minnesota, the movie has fun with state stereotypes. In Minnesota, a restaurant is named "Shorty and Swede's." A cheesy cowgirl welcomes visitors to Tennessee, and we see a giant Elvis balloon at the U. of Memphis dorm. A sign with huge ears of corn announces the

Iowa state line. After failing to catch a plane at the Des Moines airport, the couple stops at a hotdog stand shaped like a pig. On the way out of the state, they see a big billboard with cutout figures of a farmer and his wife, perhaps an allusion to Grant Wood's "American Gothic."]

Bleeding Iowa. Dir. Stephen Goetsch. Spur of the Moment Pictures, 1999. 97 min. Principals: Justin Lauer, Gretchen Morgan, Barbara Roberts, David Schultz, Heather Waters. [Son of a farmer and respected state legislator, Iowa Jackson (Lauer) ran away and ended up in prison for life, having taken money to kill a banker's son. Now an FBI agent has allowed him to escape for two days to find a stash of money hidden in a creek near the old family farm. Ellie (Waters), daughter of a workaholic farmer, chooses to join forces with Iowa, even knowing the dangers, rather than stay home, safe but bored. This film's state of Iowa foregrounds dirt roads, trucks, farmsteads, farmers with guns, and acres of corn. Iowa's closest friend in his hometown of Jackson Junction is an African-American woman, Mama Joe Roberts, whose café full of antiques has the slogan "Eat and Reminisce"—fitting for a film that associates Iowa squarely with the farming past. The film blends pastoral and anti-pastoral views of Iowa. "Bleeding Iowa" may refer to the film's violence, to the damaged hearts of the romantic pair on the lam, or to the state's economic anemia. "I will not allow the bleeding of Iowa to continue," Iowa Senator Brice repeats as his campaign slogan, but he is only interested in winning the election, not saving his beautiful, tragic state.]

Take My Advice: The Ann and Abby Story. Dir. Alan Metzger. Freyda Rothstein Productions, 1999. 90 min. Principals: Robert Desiderio, Kip Gilman, Wendie Malick. [This Lifetime movie about the two rival advice columnists, identical twins Ann Landers (Eppie) and Abigail Van Buren (Popo), begins in Sioux City when they were 20 and ends at their 40th high school reunion there. Filmed in Portland, Oregon, the real Sioux City Central High School, known as the Castle on the Hill, looks nothing like the ordinary elementary school in the movie. The film has a few local details: it refers to the girls' college newspaper column "The Campus Rat," which they wrote while Morningside College students, and establishes that they were part of a significant Jewish community in Sioux City in the 1930s by showing their double wedding and their mother's funeral performed by a rabbi. Wendie Malick plays both twins, nicely distinguishing the two, even in their early years when their sameness was their uniqueness. As the film develops,

103

the screenplay focuses more on Ann, the differences wealth and poverty made in the twins' early adulthood, the rivalry between the sisters as columnists, the success and importance of their columns, and Ann's marriage eventually falling apart. Esther Pauline and Pauline Esther Friedman are two of Iowa's celebrity successes.]

Whiteboys. [Alternate title: *Whiteboyz*]. Dir. Marc Levin. Offline Entertainment, 1999. 89 min. Principals: Eugene Byrd, Danny Hoch, Dash Mihok, Piper Perabo, Mark Webber. Source: based on characters created by Danny Hoch. [White boys wearing hip-hop fashion and rappin' about ghetto life in rural Holyoke, Iowa, are surrounded by the usual icons of pickup trucks, corn, abandoned barns, and gravel roads, making audiences think that they are in for a comedy, but they are wrong—about *this* Iowa and the movie. This film takes us to real Iowa that has telemarketing, factory layoffs, families on food stamps, malls, kids making college plans, kids dealing drugs, and a mix of social classes represented by various styles of homes. The trio of white rappers—trying to escape from poverty, middle class pampering, and a demeaning job at a fast food place are out of place at home. But they are dangerously so after arriving at Chicago's Cabrini Green with an affluent black friend Khalid (Bird). They want to make a big dope deal with a mere $160. More subtle and complex than it first appears, this film comments shrewdly on race and class and reveals the alienation from mainstream culture that converts so many young white boys into fans of rap music. It also makes fun of the affectation of underclass consciousness. "Even though I live in Iowa, I've still got the ghetto in my heart," Flip declares.] *NYT* 8 Oct. 1999, E22; *V* 27 Sept. 1999, 44, 46.

Cora Unashamed. Dir. Deborah M. Pratt. WGBH Boston and Alt Films, 2000. 95 min. Principals: Michael Gaston, Molly Graham, Cherry Jones, Ellen Muth, Kohl Sudduth, Arlen Dean Snyder, Regina Taylor. Literary source: Langston Hughes story, "Cora Unashamed" in *The Ways of White Folks* (New York: Knopf, 1934). [This work in PBS Masterpiece Theatre's new American Collection series was produced by Iowa native Marian Rees and filmed in Cambridge and State Center. The housekeeper Cora Jenkins (Taylor) comes from the only African-American family in fictional Melton, Iowa. Cora's belief in love and refusal to feel shame for giving birth to an illegitimate child with a white man contrast with the character of the wife and mother, Lizbeth Studevant (Jones), for whom Cora works. Mrs. Studevant's self-centeredness, social climbing, and class prejudices lead to an unsentimental tragedy for the Studevant family that Cora tries to prevent. This film pictures the growth of small towns in Iowa in 1930s—with the coming of autos, washing machines, gas ranges, dairies, and immigrants. The film exposes the same stifling sense of rigid respectability and moral cowardice beneath the surface cordiality of growing Midwest small towns that Sinclair Lewis described in Main Street (1920). A rare wisdom about human complexity underlying the film is that Cora is no saint and Lizbeth no monster: one chooses to live unashamed on her own terms; the other lives as a prisoner of her shame.] V 23 Oct. 2000, 54.

Rain [Alternate tile: *Luvia*]. Dir. Katherine Lindberg. Antena 3 Television, Cappa Films, Kinowelt Filmproduktion, 2001. 97 min. Principals: Jo Anderson, Diane Ladd, Kris Park, Jamey Sheridan, Melora Walters. [This extremely bleak portrayal of life in a rural small town in Iowa County lists Martin Scorsese as one of the producers. With arty pretensions, a slow pace, and little dialogue, *Rain* shows us a no-hope town with failing farms, polluted water, a dreary townscape, bored teens, despairing adults, and freight trains barreling past day and night. (The Casey's store is the only colorful place.) The melodramatic plot focuses on the mentally disturbed Ellen who blasts her philandering husband with a rifle at the film's beginning. Assisted by Richard Biddle, aimless son of the local sheriff, Ellen deposits his garbage bag-wrapped body in a stream. Young Richard kills and robs his despairing stepmother so he and Ellen can be together, he thinks, but Ellen, having learned that Richard is her own son, sets fire to the deserted barn where Richard is inside incinerating the car with the body of his dead stepmother. The sheriff running for mayor gives a speech to an unenthusiastic rally in which he articulates the hope that something can be done to stop corporations from destroying local farming and to give people a reason to stay. Iowa County on Richard's birth certificate is the only mention of the Iowa setting. The film won a cinematography award in Sweden and was released in Europe as well as the US.]

Real Time: The Siege at Lucas Street Market. Dir. Max Allan Collins. Troma DVD, 2001. 72 min. Principals: Michael Cornelison, Larry Coven, Rachel Lemieux, Brinke Stevens. Literary source: Max Allan Collins' story "Inconvenience Store" in *Deadly Allies II: Private Eye Writers of America and Sisters in Crime Collaborative Anthology* (New York: Doubleday, 1994). [This film is set in a Davenport convenience store and shot through security videos and police cameras that constantly provide multiple views of the scene. It depicts a dumb punks cash register robbery that turns bad when a sick cop stumbles into nervous gunfire and fires. Suddenly several customers are hostages, and the drama focuses on negotiation and escape. The tables are turned by a pregnant off-duty police detective who calmly outsmarts the two punks. This direct-to-DVD production offers angle-button perspective switches throughout the film.]

Mr. Deeds. Dir. Steven Brill. Columbia Pictures, 2002. 91 min. Principals: Conchata Ferrell, Peter Gallagher, Winona Ryder, Adam Sandler, John Turturro. Literary source: Clarence Buddington Kelland, "Opera Hat," published in *American Magazine*, 1935. [Based loosely on Kelland's story and the 1936 Capra classic *Mr. Deeds Goes to Town*, this movie contrasts the Big Apple with the small towns of Mandrake Falls, New Hampshire, Deeds' (Sandler) hometown, and Winchestertonfieldville, Iowa, where TV tabloid reporter Babe Bennett (Ryder) claims to have grown up. Really a Long Island native, Babe concocts a description of Winchestertonfieldville that, to her surprise, turns out to be partially true. It does have a corner drugstore and a white house with a red door, blue shutters, and a tire swing. Deeds and Babe's Iowa alter ego "Pam Dawson" fit the small town model: he hugs, writes corny greeting cards, punches out muggers and snobs, and shows kindness and tolerance. "Pam" is a school nurse who doesn't drink; she doesn't even eat rum raisin ice cream. The film shows small town people as uncultured. In contrast, the New Yorkers are shown as greedy, slick, scornful, snobby, and sleazy. As in the more inspired original, small town values prevail.] AFIs. *NYT* 28 June 2002, 1; *V* 17 June 2002, 23, 48.

A Cop's Christmas. Dir. Dan Nannen. Walnut Creek Community Church, 2003. Approx. 60 min. Principals: Dave Andorf, Becky Crane, Mike Fry, Doug Olson, Rod Van Raden. This Iowa-made film with local actors blends parody of *The Andy Griffith Show* with a message about accepting Christ into one's life. Clumsy, lonely loser "Benny Rife" barely passes his police cadet training and begins his law enforcement career in Dunnville, Iowa (actually Adel), under the mentorship of Chief "Sandy Taylor" who is amazed and irritated by his mistakes but refuses to fire him. Instead, she befriends him, takes him to church, and shares her Christian beliefs with him. Combining humor with Christian evangelism, the film has references that clearly establish the Iowa setting, and the Adel shooting location is recognizable. The film's view of Iowa is predominantly pastoral, but the turning point for Benny is the explosion of a meth lab, indicating realities in small town Iowa.]

Cutter. Dir. Charlies Matthes. Matthes and Harlow, 2003. 81 min. Principals: Charlie Matthes, Mike Doyle, Kristen Gass, J. P. Richardson, Aaron Smith, Steve Pilchen. [This adult comedy depicts a rivalry between lawn companies for the contract at a large Midwestern mall, that physical role being played by Southridge Mall in Des Moines. The scenes look generic Midwestern, and no effort is made to indicate that events are happening in Iowa. Joe Watson (Matthes) is the honest, clean living proprietor of Turfs Up (the name of an actual Des Moines enterprise), and he has happy customers. Kenny Whitehead (Pilchen) is the profane, cigar smoking, dressed-in-black Mr. Big who aspires to a five-state dominance. He is willing to cheat, undercut on price, and hire off-the-street laborers to kill Turfs Up's chances for the big mall contract. "You mess with the bull, you get the horns," he remarks about his despicable tactics. Clean and true Joe wins here, and the extra prize is some romantic fulfillment between Joe and Jackie (Gass). Another bonus is that Joe's alcoholic, Hollywood star brother does real work for a change in the big mowdown at the mall.]

Lost/Found. Dir. Scott Beck. Bluebox Limited., 2003. 70 min. Principals: Greg Bouljon, Ken Lue, Christina Lundt, Justin Marxen, Travis Shepherd. [Shot in all four of the Quad Cities, this video begins with recognizable scenes from the area, and throughout the film we see the Mississippi River as a backdrop for scenes showing despair and redemption. The central character, Keith Johnson, who at eight lost his parents in an airplane crash, is a would-be writer who spends his days on a park bench writing his observations but never connecting with anyone. A red-haired stranger begins giving him envelopes with artifacts and advertisements that lead Keith to find depressed people who are haunted by their interconnected past lives. By listening and making a suggestion or two, Keith leads most to take steps to reconnect with important people in their lives—and, in the process, he finds hope for his own life. The picture of life in the Quad Cities acknowledges real problems that Iowans and people everywhere face: grief, disillusionment, drugs, divorce, abuse, violence, isolation, and despair.]

The Music Man. Dir. Jeff Bleckner. Touchstone Television/Walt Disney Pictures, 2003. Principals: Clyde Alves, David Aaron Baker, Matthew Broderick, Kristin Chenoweth, Victor Garber, Cameron

Monaghan. 150 min. Literary source: Meredith Willson and Franklin Lacey, *The Music Man* (New York: Putnam's, 1957). [This Disney edition of Willson's popular musical was filmed in Canada, but the producers developed the River City setting through study of photographs from early twentieth-century Mason City. The group dancing and singing are graceful, and the stars playing Harold Hill (Broderick) and Marian Paroo (Chenoweth) are energetic; production values reflect the $15 million investment. The film retains Iowa's stiff-necked provincialism and gullibility that let the outsider-con man work redeeming magic on the natives, while, at the same time, undergoing a transformation himself.]

For Always. Dir. Byran Woods. Bluebox Limited, 2004. 76 min. Principals: Melissa Goode, Ian Klink Justin Marxen, Ian Klink. [This film jumps back and forth between two storylines. David is an unhappy, insecure, often harassed teen with a crush on a girl. Andrew's parents were killed three years before, and his girlfriend has left him. He receives 13 photos of a crime scene that lead him to confront the murderer—and himself. The film was shot in Bettendorf, Davenport, and West Branch in a style that pays homage to Alfred Hitchcock and M. Night Shyamalan.]

Her Summer. Dir. Bryan Woods. Bluebox Limited, 2004. 80 min. Principals: Justin Marxen, Travis Shepherd, Shane Simmons. [This straight-to-DVD, low budget film, shot in Davenport and Bettendorf, was written by the director, Bryan Woods, with improvised or paraphrased dialogue, especially between the two friends, Mark (Travis) and Greg (Simmons), who decide to explore Greg's policeman-father's box of case artifacts while hanging out. The case, based on true facts, involves a rookie cop, Ethan Crowe (Marxen), who discovers two of his brothers murdered in a shed and stays on the crime scene all night. He is never seen again. While it appears the mystery/suspense reconstruction is the primary plotline, by the end we appreciate Mark and Greg's friendship—the banter, the silliness, the sarcasm, the real feeling underlying it all.]

Lights, Camera, Kill! Dir. Insane Mike Saunders. Prescribed Films, 2004. 82 min. Principals: Jeff Alexander, Jill Emmert, Angie Lellig, Jacob Pollman, Chris Simmons, Trevor Swaim, Steven Tracy. [In this low budget horror/slasher film, the young adults Hawk (Tracy) and Kyle (Pollman) steal a video camera. They play the camera's filmed video, discovering a snuff film in which a young woman is stripped and stabbed to death. The Killer has an uncanny knowledge of where the thieves and their family members are, stalking and killing them in a series of stabbings, axings, and tortures that are all premised on his repeated statement that "theft is wrong." All crimes are recorded and used to terrify new victims. The Killer triumphs over everyone who has tried to stop him as well as their relations. The film was shot in Ottumwa.]

The Talent Given Us. Andrew Wagner. Daddy W. Productions, 2004. 98 min. Principals: Judy Dixon, Allen Wagner, Emily Wagner, Judy Wagner, Maggie Wagner. [With actors portraying themselves with the same names and the director as son in this articulate, semi-functional NYC Jewish family, is this a documentary or a fictional film? It feels like the latter. Allen, a retired stockbroker with serious medical problems, and Judy, a still lively Bennington graduate who never fulfilled her dreams, impulsively hijack their two adult daughters on a road trip to Los Angeles to find out why they haven't heard from their screenwriter son. When they get to Iowa, they pick up a family friend, Bumby, a manic-depressive just fired from a *Field of Dreams 2* production. Judy exclaims over the beauty of Iowa and the pure, simple life, though the cows scare her. Allen notes the absence of theatres and museums. The family stops at a veteran's hospital to get replacement pills for Allen, and we see a Mt. Pleasant water tower. This articulate, amazingly honest family has serious dysfunctions but shares love and a common past. Andrew Wagner presents his family and the cross-country landscapes with realism and humor.] AFIs. *NYT* 17 June 2005, 13; *V* 26 July 2004, 13.

University Heights. Dir. Scott Beck. Bluebox Limited, 2004. 95 min. Principals: Lindsey Husak, Justin Marxen, Sabien Minteer, Shane Simmons, Travis Shepherd, Jim Siokos. [This straight-to-DVD film premiered June 26, 2004, in the Quad Cities. Filmed in Iowa City, Coralville, and the Quad Cities by a nineteen-year-old writer/director/co-producer on a budget of $300, the movie successfully weaves together the stories of four men at a university struggling to come to terms with their identities. There is a philosophy teacher with a dead wife and guilt over his former drug dealing; a young man torn between peers interested in drink, drugs, and sexual conquests and a new love who expects better treatment; a closeted teacher tortured by his own homophobia; and an insecure rebel too much influenced by his Iago-like friend's poisonous racism and homophobia (the friend most likely a voice in his own head

109

he cannot control). All face ethical decisions. The scenes have recognizable Iowa City landmarks such as the Oasis bar and the Iowa River flowing through campus, but the storylines could take place at Any University, USA. The view of Iowa is hardly pastoral: we see an Iowa City that has violence and drug trafficking and residents who are full of hate and self-loathing. Yet we also see ordinary people who are intelligent, decent, and kind.]

The Bag Man. Dir. Insane Mike Sanders. Prescribed Films, 2005. 96 min. Principals: Jill Emmert, Lindsey Husak, Chris Simmons, Steven Tracy. [This film is a contribution to what might be called the screwball horror genre. Walter (Simmons) is an abused, nerdy video clerk who is exploited by a lazy, mooching roommate (Tracy). After numerous humiliations, Walter hits on the idea of becoming a serial killer as his route to power, fame, and sexual love. Jack the Ripper (Emmert) appears to him as a mentor who promises to help him kill. Despite Walter's evil intentions, each murder situation makes him popular with the public as he inadvertently brings about the death of drug dealers, shoplifters, rapists, and a right wing evangelist pedophile. His popularity finally brings sexual success with his friend Ann (Husak). This film, with casual costumes and friends as actors, was shot in Iowa City and Oskaloosa.]

Boone Style. Dir. Mas Gardner. Young Blood Films, 2005. 86 min. Principals: Stephanie Brown, Kim Duede, Mas Gardner, Steve Gardner, Katie Hermanson. ["Your typical, semi-dysfunctional Midwestern family reunion" is the tagline for this humorous, all too real film set in Des Moines. As five generations gather from the local area and California, confident, eight-year-old Ruby is a keen observer of all that happens, eventually using both kindness and assertiveness to heal the frays in individual psyches and in the fabric of the family as a whole. The film takes place in one house and yard, so we don't see much of Des Moines, but we are reminded we are in Iowa by a glimpse of the *Des Moines Register,* Iowa shirts, and occasional references in the dialogue. Character details make the film resonate with anyone who has been part of an Iowa family reunion. Besides the heaps of Iowa foods (Ruby remarks Iowa consumes more Jell-O than any other state), we see Great-Grandpa peeing in the bushes, a toddler swooping around in a Batman-style cape, Mom trying to organize everyone's life according to her plan (hiding her despair over her husband's stony silences), the men hovering over the barbeque grill while the grandmas and great-grandmas preside over the kitchen, and the young adults angsting over their vocational and life choices, wondering what they really want and what they owe family.]

Invasion Iowa. Dir. Brendon Carter. GRB Entertainment, 2005. 230 min. Principals: Garz Chan, Desi Lydic, William Shatner, and Kirk Ward. [This reality TV mini-series, aired on the Spike Channel, brought William Shatner with a cast and crew to tiny Riverside, Iowa, the self-proclaimed birthplace of Captain James T. Kirk, to make a low-budget science fiction movie. The locals, some of whom were cast in the movie or recruited for the crew, did not know the movie was a fake and they were part of a reality TV show. The mini-series created side spoofs to capture the town's reactions: distributing Shat hats, requesting the local priest to allow his church's beautiful stained-glass windows to be smashed by a Gerclon Emperor, changing the town sign from Riverside to Billville, asking the local women for reactions to a children's book about a penguin that gets a boob job and finds happiness. Although viewers may wonder that a whole town could be so easily fooled by the fake filmmakers, the Iowans displayed niceness throughout and kept quiet or tactfully made common sense suggestions when in doubt or confronted with fake Hollywood craziness and "drama." With the possible exception of Don Rath who shares his good luck raccoon penis with Bill, the townspeople seem pretty normal, not eccentrics. There are moments of sentiment— for example, when Shatner visits the grave of Don Rath's beloved wife and when he gives gifts to the local cast and crew and to the town after the revelation that the movie is a fake. The series ends with the edited science fiction film, which is especially humorous since the audience has come to know the actors and has seen the shooting.]

Iowa. Dir. Matt Farnsworth. Full Fathom 5, 2006. 97 min. Principals: Rosanna Arquette, Matt Farnsworth, Diana Foster, John Savage, Michael T. Weiss. [This methamphetamine movie filmed in Centerville, Iowa, certainly presents an antipastoral view of Iowa, despite familiar imagery—hilly gravel roads, town square, cornfields, flags, water towers, family photos. Donna (Foster and Esper's (Farnsworth) love story becomes a horror story when Esper's father, a meth dealer, dies in a car crash. They try meth at the father's deserted house and soon have their own lucrative operation. A corrupt parole officer plots with Esper's sleazy mother to kill Esper, and the officer viciously rapes Donna. Esper's boyhood friend Nick ("Tweaker") goes crazy when he takes too much meth and kills himself after nearly killing Donna. Esper loses a finger in a bar fight. Esper and Donna's attempt to escape to Mexico ends up with a shootout near the Missouri border. The film is part cautionary tale and part love story, with lots of sex, drugs, violence, and a music soundtrack by Iowan Greg Brown.]

The Bride Wore Blood: A Contemporary Western. Dirs. Scott Beck and Bryan Woods. Bluebox Limited, 2006. 60 min. Principals: Justin Marxen, Travis Shepherd, Shane Simmons, Jim Siokos, Christy Sullivan. [Scott Beck and Bryan Woods, who in 2006 were 22-year-old University of Iowa Communications majors, sold the television set they won in an MTV filmmaking contest to finance this "contemporary western" in the style of Sergio Leone and John Ford. Using non-chronological scenes, Beck and Woods (also the screenwriters) tell the story of two hired guns involved with a bride killed on a railroad track. The mystery/suspense film allows the viewers gradually to piece together what really happened and why. The film's rural and urban locales include Davenport, Bettendorf, Iowa City, and McCausland. Quad Cities musician Scott Morschhauser created the musical score.]

Farmlands. Dir. Richie Vomit. Vomit Films, 2006. 72 min. Principals: Sarah Brown, Anna Dickson, Ryan Hovde, Lexi Lutter. [This video production, showing "twisted, corn fed, backwoods Midwestern Inbreeding at its finest," was made on "a forty dollar budget, with a video camera, and a bunch of (expletives removed) Iowans." At a party on a hot summer night in the Sioux City area, Margie makes a date with the tattooed Johnny, provoking teasing by her friends. In the early hours of the morning after the date, the friends decide to descend on the couple at Johnny's rural farmhouse, partly to tease her and partly to see if she is all right. They walk in on a couple of mutilated corpses, including Margie's, and the bloodbath begins, leading up to a surprise ending. Life for this group seems to center on drinking beer, hanging out, sex talk, porno, and a little backgammon. The dialogue appears to be mostly improvised. The film announces its Iowa setting at the beginning: we see an Iowa Hawkeyes tee-shirt, and the camera captures some Sioux City scenes.]

Haunting Villisca. Dir. James Serpento. AriesWorks Entertainment, 2006. 115 minutes. Principals: Chelsea Long, Darwin Lin, Francisco Rodriguez, James Serpento, Kerry Skram, Greg Alan Williams. [Residents of the southwest Iowa town of Villisca are still haunted by the 1912 axe murders of the Moore family and two young girls who were staying overnight with them. The case has never been solved. The community debates both the murder and whether paranormal activity shadows the Moore House, now a museum. The film intersperses reenactments of the original trial testimony with the story of a psychology professor, Dave (Serpento), ridden with guilt for having an affair with a student that led his unstable wife to commit suicide. Fate seems to lead the professor, and later his girlfriend, to Villisca, where his car breaks down and he sees a figure in the town's famous haunted house. His encounters with ghosts in the haunted house eventually help exorcise his guilt. We see the usual rural/small town images, although Dave hallucinates two bison along a rural road. The talkative auto mechanic refers to attending a Renaissance Festival in Des Moines, and a cynical TV reporter remarks that "there is no eye candy in Iowa, only piggies and insurance agencies."]

Arnolds Park. [Alternate title: *Carousel of Revenge*]. Dir. Gene Teigland. Picture Factory/B. Sting Entertainment, 2007. 103 min. Principals: Jim Detmar, Tac Fitzgerald, Maitland McConnell, Jessica Stier. [This mystery, set mainly in Arnolds Park, is rooted in events of three years previous: the murder of a pregnant teen and the apparent suicide of the apparent killer, a fat teenage boy, Francis, bullied by his peers. Now strong and buff, Frank (formerly Francis) returns with his uncle to get revenge and expose the real killer. The film provides various suspects, a surprise ending, and romantic tension. Will Frank marry a beautiful blonde lawyer's daughter who witnessed the original murder or the spunky brunette daughter now managing the Arnolds Park Amusement Park purchased by Frank's uncle? The landscape and culture of the Okoboji area provide an unusual Iowa background. The DVD provides an alternate ending.]

The Final Season. Dir. David M. Evans. FOBIA/Final Partners, 2007. 119 min. Principals: Tom Arnold, Sean Astin, Powers Booth. [A sunrise over cornfields. A red barn. Cows. A windmill. A gravel road. A flag. This series of opening images proclaims, "You are in Iowa." Then Kent Stock (Astin) drives into Norway, Iowa, where he sees a sign that says, "Welcome to Norway. A nice place to come home to"—a hint that, once again, Iowa and baseball would join hands. This movie seems like a typical underdog triumphs sports fantasy with every romantic "Iowa nice" and baseball cliché ever, yet it is the true story of the 20th and last season of the Norway Community HS baseball season. The school would thereafter become consolidated, despite citizen protests. The setup is that the crusty, kind-hearted, smart coach that won the school 19 straight state championships has involuntarily retired. Kent Stock, hired by the principal to fail, guides the team to a 20th championship, the last game played against a team with a pitcher headed for the major leagues. Norway-style baseball (strong defense, few errors, community support) wins the day in a suspenseful final game. The subplots are predictable but handled with humor and more appreciation for Iowans than shown in *Field of Dreams*. The true story behind the film, as well as Iowa's love of sports, makes this one of the "most Iowan" Iowa films. A Dallas Center man, Tony Wilson, despite no filmmaking experience, served as producer and persisted until the film was made—as unlikely a victory as the team's. Tom Arnold, of Ottumwa, played the estranged father of a player.] AFIs. *V* 8 Oct. 2007, 56.

Hall Pass. Dir. Eric Frodsham. Blank Action Productions, 2007. 90 min. Principals: April Baker, Jamyl Dobson, Roschell Lloyd, Ryan Palmer, Candice Wuehle. [This dark film is set in a small town in Johnson County and was filmed in Iowa City. Sarah, a foster child, moves to a new town, Midland, where she is taken in by religious foster parents. When her foster father attempts to sexually assault her (after asking God for advance forgiveness), she turns to two teachers who have their own agendas; both claim they want to help her, but in abusive ways—by drinking with her and seducing her. The film begins with iconic Iowa images: a two-lane highway, a flag, fields of corn. The school principal starts the movie with a speech to the teachers about the importance of recognizing sexual abuse, but then simply hands the teachers a brochure, seeming to feel that sexual abuse in unlikely in an "close knit community" like Midland. Neither he nor the state social worker is effectual in dealing with Sarah. The Iowans we see are either unable to help or cruel. Sarah's real father is a violent drunk. A janitorial crew supervisor, Donald, verbally and physically abuses his mentally challenged brother. The local cops look like thugs. The male faculty member, Friday, and Donald have a history of preying on troubled students. This Iowa is not a safe place and is especially hard on foster children.]

The Hideout [Italian title: *Il nascondiglio*]. Dir. Pupi Avati. Duea Films, 2007. 100 min. Principals: Laura Morante, Rita Tushingham, Burt Young, Treat Williams. [This Avati mystery-thriller is about an Italian woman, who, having spent fifteen years in a mental institution after her husband's suicide, opens a Davenport restaurant in a mansion known as Snakes Hall, once a mental institution. The woman discovers that in 1957 several people were killed there and two others disappeared. *Variety* reports that exteriors were shot in Davenport, with interiors staged at Cinnecita in Rome.] NS. *V* 14 Jan. 2008, 1.

Indelible. Dir. Rick Amundson. BravoRomeo, 2007. 107 min. Principals: Paul Cram, Tess Gill, Joe Leonardi, Charlie Matthes, Michelle Tomlinson. [Adorned with tattoos representing his life and released from eight years in prison after surviving a failed drug deal that killed his best friend and two other men, Donnie (Matthes) checks into the Hawkeye Motel, determined to reconnect with his twelve-year-old daughter and reconstruct his life. Luckily, he meets an artistic tattooist, Maggie (Tomlinson), a survivor who sees the good in Donnie, and he finds his daughter, Grace, another survivor, is not permanently damaged from living in a trailer with her meth-addicted mother and her violent, drug-pushing boyfriend. Bad luck for Donnie takes the form of pressure from his former boss to resume dealing drugs, then bitter hatred from a local cop, and finally the violent life of his ex-wife that threatens his daughter. The film shows a bleak side of Iowa life—drugs, domestic violence, and a cycle of poor fatherhood—and yet, as the DVD jacket proclaims, the film shows that even a troubled ex-con can experience "the power of redemption and the gift of grace." The film was shot in Des Moines, but it has few Iowa references.]

The Prairie Pirates. Dir. Jamey Durham. Durham Studios, 2007. 80 min. Principals: Amy Kate Anderson, Karen Barker, John Hubers, Drew Schmidt. [This humorous, Christian-oriented pirate movie for children announces that it is set in the "most unlikely place," Iowa, "thousands and thousands of miles away from an ocean." While the town is identified as "Prairie City," a real small town east of Des Moines, and the film features a news broadcast from Des Moines, the real locations are the Lewis and Clark Center in Sioux City and Orange City, identified by the Sioux County Sheriff's car, the town's Dutch heritage, the beautiful landscaping, and various Orange City buildings. The film intersperses silent movie scenes of a pirate finding and hiding treasure circa 1800 and contemporary scenes of four brothers and sisters expecting a boring summer vacation and instead finding a map with a riddle pointing to the location of pirate treasure. Times are hard in Iowa. The kids' father has lost his factory job, and later the father's boss loses his job as well. The kids learn that the dirty Mrs. Meanley Greenly and her weird son, Billy, 27 going on 7, are the owners of the treasure. After some Bible teaching from Mom, the kids raise money by cleaning windows, cars, and dogs. Then they clean and landscape Mrs. Greenly's rundown house and yard, with the result that she gives the treasure to the kids—that is, after they all scare off Sneevly, a modern day pirate who wants to ruin their town by foreclosing on homes and farms and building a casino. Giving the treasure away is what breaks the pirate's curse. The film has some nice bits of local humor. An irate red hat lady, in full red and purple regalia, tracks down Sneevly in Prairie City to recover her precious car stolen in Sioux City.]

Through the Night. Dir. Insane Mike Saunders. Prescribed Films, 2007. Principals: Ryan Karloff, Lisa Kanning. [This might be called a "farmhouse slasher" variant within the horror genre. Sam (Karloff) and Tabitha (Kanning) live unhappily at a farm place. Sam was supposed to become a famous artist, but he can't sell anything, and resentful Tabitha, who works as a waitress, hoped to go to New York riding his fabulous success. She nags relentlessly about his failure, lack of telephone, and crappy car. A group of friends is coming for a reunion at their place, and, along the way, they hear about a nearby mental institution that had an explosion accompanied by the escape of injured inmates. After signs of the inmates' presence, Sam and Tabitha's group want to leave in the car with slashed tires. Eventually the bloodied inmates show up, obviously wanting to kill them. Traditional horror genre moralism drives the murders. Doomed are the obnoxious, exploitative, or sexually unfaithful. Sam actually cares about others and in a gender reversal becomes the genre "final girl" who survives. Credits indicate that the film was shot in Iowa City and Ottumwa.]

Beneath the Mississippi. Dir. Lonnie Schuyler. Mississippi Films, 2008. 114 min. Principals: Ariadne Schaffer, Jon Hazell, Chris Sweeney, Nick Murray, Sonja Soriano. [In this existentially dark story with physical settings along the Mississippi River, Elly (Schaffer), a documentary filmmaker, hires a crew to help her study an area where many have disappeared. Unknown to the crew, her father was one who drowned and she a child survivor of the incident. An oppressive atmosphere hangs over the enterprise, and the film's lighting is characteristically shadowy and gray in the day or pitch black at night. The soundscape amplifies the sound of rushing undertow, with the loud thumping sounds—suggesting bodies—colliding with the boat's hull. Conditions in the island camps are miserable with mud, leeches, and swarms of mosquitoes that bite relentlessly. Within a few days antagonisms break out, and the crew quickly degenerates psychologically; Eva (Soriano) becomes catatonic and is abusively force fed. Matt becomes violent and has to be tied down. Overall, this film presents the least attractive image of Mississippi River travel ever created. Burlington is listed as an Iowa shooting location, but that geographical fact does not figure in the story, which is more about the terrifying riverscape with its shadows, snakes, spiders, and dead bodies roiling beneath the surface.]

Legend Has It. Dir. Insane Mike Saunders. Prescribed Films, 2008. 93 min. Principals: Rich McNinch, Stephanie McNinch. [This is comic meta-horror, a film in which the leading character Al Cunningham (R. McNinch) aspires to be a horror film writer. With his girlfriend, Heather (S. McNinch), he decides to go for a weekend holiday in the woods with friends, most of whom are very horny. After hearing the legend of a local "plant monster," who kills humans as revenge for eating plants, Al is scared. His familiarity with horror films suggests to him that anyone who has sex will soon be killed. Al also senses that there is a screen separating him physically from a film audience, and he begins to point out to the audience and to other members of his group that they are trapped by a script. The only escape is for him to write another script that defies *Friday the 13th*'s sex-followed-by-death formula. Alas, hormones trump, and by film's end almost all are dead. Survivors are Al and another girl from space, who has unexpectedly burst through "a portal" from a sci-fi film; together they kill the leafy monster with herbicide. Even though they didn't have sex, they are now threatened by Al's now undead, bloody former friends. Al and the space girl become aware of a green screen on their horror film, which, when slashed, opens a portal into a black and white B-western. Throughout the film Al talks about genre expectations and filmic conventions such as mysterious doors, improbable lighting, and manipulative music, and he criticizes the audience for having such predictable and easily satisfied desires for horror. Credits at film's end acknowledge "*Friday the 13th, Return of the Living Dead*, and *The Purple Rose of Cairo* for inspiration." The film was shot in Ottumwa and Iowa City, the script at one point acknowledging that the action is in Iowa.]

The Poker House. Dir. Lori Petty. The Poker House, 2008. 93 min. Principals: Sophi Bairley, Selma Blair, Jennifer Lawrence, Chloe Grace Moretz. [Based on Lori Petty's growing up years, the movie, filmed in Illinois and set in Council Bluffs, shows three remarkably intelligent, resourceful sisters in a house with their cocaine-addicted mother who is a prostitute (Blair), the mother's pimp, other prostitutes, and assorted gamblers, druggies, and johns. The oldest sister, Agnes (Lawrence), an A student and basketball star, tries to take care of her sisters and live one day at a time. All three sisters know their way around the streets and have survival skills beyond their years, but we see their vulnerability. Agnes is just barely 14, confused about love and sex, and smokes the occasional joint. When raped by her mother's pimp, she is shattered, especially by her mother's clear allegiance to the pimp, not her own daughter. Yet that same evening she wins her school's semi-final basketball game, and, after the game, the three sisters sing loudly to the radio ("There ain't no mountain high enough") and head out to blow Agnes's paycheck on a decent meal. The film definitely presents a gritty, anti-pastoral view of Iowa, exposing the drug use, abuse, and prostitution that are a reality in too many Iowans' lives.] *V* 25 June 2008.

Sister Patchouli. Dir. Scott R. Thompson. My Town Pictures, 2008. 111 min. Principals: Margaret Clair, John Alex Grant, Tom Todar, Sondra Ward. [This sophisticated script pokes fun at Iowa and outsiders' views of Iowa but is really a valentine to Fairfield, which, as the film within the film points out, is both a typical Iowa town (with its square and surrounding farms) and a unique place (with Maharishi University and the T.M. community). "There has never been a town like Fairfield." Margaret, known as Sister Patchouli or Patch (Ward), is sought after everywhere she goes for solace, counseling, advice, and love. She has a giant heart, but is tormented by her mother's withering disapproval that she never made anything of her life. When outsiders—two Californians, two event planners who scorn Iowa taste, and her sisters who left Fairfield—descend for the "surprise" party Patch's mother organized for herself, Patch learns to accept who she is and her value. She also finds love with a Californian plastic surgeon turned Fairfield farmer, Jake (Todar). The film has an amusing segment in which Jake's friend Ray tries to shake Jake out of his rose-colored view of Iowa through a string of typical bicoastal insults: the cows use the land as a litter box; the locals can't tell the difference between Shakespeare and Larry the Cable Guy. The film gently pokes fun at the outsiders and the locals but shows Ray that Fairfield is not what he expected. The scenes let us see Fairfield—shops, homes, the domes in the distance. At the local radio station, a poster for the film *King Corn* is posted on the wall. At the end, we learn in passing that Patch is a meditator.]

Diary of a Superhero. Dir. John-Michael Rohret. Rohret Productions, 2009. 96 min. Principals: Casey Boland, Nigel Brown, Luke Christensen, Andrew MacKay. [A sixteen-year-old would-be superhero Theo (Christensen), a Ninja, and a cop join forces to recapture the Book of Bizarre and save the world from nuclear destruction. They encounter a greedy human in a yellow body suit, cyborgs, zombies, a half-man/half gorilla, and Theodore's father and brother in the land of the bizarre after they travel through a rift in space located at a sleazy porn place called the Boner Bar. Shot in Decorah and Iowa City by a film student, the movie won the Best Student Film award at the Cedar Rapids Film Festival. An Iowa Hawkeyes shirt, a Highway 1 sign, and other local sites can be glimpsed in the film.]

Fanboys. Dir. Kyle Newman. Trigger Street Productions, 2009. 90 min. Principals: Jay Baruchel, Kristin Bell, Dan Fogler, Sam Huntington, Chris Marquette. Cameos: Carrie Fisher, William Shatner. [In 1998, four rabid *Star Wars* friends from Ohio, estranged since high school, reunite to take a road trip to break into Lucas Ranch in Marin County to try to see *Star Wars Episode 1: The Phantom Menace* before its release. En route they stop at Riverside, Iowa, where they scrap with their natural enemies: Trekkers. After destroying a statue of Kirk and Khan, their van breaks down in rural Iowa, where they come upon a biker bar that turns out to be a gay bar. Instead of bashing the boys, the bikers force them to do a strip act. "Chief" fixes their van, gets them high, and gives Linus, dying of cancer, a package of peyote that, later on, lands them in jail. Riverside is, of course, the self-proclaimed birthplace of the fictional James T. Kirk. The film may surprise outsiders who associate Iowa with corn, pigs, and naive, old-fashioned white people—not with bikers, drugs, Native Americans, and gay bars.] AFIs. *NYT* 6 Feb. 2009, C8; *V* 4 Aug. 2008, 31.

Peace Patch. Dir. Scott Thompson. My Town Pictures, 2009. 90 min. Principals: Hannah Anderson, Sam Bass, Laura Carpenter, Marcus Dalton. [This community film by Scott Thompson features an ensemble cast playing Boone neighbors. The drama explores whether peace is possible or desirable. Two neighbors with their dueling lawn mowers fight over their property boundary line. Soon all the men in the neighborhood have their measuring tapes out. This fight is only one of many among the families and marriages in the neighborhood. When guitar-playing Ben suggests the feuding neighbors let the disputed patch of lawn just grow, they and all the neighbors who stand on it suddenly become loving toward each other—to one cynical observer, almost sickeningly so. When a son comes home and unknowingly mows the peach patch, the fighting breaks out again until one of the wives concocts a scheme to restore peace. The Boone locale is shown through several Boone and ISU tee-shirts and an Iowa cup. The cynic points out the patch is "not the Field of Dreams," to which Ben replies, "If you build it, . . ." Ben's opening and closing song, "Down by the Riverside," advocates studying war no more—and the film's aim, ultimately, is to promote peace.]

Sam Steele and the Junior Detective Agency. [Alternate title: *Junior Detective Agency*]. Dir. Tom Whitus. Silver Hills Pictures/Zingraff Motion Pictures, 2009. 87 min. Principals: Jacob Hays, Daren Kennedy, Jilanne Klaus, Katherine McNamara, Luke Perry, M. Emmet Walsh. [Thirteen-year old Sam Steele, Jr. (Hays), styles himself as a 1940s private eye, with trench coat, fedora, wise-cracking receptionist, faithful dog, and inner monologues. When he botches a stolen bicycle case, his father, a Des Moines policeman, and mother shut down the agency. His partner, Lenore, and her dog move to St. Louis but leave him a clubhouse for his office, should the agency revive. A new family with a daughter, Emma (McNamara), moves in down the street and inherits from the West Des Moines Fire Department a dog named Doug. Sam, Emma, and Doug secretly reconstitute the agency and crack the case of recent art burglaries perpetrated in Des Moines and West Des Moines by the Cat, an elusive Frenchman that the police, including Sam, Sr., have failed to catch. The movie was shot in Des Moines and makes reference to Windsor Heights, Polk County, and Des Moines' French sister city. Des Moines seems to be full of fine art: the Cat steals a Rembrandt, Leonardo Da Vinci drawings, a Ming vase, and a Michelangelo. The families in the film are wholesome, neighborly, and capable of lovingly disciplining their children when needed. The Cat refers to Des Moines as a "quaint little town."]

Something Blue. Dir. Sean Gannon. Blort Pictures, 2009. 94 min. Principals: Mike Kreissl, Kate Mortimer. [Sean Gannon says on his website that this "ultra-low-budget movie" was shot entirely in Polk County, where he grew up. A theatre professor helped with casting, friends played supporting roles, and his mom catered. This documentary-style scripted film follows a happy young Iowa couple, Michael and Jackie, who have not known each other long enough, as they embark on a year-long journey to matrimony. The usual minor skirmishes turn

into heart-wrenching agony, especially as Michael's grieving and dysfunctional family's bad behavior exposes the couple's insecurities and
inability to stand up for themselves and each other. The film won Best
Picture and Best Produced Screenplay at Des Moines' Wild Rose Film
Festival.]

Star Trek. Dir. J. J. Abrams. Bad Robot, 2009. 127 min. Principals:
Eric Bana, Leonard Nimoy, Chris Pine, Zachary Quinto. [This prequel
to the *Star Trek* series begins with the birth of James T. Kirk in space
after a Romulan attack on his father George's spacecraft. George Kirk
saves hundreds of people, including his wife and just born son, at the
cost of his own life. The film moves to Iowa, where we see a wild young
boy (Kirk) driving a fast car, flying down a country road and nearly
careening into a canyon (in Iowa?). A few years later we see teenage
Kirk fighting drunken bullies after being called a farm boy and a hick
and accused of having sex with farm animals. He rides a high-speed
motorcycle recklessly (without helmet). We also see him trying to pick
up a young Uhura, who rejects him for young Spock. By 2009 Riverside
is clearly established as the "hometown" of Captain Kirk in *Star Trek*
mythology, from where he leaves to train as a Starfleet officer. As a
traveling Iowan throughout the galaxy in the TV and movies series,
Kirk shows the kind of heroic leadership associated with Iowa in World
War II films: fearlessness, ethics, determination, practicality.] AFIs.
NYT 8 May 2009, C1; *V* 22 Apr. 2009.

Sugar. Dir. Anna Boden and Ryan Fleck. SONY/HBO Films, 2009.
118 min. Principals: Richard Bull, Andre Holland, Rayniel Rufino,
Algenis Perez Soto, Ann Whitney. [This well received baseball film is
more than a story about a teenage pitcher from a poor family in the
Dominican Republic becoming a major league star. It also shows us
baseball recruitment and the farm team system, the immigrant experience, and a boy, Sugar (Soto), who has a family depending on his
baseball success in the United States. Sugar's extended family is elated
when he is chosen by the Kansas City Knights to train in Phoenix and
then assigned to a farm club in Bridgetown, Iowa. Sugar lives with a
Presbyterian farm family who understands the pressures on him as
little as he understands their language, but they are kind to him, and
he doesn't want to let them down. When he arrives in Iowa, Sugar does
not understand how to order eggs, who Babe Ruth is, or what to make
of a Protestant church service. When he kisses his host's very friendly
granddaughter (Whitney), she confuses him with her uncomfortable

response. Partially filmed in Burlington and Davenport, the Iowa landscape has the usual rural images—fields of corn, windmills, hilly gravel roads—but also Davenport stores and signs. The film turns out to be less about winning and losing at baseball and more about a sweet-natured young man who is one of the many from Central and South America who do not end up as rich superstars. When an injury, competition, and the cultural discomfort of Iowa becomes too much, Sugar makes a life and friends in NYC near Yankee Stadium.] AFIs. *NYT* 3 Apr. 2009, C1.

16 to Life. [Alternate title: *Duck Farm No. 13*]. Dir. Becky Smith. Duck Farm, 2010. 100 min. Principals: Shiloh Fernandez, Hallee Hirsh, Mandy Musgrove, Theresa Russell. [This independent film, which won festival awards, was set and shot in McGregor, with the action taking place at an ice cream stand along the Mississippi on a single day in late summer/early fall, during bookish Kate's (Hirsh) 16th birthday. The landscape is like a character in the film: the boats on the river, sky, fall trees on bluffs overlooking the river, corn harvesting, main street, and flocks of birds "pooping their way south" for the winter. The ice cream stand gives a picture of the residents of McGregor, both the natives and the rich folks closing up summer cottages. The characters are funny, individualized, and very real—not the usual Iowa stereotypes. The ice cream workers are all searching for love—in Kate's case, a first kiss—and all find what they want during the course of the day and evening. Kate reads intermittently during the day from a book about China's Cultural Revolution and fantasizes herself in a China that disapproves of her desire for love rather than making China great for Chairman Mao.] *V* 22 Aug. 2010.

2001 Maniacs: Field of Screams. Dir. Tim Sullivan. Tax Credit Finance/Social Capital/Ambergreen Entertainment, 2010. 84 min. Principals: Bill Moseley, Asa Hope, Katy Marie Johnson, Lin Shaye. [Filmed in Council Bluffs on a low budget, this comic horror film is a sequel to director Sullivan's 2005 remake of Herschell Gordon Lewis's 1964 cult film *Two Thousand Maniacs*. The premise is that Dixie zombie cannibals from Pleasant Valley, Georgia, annually avenge the death of Southerners during the Civil War. Since the Northerners will not come to their their Guts 'n' Glory Jamboree in Georgia, the host group heads off in a yellow school bus to Iowa where they encounter a crew of shallow Hollywood types looking to make a reality show. The film is a string of inventively gory killings of the Hollywood cast and crew, interspersed with sex/nudity scenes and a string of tasteless anti-PC jokes targeting Jews, gays, blondes, black slaves, Mexicans, redneck Southerners, Hollywood, and the elderly. The dialogue is crude and corny: Major Buchman, for example, refers to the "Anals of History." The title, of course, alludes to the iconic Field of Dreams in Dyersville.]

Ash. Thomas Geraty. Big Field Productions, 2010. 98 min. Principals: Stephanie Brown, Tim Decker, Thomas Geraty, Kevin R. Kelly. [Des Moines Police officer and devoted husband and father Dan McBurney (Decker) quits his job after one too many cases of child abuse and domestic violence. Two years later he accidentally comes upon a rapist/abductor near his storage business and locks him up in one of his units after seeing that the two boys held in cages are freed. His conversations with the perpetrator, and a visit to the rural area where one of the boys was abducted, cause him to wrestle obsessively with his own childhood demons. The film gives a glowing picture of family life in the heartland but also shows that abuse can cast long shadows, especially when hidden by silence. Two ash trees and a bat made out of ash become symbols of survival. The ending seems to support vigilantism in that McBurney sets up the abductor for murder by one of the abducted boys' fathers and is suddenly reconciled with everyone who urged him not to do it. The film has identifiable Des Moines markers such as a copy of the *Des Moines Register* and the state capitol building. Some scenes take place in a rural Iowa small town.]

The Crazies. Dir. Breck Eisner. Overture Films/Participant Media, 2010. 101 min. Principals: Joe Anderson, Radha Mitchell, Timothy Olyphant. [When the water supply of Ogden Marsh, Iowa, near Cedar Rapids, is contaminated by a biological agent carried in a crashed plane, the residents turn into violent psychopaths, the government imposes a brutal cover-up, and the Sheriff, his pregnant wife, the Deputy, and another young woman attempt to escape. The horror scenes take place in small town Iowa settings: a baseball game, a baby's nursery in a farm house, a car wash, and a truck stop. The film, shot in Georgia, is a remake of a 1973 George Romero film with the same title.] *NYT* 26 Feb. 2010, 10; *V* 1 Mar. 2010, 19, 21.

Dead Awake [Originally titled: *Dylan's Wake*]. Dir. Omar Naim. Tax Credit Finance, 2010. 93 min. Principals: Kim Grimaldi, Brian Lynner, Rose McGowan, Ben Marten, Amy Smart, Nick Stahl. [A funeral parlor employee and depressed loner, Dylan (Stahl), is haunted by a fatal taxi car accident on a bridge ten years before—and by his former high school girlfriend, Natalie (Smart), a nurse now engaged to someone else. Dylan's boss (Lynner) wagers him that if they stage a funeral for him, people will come. Two people show up: Natalie and a female druggie named Charlie (McGowan). This experience launches Dylan into a mystifying state in which he and viewers are not at all sure who and what are real. Are the "dead awake" those who cannot work through Kubler-Ross's stages of grieving, or are we literally haunted by ghosts? Is Dylan himself dead or alive? The film was shot in Des Moines. The lighting and film editing give the city a mysterious, not-of-this-world feel.]

The Experiment. Dir. Paul Scheuring. Inferno Entertainment/ Magnet Media Productions, 2010. 96 min. Principals: Adrien Brody, Forest Whittaker. [A remake of the 2001 German film *Das Experiment*, this version of a psychological experiment gone wrong (based on Stanford's 1971 Zimbardo experiment) is set in a leased prison facility surrounded by cornfields. The locale is not identified as Iowa, but the psychologically and physically battered men walking out of the facility into the grass surrounded by cornfields at the end of the movie is an ironic allusion to *Field of Dreams*. Twenty-six men are promised $1000 a day for 14 days to participate in a supposedly closely monitored experiment in which some become guards and more become prisoners. The quick-tempered pacifist prisoner Travis (Brody) argues for rationality and humanity but ends up leading the resistance and pounding the face of the brutal leader of the guards, Barris (Whitaker), a conformist momma's boy of 42 before the experiment revealed to him the sexual charge of power. The film was shot in Des Moines and Alleman, Iowa.]

Fell. Dir. Marcus Koch. Chemical Burn Entertainment with Manic Entertainment and Modern American Cinema, 2010. 80 min. Principals: Jeff Dylan Graham, Katie Walters, Kristian Day, Barron Christian. [Shot in Des Moines, this claustrophobic, low budget horror film explores psychological degeneration, psychiatric medications, and a resulting murder. Bill (Graham) is a dropout from a punk band who then took up bartending but was fired. When we encounter him, he is self-mutilating, is medicating with an array of prescriptions, and he has a facedown dead woman in his bathtub. What to do about it? He desperately calls Jenny (Walters), an ex, and begs her to come be with him. He refuses to leave his apartment, sleeping stoned on his medications and weeping when awake. A band friend Derrick (Day) eventually comes by, smells the corpse, and asks Bill, "Who??" and whether he wants help in disposing of it. Bill dithers, cries harder, and burns incense in the bathroom to mask the smell. Jenny finally comes by and takes a consoling, therapeutic approach. By film's end, we realize that much we think we have seen is hallucination. A flashback shows that Bill, before the film's beginning, had bashed Jenny in response to her caustic nagging about his life. The film does not signal that we are in Des Moines or in Iowa. In terms of the story, the seedy apartment where almost all the action occurs is simply the place where Bill falls apart.]

Fortnight. Dir. Scott R. Thompson. My Town Pictures/Joventure Productions, 2010. 86 min. Principals: Laura Carlson, Ty Kamerman, Susan Wynne Lunning, Jim Morrill. [Having achieved an impressive suburban house and her own (ridiculously unsuccessful) greeting card business, Edmé wants manners, culture, and travel in her life. She invites a well-traveled husband and wife she meets on an online travel club to stay for a fortnight with her. Her own family consists of a college-flunking sister and her loving husband who feels estranged because he prefers laughter and spontaneity to cultural pretension and Iowa to foreign travel. The guests' public toenail cutting, unusual clothes, and shifting accents disgust Edmé who enlists friends and family to get them to leave the community. A revelation at the end causes Edmê to reassess her marriage and priorities. The movie has a quirky humor combined with a pro-Iowa/Midwest message. The film was shot in West Des Moines and presents Iowa suburban culture. Mentions are made of Ottumwa and Decorah.]

Janie Jones. Dir. David M. Rosenthal. Unified Pictures/Industrial Entertainment, 2010. 107 min. Principals: Abigail Breslin, Frances Fisher, Allesandro Nivola, Elisabeth Shue, Brittany Snow. [Janie Jones's mom (Shue) had a fling. Thirteen years later, mom, now a meth addict heading for rehab, abandons Janie to Janie's father, Ethan Brand (Nivola), on a rock tour that is not going well. An Iowa cop pressures Ethan to take Janie (Breslin) on tour, which he does, strongly against his will. A guitarist and singer-songwriter herself, Janie watches her dad's drinking and bad temper break up the band and alienate his manager. After father and daughter perform together for the first time, Dad lands himself in jail for fighting. Janie bails Ethan out by pawning their guitars, and thus begins Ethan's redemption as a human being and reconciliation with his rich mother, whom he has resented all his life, and with Janie's mother, who has been clean for a month. It appears that Janie and her mother may be from rural Iowa—there is a cornfield outside their house. Several scenes take place in Des Moines. The Interstate 35/80 sign suggests a crossroads: in Des Moines the band breaks up, and, later, this is where Janie pawns the guitars and moves Ethan down a new road to responsible and loving fatherhood. The Iowa portrayed in this film is not heaven.]

Butter. Dir. Jim Field Smith. Radius-TWC, 2011. 91 min. Principals: Ty Burrell, Rob Cordry, Jennifer Garner, Ashley Greene, Yara Shahidi, Alica Silverstone, and Hugh Jackman. The Iowa State Fair Butter Cow is perhaps the state's most distinctive icon. This comedy about a butter sculpture competition shows greed, racism, political hypocrisy, and out of bounds sex by an entire family. An African-American foster child, Destiny (Shahidi), upsets the butter dynastic dreams of unscrupulous, conservative Laura Pickler (Garner). Her husband, Bob (Burrell), originally from Battle Creek, has been forced to retire after fifteen years of champion sculptures that recreated *Schindler's List* and da Vinci's *The Last Supper*. When Laura's praying hands at the dinner table loses out to Destiny's Harriet Tubman sculpture at the Johnson County competition, Laura uses sex and lies to force a rematch at the Iowa State Fair. There Destiny's rendition of her dead mother and herself gets partially melted, thanks to a masked intruder with a blow torch. Regardless, Destiny triumphs at the fair. She is adopted by "the whitest people she has ever met," a loving, liberal couple, and she behaves better to Laura than Laura deserves, telling her "butter is not all she's got." This inspires Laura to run for Governor of Iowa, though her campaign spreads the rumor that God told her to run. The film is set in Iowa City with Destiny as student at a Country Day School and at the Iowa State Fair with its midway and 100+ degree temperatures. The political remarks in the film suggest the political spectrum in Iowa from left to right. The film locations are identified as in Louisiana.] V 5 Sept. 2011.

Cedar Rapids. Dir. Miguel Arteta. Ad Hominem Enterprises, 2011. 87 min. Principals: Anne Heche, Ed Helms, John C. Reilly, Sigourney Weaver. [In this comedy filmed in Ann Arbor, Michigan, Tim Lippe (Helms), a naive good boy from Brown Valley, Wisconsin, leaves his mothering lover for his first airplane trip to the big city of Cedar Rapids, Iowa, for a Christian-oriented insurance company's convention. The weekend delivers one shock after another as he meets a prostitute, imbibes alcohol and drugs for the first time, is seduced by a soccer mom insurance agent from Omaha, swims almost naked in the hotel pool, gets in a fight at a party in rural Iowa, and discovers his deceased boss was both sexually and financially corrupt. Tim grows up, makes true friends, and leaves the convention with his integrity intact, ready to take his loyal clients and start a new agency. Tim is a true believer in insurance agents as helpers of those in need, like those who lost everything in the Cedar Rapids flood disaster. The film has a modern Midwest look.] AFIs. *NYT* 11 Feb. 2011, C6; *V* 24 Jan. 2011.

Husk. Dir. Brett Simmons. After Dark Films, 2011. 83 min. Principals: Devon Graye, Wes Chatham, C. J. Thomason, Tammin Sursok, Ben Easter. [This horror film finds its setting in the Iowa countryside near Roland. The minimal setting is defined by a gravel road, a tall dense cornfield, and abandoned houses filled with dusty rubbish. A group of young people is driving toward a holiday destination when several ravens smash their windshield, causing the car to crash. They are somewhat disoriented, distrustful of one another's plans, and Johnny (Easter) is the first to wander away. A pair of them, Chris (Thomason) and Scott (Graye), discover a menacing scarecrow with a sewn burlap face and a nearby farmhouse, which has a lightbulb that pops on and off and doors that open, close, and lock themselves. The house is revealed to be the site of a ritual in which members of their group will be seized and zombified and sew their own burlap masks before going out to seize and zombify others. Scott alone, assisted by visions of a previous Cain and Abel type murder at the farm place, figures out a strategy (apparently) for escaping from the chain of zombification.]

Lucky. Dir. Gil Cates, Jr. Ten/Four Pictures/Tax Credit Finance/ Mirabelle Pictures, 2011. 103 min. Principals: Ann-Margaret, Ari Graynor, Colin Hanks, Jeffrey Tambor. [In this dark comedy, mild-mannered Ben Keller (Hanks) will do anything to win Lucy (Graynor), who ran away when he kissed her as a child. She is not interested in Ben as an adult until he wins $36 million from an Iowa Lottery ticket he stole from a woman he murdered because she looked like Lucy. (She is only one victim of the "Council Bluffs Killer.") Ben and Lucy marry, but Lucy learns the truth on her honeymoon, leaving her conflicted about whether to flee before the next lottery payment arrives. The plot twists several times before Ben finally has Lucy where he wants her—incarcerated for his crimes and desperate enough to welcome his visits.]

Sick of Larry. Dir. Scott R. Thompson. My Town Pictures, 2011. Principals: Kim Grimaldi, Kiera Morrill, Andrea Cunningham, Jess

Musgrave, Gretchen Skellenhagen, Jay Villwock, Matt Eastwold. [The recently widowed Imogene (Grimaldi) cannot bear her loneliness and has constant visits from the bizarre Larry (Villwock) and her solicitous stepson William (Eastvold). She decides to take in renters for companionship and quickly takes in Clementine (Morrill), Josie (Cunningham), and McKenzie (Skellenhagen). Clementine is haunted by the death of her mother and sleepwalks, Josie is overtly erotic, and McKenzie, a pre-law student, is fanatically organized. Yet they all agree that Larry is repulsive—he believes that "our saliva is our salvation," shares his spit at the dinner table, and sneaks a drink of Josie's bathwater when requested to fix the drain. Imogene becomes sicklier, and the girls conclude that Larry is poisoning her with strange fluids. To protect Imogene they decide to kill him and contrive a situation where he seems to die of fright. With the help of boyfriends, they leave dead Larry propped at a picnic table in the park. By film's end, all that we think we know from this tense narrative is cleverly upended. This film was shot in Ames and Des Moines.]

Ticket Out. Dir. Doug Lodato. Disparate Films/Minds Eye Entertainment/Moving Images, 2011. 90 min. Principals: Billy Burke, Alexandra Breckenridge, Colin Ford, Ray Liotta, [Jocelyn (Breckenridge) loses a custody battle when she keeps her son from testifying against his brutal father. With the help of Jim (Liotta) and an underground network, she and the children begin a journey that ends with their flying out of Canada to freedom, minus Jim, who has been shot. One of their stops is Willow Creek, Iowa, an island in the Mississippi River. After crossing the Mississippi, they make stops in Iowa and then cross the Missouri into the Dakotas and Canada, chased by law enforcement and then the husband's private detective. For reasons not entirely clear, the FBI involves itself in the case on the side of Jocelyn and Jim, who turns out to be an FBI agent. The ending leaves viewers with unanswered questions. Since the family is keeping a low profile, their stops tend to be small towns, truck stops, and isolated farmhouses. This movie was filmed in various Iowa locations including the Newton Courthouse, Mercy Capitol Hospital in Des Moines, the Adel town square, and an A&W restaurant in Indianola.]

Twelve Thirty. Dir. Jeff Lipsky. Twelve Thirty Productions, 2011. 120 min. Principals: Barbara Barrie, Reed Birney, Jonathan Groff, Mamie Gummer, Portia Reiners, Rebecca Schull, Karen Young. [Throughout the film we see Iowa City scenes, but the focus is not on place but on articulate, troubled people: an agoraphobic mom who sells furs from her home, her two daughters, her bi-sexual ex-husband, an aspiring young architect who is still a virgin until he has sex with both daughters and the mom within one week, and two British ladies, one dying, with remarkable lives. The director exposes the characters physically and emotionally in a series of memorable scenes. After the young man has sex with one of the sisters, despite her protests, in a dark closet at a party, the isolated family members unite to confront him and begin to open up to each other.] AFIs. *NYT* 13 Jan. 2011, C12.

At Any Price. Dir. Ramin Bahrani. Black Bear Pictures/Treehouse Pictures, 2012. 104 min. Principals: Clancy Brown, Kim Dickens, Zac Efron, Heather Graham, Dennis Quaid, Patrick W. Stevens. [Filmed in and around Dekalb, Illlinois, the film is a morally complex Iowa tragedy revealing that success at any price brings its own harvest of stress and sorrow. Henry Whipple (Quaid) farms 3000 acres of corn and is top salesman for Liberty Seeds in seven counties, but his greed and arrogance have alienated neighbors and his own sons. A former ISU football player, Grant (Stevens) has fled to Argentina to climb a summit to impress the father he resents, and young Dean (Efron) dreams of NASCAR stardom, not life on the family farm. Both Henry and Dean cut corners ethically. Pressured to succeed or else by his resentful father, who thinks Henry has it easy with his big harvester with AC and computerized technology, Henry buys 200 acres for Grant, ignoring the tenant family who will lose their livelihood, and hopes Grant will return to farm. He also cleans and resells copyrighted seeds and cheats on his wife. Son Dean, cocky and charming but weak like his Dad, steals a part for his racing car and self-indulgently takes out his big race failure on his girlfriend and family. The traditional Iowa icons are there (flags, the national anthem, a church service, gravel roads, acres of corn, familiar townscapes), but we know that this is not grandpop's rural Iowa. We see, for example, cell phones, the giant turbines that dot the Iowa landscape, and how the economic climate of farming in the twenty-first century has set neighbor against neighbor, despite surface friendliness. Dean's girlfriend has a dad in prison and a mom making meth. Zac remarks early on that there is nothing to do in Iowa but does settle down in the end to follow in his father's footsteps. Having climbed his mountain in Argentina, so high he could see Iowa, Grant will return. But the family—like the community—is morally compromised, as are the agribusinesses that operate in the country's heartland.] *V* 30 Aug. 2012.

Black Web. [Alternate titles: *Easton's Article; Router*]. Dir. Tim Connery. Flood 93 Productions/DreamCatcher Productions/Double Dubuque Productions, 2012. 89 min. Principals: Dan Flannery, Kristina Johnson, Chad Meyer. [In this science fiction-thriller-romance, Dubuque provides the setting. Easton Denning (Meyer) grew up there. When he was younger, his friend Tom drowned when the Mississippi River ice gave way after the two had fought over Hayley (Johnson), Easton having just told Tom that he and Hayley were forming a relationship behind Tom's back. Years later Easton, now a computer repair technician in Chicago, receives his own obituary and a set of instructions on his 1997-era computer along with a barrage of corrupted files. Following the instructions leads him back to Hayley, now a divorced elementary teacher. Together they try to avoid the seemingly certain future. Like many young Iowa directors, Tim Connery also wrote the screenplay for the film. The shots of wintertime Dubuque are full of recognizable landscape features. The Mississippi River's 1993 flooding is used to explain how the future may have slipped into the present on Easton's computer.]

Dropping Evil. [Alternate title: *Resist Evil*]. Adam Protextor. Roklaf Studios, 2012. 82 min. Principals: Rachel Howell, Zachary Eli Lint, Cassandra Powell, Armin Shimerman, Tom Taylor. [This horror movie was filmed partly in the Iowa City/Cedar Rapids area. Judging by the landline phones and older cars, the film was made before 2012 or set in an earlier era. A teen couple invites along two other teens for a weekend camping trip: the plain Becky (Powell), who brings along LSD and seems to be a spy for a mysterious corporation, and the much bullied, nerdy, religiously judgmental boy named Nancy. When the three slip Nancy some LSD in his juice as a joke, he thinks he sees them as they really are and goes on a righteous killing spree. All this is monitored by the mysterious corporate entity associated with "the gods" who need a morale booster. We learn that the corporation monitors unusual pregnancies that might indicate divine births. The end of the film leaves much unanswered, but we get a preview of *Dropping Evil 2*, which promises to answer some of our questions and develop the story further.]

Finding John Smith. Dir. Marlo Bernier. Smart House Films, 2012. 92 min. Principals: Jennifer Fontaine, Dominique Joelle, David Mattey, Lydia Blanco. [TV glam journalist Jodi (Fontaine) and her seven foot, teddy-bear cameraman Jake (Mattey) are in Iraq during the 2003 invasion to develop background on Gulf War Syndrome (GWS), associated with the 1990 Gulf War. In a firefight they grab a terrified girl, Aasemah (Joelle), who has fallen in the street after an explosion. Out of humanitarian instinct, they smuggle her back to the Midwest, partly because with the few English words she knows, she states her belief that her father is a soldier in Iowa named John Smith. With just that information, the journalists set off to find him so that Aasemah can be part of a family. Their search takes them to a somewhat demented elderly widow, an attorney who turns out to be a Korean War vet, a leering under-the-car hillbilly mechanic who is a Gulf War vet but was sterilized fifteen years before, and a gay veteran who can speak Farsi. The real father turns up as a mentally vacant GWS victim in a VA hospital. Jodi and Jake fulfill the opposites attract romantic formula and will become the parents of Aasemah, who has gained asylum through the Korean vet's assistance. The film shows Iowa's country roads handsomely and includes recognizable destinations at Strawberry Point and "Carter's Amazing Maze" near Princeton.]

Smitty. Dir David M. Evans. Tricoast Studios, 2012. 94 min. Principals: Peter Fonda, Louis Gossett, Jr., Jason London, Brandon Tyler Russell, Mira Sorvino. [Filmed in Dallas Center and Des Moines and set in fictional Summit Town (near Fort Dodge), this family movie focuses on a Chicago 13-year-old boy, Ben (Russell), who has gotten into trouble through a bad choice of friends. A court decision transplants him to an Iowa farm ("three years in juvenile detention or three months in Iowa") to live with a taciturn grandfather (Fonda) who is estranged from Ben's overworked single mother (Sorvino). Knowing he will need to use tough love on the kid, the grandfather provides Ben with a smart, loyal dog from the locale rescue shelter to be his friend. At first, the kid resists the dog, chores, making his own meals, and summer vacation study time. He tries to guilt his grandfather into buying him a used electric guitar. Over the summer Ben learns, sometimes the hard way, to be responsible, hard-working, and loving. He takes a job with his grandpa's friend Smitty (Gossett) to dig out an old tree stump to earn the money for the guitar. His mom, now with a nice veterinarian boyfriend, reconciles with her father toward the end of the summer, and they all go to the county fair in Fort Dodge. Ben and the now much loved mutt return to the city at summer's end. The crusty grandpa has proven to have a heart of gold. Ben has had to face Smitty's death and the near-death of the dog. The film has beautiful Iowa sky shots.]

The Wedge. Dir. Joe Clarke. Backrow Studios, 2012. 79 min. Principals: Thomas Beecher, Isai Rivera Blas, Jamie Schiller, Mike Schminke. [This farce filmed and set in Iowa City depicts the worst July 4th ever for Flint Schminke (Schminke), delivery boy for The Wedge pizzeria. Early frustrations include getting dumped by his girl-friend and putting up with idiotic roommates, a suck-up colleague, and bosses who think they are hilariously funny (not). Flint later witnesses a murder by an impatient, trigger-happy Asian thief planning a casino heist with his nephew and several short-lived henchmen. While steal-ing cars to escape his pursuers, Flint unknowingly kidnaps a cheerful baby and later three rowdy boys who dispense Dr. Phil advice to him about his love life. Fortunately, the police chief is so wacky that he can understand and empathize with all that has happened to Flint. The screenplay features funny dialogue and situations (e.g., the computer whiz nephew uses a Windows 95 operating system) and occasional Iowa references and landmarks. As a whole, the Iowans in this film are not too bright and prone to impatience and fighting—or to slacker/stoner behavior.]

Winning Favor. Dir. Jamey Durham. Engine 15 Media Group/ O.C. Basketball Productions, 2012. 70 min. Principals: Matthew Ashford, Bonnie Johnson, Dallas Mix. [In 2005 two Orange City high school boys' basketball teams won their respective divisions in state champi-onships, the first time a community under 100,000 had achieved that feat. Four boys played basketball together as kids with a dream of win-ning the state championships, two eventually going to MOC (Maurice-Orange City) Floyd Valley high school and two to Unity Christian high school. The film focuses on "the Dutch," the MOC team, and player Chris Vander Berg. In fall 2004, the coach takes Chris from the starting lineup, and Chris quits, his pride injured. His grandmother, formerly a fierce defensive player in half-court girls' basketball, convinces him to ask the coach to take him back. The coach and Chris's teammates—influenced by a God-centered team mission statement—welcome his return, and Chris later shoots the winning free throw in the state championship, even though his beloved grandma died shortly before the game. Based on a true story, the film is more concerned with life lessons than actual basketball scenes. The film carries a strong sense of place: Orange City's windmills, gardens, homes, schools, a hospital, as well as Orange City and U of Iowa tee-shirts.]

The Formula. Dir. Thomas Beecher and Joe Clarke. Backrow Studios, 2013. 90 min. Principals: Brandon Baker, Katie Goebel, Sasha Jackson, Mike Schminke, Reginald VelJohnson. [Romantic Quinn (Baker) and would-be womanizer Graham (Schminke) are engineering graduate students who share an apartment and a less than impressive track record with women. They develop an implausible mathematical formula to make them irresistible. Despite their advisor's ridicule and disapproval, they test the formula—and it works, though not as well with the women they really like. With recognizable landmarks in Iowa City and Cedar Rapids, this comedy presents a humorous view of college life and the seemingly insurmountable communication barrier between men and women when it comes to love. Joe Clarke wrote the screenplay, but some dialogue was improvised by the actors.]

II. Iowa Settings, Historical Films

The Law Commands. Dir. William Nigh. Crescent Pictures, 1937. 58 min. Principals: Matthew Betz, Bud Buster, Robert Fiske, Lorraine Hayes, Tom Keene, John Merton, David Sharpe, Marie Stoddard, Carl Stockdale. [This is a B-western set in Johnson County, IA, before passage of the Homestead Act in 1862. Squatters in the territory are threatened by "land sharks" who use night riding tactics to terrorize farmers so that a single owner John Abbot (Fiske) can monopolize the entire county in advance of the Homestead Act. The settlers disagree about the right tactics—whether to fight with guns or establish the rule of law through the creation of a Johnson County Claim Association, a kind of court to adjudicate and enforce land claims. Doctor Keith Kenton (Keene) emerges as a leader favoring legal action but is ostracized after the president of the new association is murdered by one of Abbot's thugs. Abbot then cunningly creates a Johnson County Protective Association, ostensibly to protect the settlers, but signing the agreement swindles them out of their land. Kenton persists in seeking legal resolutions and persuades the Governor of Iowa to appoint him as a special agent. Kenton and his specially appointed judge eventually prevail over the gangs. Events depicted in the film do not match precisely with documented history, though there was a Claims Association of Johnson County that functioned for four years prior to 1843. Physically the film looks as if it were shot at one of Hollywood's studio ranches on the edge of Los Angeles. The film is an excellent example of a particular kind of "History by Hollywood," which can spin a few facts into an exciting story.] AFI. *V* 17 Aug. 1938, 23.

Union Pacific. Dir. Cecil B. DeMille. Paramount, 1939. 135 min. Principals: Henry Kolker, Joel McCrea, Robert Preston, Barbara Stanwyck, Akim Tamiroff. Literary source: the Ernest Haycox novel *Trouble Shooter* (Garden City, NY: Doubleday and Doran: 1937). Academy Award nomination: Special Effects. [DeMille's splendorous movie combines adventure and romance in depicting the efforts to push the transcontinental railroad across the frontier from Council Bluffs to California, while financial schemers attempt to delay the project. Two former Civil War buddies are rivals for the engineer's daughter, Molly Monahan (Stanwyck). Council Bluffs commemorated the world premiere in Omaha with a 56-foot concrete golden spike that remains on display at South 16th Street and Ninth Avenue.] AFI. *NYT* 11 May 1939, 31; *V* 3 May 1939, 16.

Brigham Young–Frontiersman. [Alternate title: *Brigham Young*]. Dir. Henry Hathaway. Twentieth Century-Fox, 1940. 114 min. Principals: Mary Astor, John Carradine, Linda Darnell, Brian Donleavy, Dean Jagger, Tyrone Power, Vincent Price, Jean Rogers. [During the mid-nineteenth century, Mormons moved several times to escape persecution. After moving from New York to Illinois, they are again attacked. When Joseph Smith (Price), the founder, urges them to take up arms, he is accused of treason, imprisoned, and killed before he can be tried. Brigham Young (Jagger) decides to lead the Mormons in a westward direction, crossing the Mississippi into Iowa. From there, the group treks on to Council Bluffs, where some choose to stay and others cross the Missouri and head toward Utah in a long march on foot.] AFI. *NYT* 21 Sept. 1940, 13; *V* 28 Aug. 1940, 16.

The Sullivans. [Alternate titles: *The Fighting Sullivans; The Five Sullivans.*] Dir. Lloyd Bacon. The US Sullivans, Inc./Fox, 1944. 111 min. Principals: Anne Baxter, Ward Bond, Bobby Driscoll, Thomas Mitchell, Addison Richards, Selena Royle. Academy Award nomination: Writing (Original Story). [This amusing and touching film begins with the christening of the Sullivan boys, one by one, and ends with the christening of the navy destroyer USS *The Sullivans*, named in honor of the five brothers who died together on a cruiser ship near Guadalcanal in World War II. The film shows their rough and tumble Irish Catholic boyhood in Waterloo, IA. The boys are no saints, but they have an instinctive devotion to church, to nation, and especially to family. The wife of the youngest knows her husband would be miserable separated from his brothers, so she urges him to fight, even though they have a baby. As the ship sinks, four refuse to leave without their injured brother. This Iowa family celebrates duty and stoical self-sacrifice. When the officer comes to announce the death of the brothers, Mr. Sullivan goes to his job as a freight conductor for the Illinois Central because he hasn't missed a day in 33 years.] AFI. *NYT* 10 Feb. 1944, 19; *V* 9 Feb. 1944, 12.

The Rock Island Trail. [Alternate title: *Mississippi-Express*]. Dir. Joseph Kane. Republic, 1950. 90 min. Principals: Bruce Cabot, Lorna Gray, Adele Mara, Forrest Tucker, Chill Wills. [In this action-packed Western, Reed Loumas (Tucker) is determined to build the first railroad bridge over the Mississippi from Rock Island to Davenport and then extend the railroad across Iowa and into the West. He faces determined opposition from the stagecoach and steamship lines. Loumas is loved by a banker's daughter, Constance, and an Indian princess, Aleta. The World Premier of the film was in the Quad Cities on 27 Apr. 1950. It included Republic stars such as John Wayne, Roy Rogers, and Dale Evans parading from Silvis, the home yard of the Rock Island Lines, to the theatre in Rock Island.] *NYT* 28 June 1950, 19.

Bonnie and Clyde. Dir. Arthur Penn. Warner Brothers, 1967. 111 min. Principals: Warren Beatty, Faye Dunaway, Gene Hackman, Estelle Parsons, Michael J. Pollard. Academy Awards: Supporting Actor, Supporting Actress, Most Promising Newcomer, Cinematography, Screenwriting, and Screenplay. [This violent film presents the strange romance and bank-robbing adventures of Clyde Barrow (Beatty) and Bonnie Parker (Dunaway). The pair were fated to be ambushed in a shootout with law enforcement officials at Dexter, Iowa. They did not die there, however, but escaped to Louisiana where they were later killed.] AFI. *NYT* 14 Aug. 1967, 36; *V* 9 Aug. 1967, 6.

The Buddy Holly Story. Dir. Steve Rash. Innovisions, 1978. 113 min. Principals: Gary Busey, Conrad Janis, William Jordan, Maria Richwine, Charles Martin Smith. Literary source: Based on the book *Buddy Holly: His Life and Music* by John Goldrosen (Bowling Green, OH: Popular Press, 1975). Academy Award: Original Song Score or Adaptation; Nomination: Best Actor. [This highly acclaimed film biography of Buddy Holly's rock and roll career closes with his last concert in Clear Lake, Iowa, sponsored by "WIOA Radio." Later that night Holly, Ritchie Valens, and J. P. Richardson, Jr. (the Big Bopper) die when their small charter plane crashes. The Iowa teens in the audience that night wave their arms, clap, sing along, and cheer as Buddy sings his trademark songs, some of which ("That'll be the Day," "Not Fade Away") eerily foreshadow his death. Ironically, former band members had planned to meet him in 'Clear Lake to propose reuniting the Crickets but visited his wife, Maria, instead. The brief glimpse of the bus pulling into Clear Lake shows a large municipal auditorium. The Iowa teens are presented as typical kids of the era.] AFIs. *NYT* 21 July 1978, C 14; *V* 17 May 1978, 54.

Friendly Fire. Dir. David Greene. Marble Arch Productions, 1979. 146 min. Principals: Ned Beatty, Carol Burnett, Timothy Hutton, Sam Waterston. Literary source: C. D. B. Bryan, *Friendly Fire* (New York: Putnam's, 1976). [Gene (Beatty) and Peg Mullen (Burnett) of LaPorte City, Iowa, were farmers who lost a son to a "friendly fire" incident in Vietnam. Anger over the Pentagon's explanations and treatment of them led to their publishing a full-page protest ad in the *Des Moines Register*. As they lived their life of incomprehension and anger, they became national icons representing ordinary citizens who had left Nixon's Silent Majority and turned toward activism. The film is set in the Iowa farmscape. The narrative emphasizes the connection of the Mullens with the earth and their quickly lost innocence as they encounter the world outside Iowa.]

Bill. Dir. Anthony Page. Alan Landsburg Productions, 1981. 100 min. Principals: Dennis Quaid, Mickey Rooney, Largo Woodruff. [This is a docudrama about a profoundly retarded man, Bill Sackter (Rooney), who was institutionalized at the Faribault State Hospital from the age of seven into his fifties. Working as a dishwasher in Minnesota, Bill accidentally meets a struggling young filmmaker, Barry Morrow, who takes an interest in filming his life. Morrow eventually brings Bill to the University of Iowa after accepting a teaching post. There "Wild Bill" operates a coffee kiosk at the School of Social Work. The full story of his acceptance and flowering has been told in a book by University of Iowa Social Work Professor Thomas Walz, *The Unlikely Celebrity: Bill Sackter's Triumph Over Disability* (Carbondale, IL: Southern Illinois UP, 1998). Rooney earned Emmy and Golden Globe awards for his fine performance as Bill. Clips of the real Bill Sackter appear in both films.] *NYT* 22 Dec. 1981, C15.

Bill: On His Own. Dir. Anthony Page. Alan Landsburg Productions, 1983. 100 min. Principals: Helen Hunt, Dennis Quaid, Mickey Rooney,

Largo Woodruff, Teresa Wright. [In this sequel to *Bill* (1981), we learn about Bill's (Rooney) struggles in Iowa City when his mentor and protector, Barry Morrow, leaves Iowa City for Los Angeles. Bill is watched over in his transition by a tenacious but impatient social work student, Jenny Wells (Hunt). He works toward celebrating his Bar Mitzvah after accidentally discovering a Jewish heritage. This film explores departmental and university politics at Iowa as they affect the advocates for Bill.] *NYT* 9 Nov. 1983, C20.

Who Will Love My Children? Dir. John Earman. ABC Films, 1983. 100 min. Principals: Ann-Margret, Cathryn Damon, Frederic Forrest, Donald Moffat. [This TV docudrama tells the story of Lucile Fray (Ann-Margret), a 1950s Iowa mother of ten children. She lives a hard life in rural Iowa with an arthritic and alcoholic husband (Forrest) whom she cannot trust as a primary caregiver for her children. After discovering that she has terminal cancer, she works on finding loving homes for her children, insisting that she visit each one before placing her child with them.] NS. *NYT* 14 Feb. 1983, C15.

La Bamba. Dir. Luis Valdez. New Visions, 1987. 103 min. Principals: Rosanna DeSoto, Esai Morales, Joe Pantoliano, Elizabeth Pena, Lou Diamond Phillips, Danielle von Erneck. [The film is based on the true story of Mexican-American rock and roll singer Ritchie Valens, who died with Buddy Holly and the Big Bopper in an airplane crash after a concert at Clear Lake, Iowa. Only 17 at his death, Ritchie, formerly a farm laborer, was already beginning to succeed, having recorded a handful of hits and appeared on *American Bandstand*. The film focuses on his relationships with his Anglo girlfriend, Donna, and his troubled, alcoholic brother, Bob. Just prior to winning the coin toss to take the "Clear Lake Charter Service" plane rather than the bus, the sick and very cold Ritchie had reconciled over the phone with his brother. Before leaving California for the tour, he and Donna had declared their love for each other and spoken of marriage. The concert scene provides only a brief glimpse of Iowa teens on their feet swaying and cheering to the music.] AFIs. *NYT* 24 July 1987; *V* 31 Dec. 1986.

Crash Landing: The Rescue of Flight 232. [Alternate title: *A Thousand Heroes*]. Dir. Lamont Johnson. Bob Banner Productions and ABC, 1992. Principals: James Coburn, Charlton Heston, Richard Thomas. 95 min. [This film is a docudramatic recreation of the crash landing of United Flight 232 in Sioux City, Iowa, during the summer of 1989. In addition to exceptional piloting by Al Haynes (Heston), the rescue operation reflects a heroic community of ordinary people who performed miracles of logistics and medical care to save 185 passengers in a catastrophe that killed 111. The film manufactures a bit of conflict between rescue leaders for dramatic purpose and occasioned some irritation at the time of the film's premier showing in Sioux City. There was also disappointment that *A Thousand Heroes* was not the title, since that would have highlighted the community response rather than the disaster itself. The extras in the film were recruited from among the people of Siouxland—the tri-state area of Iowa, Nebraska, and South Dakota. Some rescue workers played roles in the film.]

In the Best Interest of the Children. Dir. Michael Ray Rhodes. NBC Productions, 1992. 96 min. Principals: Elizabeth Ashley, John Dennis Johnson, Sarah Jessica Parker, Lexi Randall, Sally Struthers. [Estherville, Iowa, was the scene of a late 1980s custody battle. NBC's docudrama, filmed in Iowa, fictionalizes the family names and tells the story of Callie Cain (Parker), a depressed and financially struggling mother of five who lives with a succession of abusive boyfriends. Her neglect of the children's clothing and food brings the attention of social services, which reassign her children to foster parents Patty Pepper (Struthers) and her husband Harlan (Johnson). The Peppers' inability to have children has turned Patty into an overzealous Donna Reed personality, determined to win the love of the confused children, torn between two mothers. After losing her children, Callie undergoes treatment at a state psychiatric unit and then decides that she wants to get her children back. Happy to be cared for by the Peppers on their farm, the children, caught up in Patty's crusade to keep them with her, do not want to return to Callie. A legal battle ensues.] *NYT* 14 Feb. 1992, C28.

Taking Back My Life: The Nancy Ziegenmeyer Story. Dir. Harry Winer. Lyttle-Heshty Prod. with CBS, 1992. 97 min. Principals: Eileen Brennan, Ellen Burstyn, Joanna Cassidy Shelley Hack, Stephen Lang, Patricia Wettig. [In this TV movie based on real events, Nancy Ziegenmeyer (Wettig) of Grinnell, a former bartender, is kidnapped and raped. Frustrated by the slow workings of the legal system and supported by her stoical ex-husband, Steve (Lang), and by *Des Moines Register* Editor, Geneva Overholser, Nancy goes public with her story and gets admiration for her courage. The film focuses on Nancy's relationship with Steve; it is strained when she becomes a celebrity, and it underscores the points that Iowa is not a safe place and the criminal justice system is very challenging.]

Whose Child Is This? The War for Baby Jessica. Dir. John Kent Harrison. Orange Productions with ABC Productions, 1993. 96 min. Principals: Susan Dey, David Keith, Michael Ontkean, Amanda Plummer. Literary source: Lucinda Franks, "The War for Baby Clausen: Annals of Law. (Interstate Adoption Fight between Cara Clausen Schmidt and Jan and Robby DeBoer)," *New Yorker,* 22 Mar. 1993, 56-73. [This made-for-TV film drew on the story of Iowans Cara Clausen (Plummer) and Dan Schmidt (Keith), the unmarried birth parents of baby Jessica. Clausen had agreed to give up Jessica to a middle class couple Robby (Dey) and Jan Deboer (Ontkean). Dan Schmidt had not agreed to the arrangement and insisted on getting Jessica back. The battle was ugly. The docudrama producers acquired story rights from the more stable Deboers and accordingly bestow their admiration upon them, while presenting the Iowa contenders as repulsive trailer folk whose legal rights are nonetheless vindicated by Iowa courts.] NS. *NYT* 24 Sept. 1993; *V* 4 Oct. 1993.

Wyatt Earp. Dir. Lawrence Kasdan. Tig Productions and Kasdan Pictures, 1994. 189 min. Principals: Linden Ashby, Kevin Costner, Joanna Going, Gene Hackman, Michael Madsen, Dennis Quaid, Catherine O'Hara, Isabella Rosellini. [This is the well-known saga of Wyatt Earp and includes all the usual shootings. Striving for some biographical accuracy, the film correctly places the birth and first years of Wyatt Earp (Costner) in Pella, Iowa. Pella, incidentally, has preserved the Earp home, which has earned a place on the National Register of Historic Buildings.] AFIs. NYT 24 June 1994, C10; V 20 June 1994, 41, 44.

The Tuskegee Airmen. Dir. Robert Markowitz. HBO, 1995. 106 min. Principals: Andre Braugher, Laurence Fishburne, Cuba Gooding, Jr., John Lithgow, Christopher McDonald, Rosemary Murphy, Allen Payne, Courtney B. Vance, Malcolm Jamal Warner. [Based on the true story of the training and combat missions of the US Army Air Corps' first squadron of African-American pilots, the "Fighting 99th" of the 332nd Fighter Group, the film focuses on Hannibal Lee, Jr. (Fishburne), of Ottumwa, Iowa. He is called "Iowa" in the film. We see Lee leave his family's loving home to follow his dream of becoming a pilot. During training at Tuskegee and later while serving overseas, Lee writes to his family daily. The Tuskegee Airmen, including Lee, face prejudice and discouragement repeatedly, within and outside the Army Air Corps. Lee's Iowa character traits—self-respect, professionalism, patriotism, good sense, and compassion—contribute to his success in training and his survival as a combat pilot. (Most of his original pals don't make it.) Lee and his fellow Tuskeegee airmen eventually win praise for their skill in the skies, never losing a single bomber they escorted.] *V* 21 Aug. 1995, 23.

The Siege at Ruby Ridge. [Alternate title: *Ruby Ridge: An American Tragedy*]. Dir. Roger Young. Victor Television Productions/CBS, 1996. 192 min. Principals: G. W. Bailey, Joe Don Baker, Laura Dern, Kirstin Dunst, Diane Ladd, Randy Quaid. Literary source: Jess Walter, *Every Knee Shall Bow* (New York: Harper, 1996). [Based on real events, this TV movie depicts a Cedar Falls area family, the Weavers, who, at first, embody stereotypical "Iowa qualities": fervent religious faith, strong family ties, cheerful neighborliness. The early Iowa scenes show Randy (Quaid) and Vicki (Dern) adopting apocalyptic religious views derived from an interpretation of Old Testament prophecy. Their fears of a "Zionist One World Conspiracy" lead them to northern Idaho where the family adopts Aryan Nation views, the children wear swastikas, and Randy gets involved in gun trafficking. Confusions among over-zealous federal agents lead to a siege in which Vicki and son Samuel are killed. A jury trial eventually exposes the government's errors as well as the family's hatred of non-whites and the government. The loyalty and love of Vicki's Iowa family, who do not share her views, is a strong theme. Randy and the remaining children return to Iowa after the siege.]

The Straight Story. Dir. David Lynch. Disney Films, 1999. 111 min. Principals: Richard Farnsworth, Jane Galloway Heitz, Jennifer Edward-Hughes, Everett McGill, Sissy Spacek, Harry Dean Stanton. Academy Award nomination: Actor in a Leading Role. [The film is based on the true story of Alvin Straight (Farnsworth), a 73-year-old resident of Laurens, Iowa, who resolves to visit his stroke-afflicted brother Lyle (Stanton) in Mt. Zion, Wisconsin. Unable to drive a car and unwilling to ride the bus, he makes the long journey on a John Deere riding mower. The quiet purpose of the slow trip is to outgrow a ten-year-old, alienating anger against his brother. Along the way he offers laconic revelations from his hard-earned wisdom to the depressed, the overwrought, some touring bicyclists (a mini-RAGBRAI?), a WWII-haunted veteran, bickering brothers, and a Catholic priest. A magical Iowa landscape is a prominent actor. Waves of golden corn stalks, the lush pastures of the hills, the brilliant stars of an unpolluted rural sky are healing agents for this spiritual pilgrim. His daughter (Spacek), afflicted with mental disabilities that led to the loss of her children, is a constant in the film—courageous, competent, and caring about her father. While not stylish or skilled as conversationalists, the Iowans portrayed have good hearts. This film was nominated for, and won, many awards around the world.] *NYT* 15 Oct. 1999; *V* 24 May 1999, 73-74.

The Coverup. Dir. Brian Jun. Roberts/David Film Production, 2008. Principals: Gabriel Mann, Eliza Dushku, John Savage, Lee Garlington, Michael Welch. [Based on a Marshalltown incident in 1983, this is the story of novice lawyer Stuart Pepper (Mann) and his decision to serve as plaintiff's attorney in a wrongful death suit. His clients are the Thacker parents (Savage and Garlington) who believe that the Marshalltown police murdered their son Kevin (Welch) after a drunken driving arrest. Pepper's legal practice is getting a slow start, and alleging criminal police misconduct can backfire against his career and young family. He is an idealist ("Socrates is my hero"), and this leads to spousal conflicts over whether they will lose their home and marriage if he persists. He is encouraged to go forward by the other woman in his life, the paralegal Monica (Dushku) who, in some ways, knows courtroom litigation far better than he. Based on forensic evidence suggesting that Kevin was killed with a police nightstick rather than a leap from a tall building, the Thackers win the jury's vote in their wrongful death and damages case against the police. However, the criminal charges against the police are not upheld, leading Pepper to create the the film to give the case a public profile. Pepper wrote the story and screenplay in addition to serving as executive producer. Shooting was done in Alton, Illinois, and an assortment of locations in Los Angeles.]

Bonnie and Clyde (TV miniseries). Dir. Bruce Beresford. Sony Pictures Television, 2013. 240 min. Principals: Emile Hirsch, Holliday Grainger, Sarah Hyland, Elizabeth Reaser, Holly Hunter, William Hurt. [At four hours, this is the most leisurely film treatment of the legend of Clyde Barrow (Hirsch) and Bonnie Parker (Holliday). Vintage news reels and news clippings intermittently root the events in period history. The film is scrupulous about the crimes' chronology, which means that there must be a visit to Dexter, Iowa, where Clyde goes to a store for bandages and ice where his blood from a Missouri shootout conspicuously drips on a store counter. The shootout occurs at the Dexfield Park campground and results in the separation from brother Buck and his wife as the more infamous pair slips away to Louisiana. The town recognizes the historical event at its Dexter Museum, which sells Bonnie and Clyde biographies and has exhibits relating to the battle. This film was shot at Louisiana locations.] *NYT* 5 Dec. 2013; *V* 4 Dec. 2013.

III. Traveling Iowans

Bill Henry. Dir. Thomas Ince. Thomas H. Ince Productions, 1919. 5 reels, silent. Principals: William Carroll, Charles Ray, Edith Roberts, Bert Woodruff. [Set in Alabama, the story presents Bill Henry Jenkins (Ray), a hotel clerk. Into his life comes a lovely lady from Iowa, Lela Mason (Roberts), who has come to Alabama to claim a farm that she has inherited. After attempted swindles and seductions by predatory locals, she turns the tables and claims the money realized by the sale of her property, which is discovered to have oil.] NS. AFI. *NYT* 18 Aug. 1919, 9; *V* 22 Aug. 1919, 77.

Crooked Straight. Dir. Jerome Storm. Thomas H. Ince Productions, 1919. 5 reels, silent. Principals: Wade Butler, Otto Hoffman, Gordon Mullen, Charles Ray, Margery Wilson. [The action focuses on the fate of Ben Trimble (Ray), an Iowa boy just arrived in Chicago. He is immediately flimflammed out of his life savings of $1000. As a result, he is coerced into a life of crime to survive. He eventually moves to the country to raise the children of a dead partner in crime. Despite many complications arising from his criminal past, he gets to marry the woman next door. This is the first film with a naive-Iowan-in-the-big-city theme.] NS. AFI. *V* 24 Oct. 1919, 60.

Stardust. Dir. Hobart Henley. Hobart Henley Productions, 1921. 6 reels, silent. Principals: Mary Foy, Hope Hampton, George Humbert, Charles Musset, Vivian Ogden, James Rennie, Edna Ross, Noel Tearle, Charles Wellesley, Gladys Wilson. Literary source: Fannie Hurst, *Stardust* (New York: Harper, 1919). [Lily Becker (Ross) has been raised in an Iowa home with a tyrannical mother who refuses to nurture her musical aspirations. Lily is compelled to marry a wealthy tyrant, Albert Penny (Tearle), who makes her miserable. Pregnant, she flees to New York, almost starves, and has a baby who dies. She meets up with a musical fellow who believes in her singing and leads her to an operatic career. The brutal husband back in Iowa dies in a railway accident, leaving her free to pursue a life with her fellow musician in the big city. At film's end she attains the pinnacle of sophistication and personal fulfillment, singing the role of Thaïs at the opera.] NS. AFI. *NYT* 6 Feb. 1922, 9.

Night Life of New York. Dir. Allan Dwan. Famous Players-Lasky, 1925. 8 reels, silent. Principals: Dorothy Gish, George Hackathorn, Riley Hatch, Arthur Houseman, Rod La Rocque, Ernest Torrence, Helen Lee Worthing. [John Bentley (Torrence), a father living in New York, hates it, while his Iowa son, Ronald Bentley (LaRocque), is bored with Iowa and wants to come to New York. Dad invites him to come but contrives so much trouble that he expects his son to go running back to Iowa. Things go awry, and the son is charged with a crime. He is saved by telephone operator Meg (Gish), who eventually becomes his bride. Dad's plan works out: Ronald does take Meg back to Iowa.] NS. AFI. *NYT* 14 July 1925, 14; *V* 15 July 1925.

A Slave of Fashion. Dir. Hobart Henley. Metro-Goldwyn-Mayer, 1925. 6 reels, silent. Principals: Sidney Bracy, Mary Carr, Estelle Clark, Lew Cody, James Corrigan, Miss DuPont, William Haines, Vivia Ogden, Norma Shearer. [Katherine Emerson (Norma Shearer) plays a restless young woman from Iowa who wants to experience big city life. As she travels to New York, an accident occurs that kills a woman whose purse she takes. In it she finds an invitation to spend time in a New York apartment. After moving in, her Iowa parents and Aunt Sophie arrive at the Park Avenue apartment and want to know what she's doing there. The daughter fabricates a yarn about being married to a man who has left for Europe. The mother is alarmed about his desertion of her and writes to the owner in Europe, urging him to come home. When he does, the daughter is exposed. However, he finds her charming enough to marry anyway.] NS. AFI. *NYT* 21 July 1925, 26; *V* 15 July 1925.

Midnight Daddies. Dir. Mack Sennett. Mack Sennett Productions, 1929. 6 reels, silent. Principals: Alma Bennett, Andy Clyde, Jack Cooper, Harry Gribbon, Addie McPhail, Rosemary Theby, Katherine Ward. [Charlie Mason (Gribbon), owner of a nearly bankrupt, big-city fashion shop, takes some of his models to the beach. There, the ex-Iowan meets his hometown cousin Wilbur Louder (Clyde), vacationing in the city with wife (Theby) and mother-in-law (Ward). Mason senses that Louder is a little dopey about the pretty girls and plots to use them in getting his money away from him. The wife figures out what is happening, gets Mason drunk, and exposes the plot. Wilbur almost kills himself, but his wife forgives him, and things go back to normal.] NS. AFI. *V* 16 Oct. 1929.

High Society Blues. Dir. David Butler. Fox Film, 1930. 10 reels, silent. Principals: William Collier, Sr., Charles Compton, Gregory Gaye, Janet Gaynor, Charles Farrell, Louise Fazenda, Hedda Hopper, Brandon Hurst, Lucien Littlefield. Literary source: Dana Burnett, "Those High Society Blues," *Saturday Evening Post*, 23 May 1925, 8-9. [A wealthy family in Iowa, the Grangers, sell their business and move to Scarsdale, New York. The son meets the daughter of the rich Divine family next door. Her family scorns the newcomers. While her mother schemes for her to marry European royalty, and the fathers feud on Wall Street, the two young people fall in love and eventually reconcile their families.] NS. AFI. *NYT* 19 Apr. 1930, 15; *V* 23 Apr. 1930, 26.

As Husbands Go. Dir. Hamilton MacFadden. Jesse L. Lasky Productions and Fox Film 1933. 78 min. Principals: Warner Baxter, Catherine Doucet, G. P. Huntley, Jr., Warner Oland, Helen Vinson. Dramatic source: the play *As Husbands Go* by Rachel Crothers, as produced by John Golden (New York, 5 Mar. 1931). [A pair of women from Dubuque, the married Lucille (Vinson) and widow Emmy (Doucet), travel to Paris. Meeting a pair of men much to their liking, they are especially irritated by their return to boring Iowa and Lucille's artless husband, Charles (Warner Baxter). When the Continental sophisticates Ronald Derbyshire (Huntley, Jr.) and Hippolitus Lomi (Oland) show up to visit in Dubuque, Ronald befriends Charles and confesses his selfish and unfriendly designs. He disappears the next day, Lucille regains her love for the dull husband, and Emmy solidifies her relationship with Hippolitus, overcoming the initial objections of her daughter.] NS. AFI. *NYT,* 26 Jan. 1934, 20; *V* 30 Jan. 1934, 12.

Men of the Night. Dir. Lambert Hillyer. Columbia Pictures, 1934. 58 min. Principals: Judith Allen, Lucille Ball, Ward Bond, Bruce Cabot, Arthur Rankin, Matthew Betz, John Kelly, Walter McGrail, Arthur Rankin, Maidel Turner, Charles C. Wilson. [This film depicts an Iowan, Mary Higgins (Allen), in Hollywood. She has come hoping that she will have a chance for movie stardom but has to take a job at a sandwich stand. A detective Kelly (Cabot) who has been watching the sandwich stand for criminals accuses her of being allied with criminals who come there, and she goes undercover for the police to prove that she's on their side. Her participation leads to her abduction by the gang. After the police retrieve her, Kelly sends her back to Iowa and then relents and fetches her back to Hollywood.] NS. AFI. *V* 4 Dec. 1934, 12.

Times Square Lady. Dir. George B. Seitz. Metro-Goldwyn-Mayer, 1935. Principals: Virginia Bruce, Robert Elliot, Raymond Hatton, Isabel Jewell, Fred Kohler, Henry Kolker, Jack LaRue, Nat Pendleton, Paul Stanton, Robert Taylor, Helen Twelvetrees. [A twenty-two-year-old Iowa girl inherits several businesses from her father, who has been a Broadway promoter in New York. When she arrives to investigate the enterprises, a nightclub, a hockey team, gambling, a dog track, everyone assumes that she's a patsy who can be bilked out of her assets. One of the swindlers, assigned to frighten her into a panic sale, falls in love with her. Then they turn a caper against the crooks who are trying to cheat her. Eventually the plucky Iowan can leave New York with her fortune and the loving criminal she has converted.] NS. AFI. *NYT* 15 Mar. 1935, 25; *V* 20 Mar. 1935, 17.

Farmer in the Dell. Dir. Ben Holmes. RKO-Radio, 1936. 67 min. Principals: Frank Albertson, Lucille Ball, Rafael Corio, Esther Dale, Maxine Jennings, Ray Mayer, Moroni Olsen, Jean Parker, Fred Stone. Literary source: Phil Stong, *Farmer in the Dell* (New York: Harcourt, 1935), also serialized in *The Saturday Evening Post* from 26 Jan. to 15 Feb. 1935. [The plot involves an Iowa farmer who retires to the Los Angeles area; his daughter craves to be in the film industry, but he, improbably, becomes a famous character actor himself.] NS. AFI. *NYT* 7 Mar. 1936, 11; *V* 11 Mar. 1936, 15.

We Have Our Moments. Dir. Alfred L. Werker. Universal Pictures, 1937. 65 min. Principals: Mischa Auer, James Dunn, Sally Eilers, Thurston Hall, David Niven, Grady Sutton. [Clem Porter (Sutton) is a bowling devotee who lives in the small town of Brattelburo with his fiancée, Mary Smith (Eilers). They are to be married soon, but his commitment to bowling requires that their honeymoon be spent in nearby Sioux City. For her, such a honeymoon is too depressing to consider, so she books passage on a ship to Europe. She tells Clem that she will come back after learning something about the larger world.] NS. AFI. *NYT* 30 Apr. 1937, 17; *V* 5 May 1937, 16.

Keep Smiling. [Alternate title: *Hello Hollywood*]. Dir. Herbert I. Leeds. Twentieth Century-Fox Film, 1938. 77 min. Principals: Robert Allen, Gloria Stuart, Jane Prouty, Helen Westley, Jane Withers, Henry Wilcoxon. [Jane Rand (Withers) is an orphan with an Uncle Jonathan (Wilcoxon), a famous Hollywood film director. Without informing him, she decides to go spend the summer at his home, and arrives to discover him drunk and losing all his possessions. Jane is befriended by Uncle Jonathan's secretary, Carol Walters (Stuart), a woman from Iowa with a fiancé, Stanley Harper (Allen), who is pressuring her to come back and marry him. With the help of Carol and Jane, Jonathan manages to get work again. Stanley has telegrammed that he's coming to take Carol back to Iowa and threatens to go straight back if she doesn't meet him at the train station. She decides to work for Jonathan again, and he decides to propose marriage to her.] NS. AFI. *NYT* 10 Aug. 1938, 15; *V* 17 Aug. 1938, 22.

The Flying Deuces. [Alternate title: *The Aviators*]. Dir. A. Edward Sutherland. Borris Morros Productions, 1939. 65 min. Principals: Oliver Hardy, Stan Laurel, Jean Parker. [Ollie is a fishmonger from Des Moines who went to Paris and met the lovely Georgette, who turned against him. As he contemplates suicide in the River Seine, a legionnaire comes by and suggests enlistment in the Foreign Legion. With Stan, he joins for life, but the service quickly becomes boring. Then they discover that Georgette was actually the wife of their superior. They decide to desert, are captured, and are sentenced to death. Hiding in a plane, they accidentally start and eventually crash it. Stan survives, but Ollie ascends to heaven and then returns as a horse.] AFI. *NYT* 24 Nov. 1939, 29; *V* 11 Oct. 1939, 13.

Let's Go Collegiate. Dir. Jean Yarbrough. Monogram Pictures, 1941. 62 min. Principals: Frankie Darro, Marcie Mae Jones, Keye Luke, Jackie Moran, Mantan Moreland, Gale Storm, Frank Sully. [Fraternity boys at Rawley University promise their girls that rowing champ Bob Terry will compete for Rawley. When Bob is drafted, they recruit a burly stranger off the streets, "Herk" Bevans, to impersonate Bob. Herk is no brain like the real Bob, but he soon charms the girlfriends and then blackmails the frat boys into helping him stay in college to be with the girls. Before the big race, two alumni come "all the way from Des Moines" to see Bob Terry row. When the biology professor threatens to keep the frat boys from rowing (their grades have taken a dive while tutoring Herk), the alums coerce the professor to relent, commenting that they have forgotten all they learned in college. Later, when the alums have seen a wanted poster for Herk, a burglar and safe cracker, they punch out and hold captive their old pal Slugger, now a policeman, until the race is over, and Rawley wins. The film features musical numbers by Jones and Storm and the popular Frankie Darro-Mantan Moreland comic duo. The film is "of its era" when it comes to portraying African and Chinese Americans.] AFI. *V* 12 Nov. 1941, 9.

Melody Lane. Dir. Charles Lamont. Universal Pictures, 1941. 60 min. Principals: Mary Lou Cook, Don Douglas, Leon Errol, Anne Gwynne, Joe McMichael, Judd McMichael, Ted McMichael, Robert Paige. [J. Roy Thomas (Douglas) represents a client, McKenzie (Errol), who advertises Kornies Breakfast Food on the radio. McKenzie wrecks every attempt to develop an ad because he always joins into any performing group. Since no one in New York will work for Thomas, he sends his aide to Yuba City, Iowa, to recruit The Gabe Morgan Rhythmeers. The group goes to New York and experiences similar frustrations with McKenzie, threatening to go back to Iowa. But romances develop, creating an incentive to battle the awkward sponsor. McKenzie is maneuvered out of the ad production, the Rhythmeers stay, and the predictable engagements are announced.] NS. AFI. *Daily Variety* 10 Dec. 1941, 3.

Navy Blues. Dir. Lloyd Bacon. Warner Bros., 1941. 109 min. Principals: Ann Sheridan, Jack Oakie, Martha Raye Jack Haley, Herbert Anderson, Jack Carson, Jackie C. Gleason, William T. Orr, Richard Lane, John Ridgely, Navy Blues Sextette. [In this musical Lilibell Jordan (Raye), a showgirl working in Hawaii with pal Margie Jordan (Sheridan), wants her alimony from her ex-husband, sailor Powerhouse Bolton (Haley), buddy of Cake O'Hare (Okie). Short of funds for a wild shore leave, the sailors take bets on the results of an upcoming gunnery contest, knowing that the current champion, Homer Matthews, is soon to be transferred to their ship. When they find out Homer's service will be up before the contest, they enlist Margie's help to seduce the shy sailor from Iowa to reenlist. Together Margie and Homer participate in Iowa-type activities such as a livestock exhibition and rowing, but Homer refuses to reenlist because he wants to marry Margie and take her back to the family corn and hog farm in Aplington, Butler County, Iowa. When the guys tell Homer Margie has been stringing him along to make him reenlist, he does reenlist—to be near her. Too depressed to shoot in the contest, Homer changes his mind when Margie flies over the ship in an airplane and shouts a hog call that convinces him she loves him. Homer wins the contest, and Lillibeth gets her alimony.] NS. AFI. *NYT* 20 Sept. 1941; 11; *V* 13 Aug. 1941, 8.

Don't Get Personal. [Alternate title: *Nobody's Fool*]. Dir. Charles Lamont. Universal Pictures, 1942. 60 min. Principals: Mischa Auer, Jane Frazee, Anne Gwynne, Hugh Herbert, Robert Paige. [A pickle millionaire, Oscar Whippet, dies in an airplane accident, and his Iowa cousin, Elmer Whippet (Herbert), inherits the profitable business. A pair of Oscar's associates first attempt (unsuccessfully) to buy the company and then try various swindles that presuppose Elmer's stupidity. Elmer sees through the schemes and fires the scheming executives.] NS. AFI. *V* 31 Dec. 1942, 8.

The Major and the Minor. Dir. Billy Wilder. Paramount, 1942. 100 min. Principals: Robert Benchley, Rita Johnson, Diana Lynn, Ginger Rogers, Ray Milland. Literary source: Edward Child Carpenter's play *Connie Goes Home* (New York: S. French, 1923) and Fannie Kilbourne's *Saturday Evening Post* story "Sunny Goes Home" (1921). [Wilder's witty comedy turns on Iowa-bred Susan Applegate's (Rogers) posing as a child ("Sue-Sue") to get half-price train fare. She must flee morally unwholesome New York City, where she has been groped and propositioned once too often. Awaiting in Stevenson, Iowa, are her jam and jelly making mom and Will Duffy, her "plain, honest, slow-witted" boyfriend who runs a feed and grain store. En route to Iowa, Susan becomes embroiled in funny situations with a Major Kirby (Milland), his fiancée, and hundreds of military school cadets attracted to Sue-Sue like moths to a flame. The screenplay positions Iowa, predictably, as the safe, dull, patriotic breadbasket. As an Iowa woman, Susan is a breath of fresh air. While objecting to sexual harassment, she is no hick and no prude. Her charm, sophistication, and risk-taking spirit—as well as her kindness to the officer and a teenage girl—ultimately lead to her marriage with the nice, dim, naive Kirby, soon to begin active military service.] AFI. *NYT* 17 Sept. 1942, 21; *V* 2 Sept. 1942, 18.

Double Exposure. Dir. William Berke. Pine-Thomas Productions, 1944. 63 min. Principals: Jane Farrar, Nancy Kelly, Chester Morris, Phillip Terry. [Pat Marvin is a female photographer in Iowa, whose work has attracted the attention of *Flick Magazine* in New York City. Editor Larry Burke (Morris) is ordered to hire Pat, who must leave her boyfriend, Ben Scribner (Terry), back in Iowa. Complicated adventures and romantic liaisons follow.] NS. AFI. *V* 20 Dec. 1944, 17.

Blonde from Brooklyn. Dir. Del Lord. Columbia Pictures, 1945. 64 min. Principals: Thurston Hall, Lynn Merrick, Robert Stanton, Mary Treen, Gwen Verdon. [Dixon Harper (Stanton) from Dubuque, Iowa, has been released from the Army and would like to resume his career as a singer and dancer. He meets a girl, Susan Parker (Lynn Merrick), who would also like to perform, and they persuade an orchestra leader to let them try something for an audience. They are successful and fall into the hands of "Southern Colonel" Hubert Farnsworth (Hall). His plan is to develop their Southern accents and mannerisms so that they can appear on the "Plantation Coffee Time" radio series. The Colonel also has a scheme to misrepresent Susan as a missing heir for a large estate. In the ensuing confusions, Dixon and Susan are alienated from one another, but reunited in the end as radio performers.] NS. AFI. *V* 27 June 1945, 16.

Bud Abbott and Lou Costello in Hollywood. [Alternate titles: *Close Shave*; *Abbott and Costello in Hollywood*]. Dir. S. Sylvan Simon. Metro-Goldwyn-Mayer, 1945. 83 min. Principals: Warner Anderson, Bud Abbott, Lou Costello, Frances Rafferty, Jean Porter, Robert Stanton. [Buzz Curtis (Abbott) and Abercrombie (Costello) work a "barbershop service to the stars" enterprise in Hollywood. As they give a shave to successful agent Norman Royce (Anderson) at his office, a singer, Jeff Parker (Stanton) from Des Moines, comes seeking help to get into the movies. He is a naive, charming crooner who has been repeatedly rejected and comes to Royce because he is an old family friend from Des Moines. Royce quickly gets him a contract. Buzz and Abercrombie are inspired by the prospect of becoming agents themselves, so they persuade the naive Parker to be their first client after Royce suddenly betrays him. When Jeff's contract is revoked, he is so discouraged that he wants to take the bus back to Des Moines. At this point, Buzz and Abercrombie scheme to disable the star who took Jeff's role and cause the usual ruckus. Jeff eventually triumphs as a Hollywood star despite the clumsy assistance.] AFI. *NYT* 23 Nov. 1945, 26; *V* 22 Aug. 1945, 20.

They Were Expendable. Dir. John Ford. MGM, 1945. 135 min. Principals: Robert Montgomery, Donna Reed, John Wayne. Literary source: William L. White, *They Were Expendable* (London: H. Hamilton, 1942). [Based on the 1942 book and on real characters, this film stars two native Iowans: John Wayne and Donna Reed. Wayne plays Lt. J. G. "Rusty" Ryan, who captains a P. T. boat, at first in Manilla Bay in 1941 and later in Bataan. The Navy underestimates the small, fast boats at first, but, under the leadership of Lt. John Brickley, the P. T. boats and their crews prove their value by shooting down enemy planes, carrying messages, and torpedoing a Japanese cruiser and later a destroyer. When Rusty's shrapnel wound leads to blood poisoning in his right arm, Brickley sends him to a hospital, where he meets a much admired nurse from Iowa, Lt. Sandy Davyss (Reed). She is brisk with Rusty at first, but a romance develops. Unfortunately, later on, Rusty has to leave on a secret mission and has only a minute on the phone to say goodbye. We never learn what happens to Sandy, but she was probably killed or became a prisoner of war. Despite appalling circumstances suggested by the film's title, Sandy is brave, professional, stoical, and quietly patriotic—typical of Iowans in World War II movies. Sandy shows her charm and femininity at an awkwardly formal meal with Rusty and his buddies, for which she wears pearls with her uniform. In a conversation with Rusty soon after they meet, Donna announces she is from Iowa, the tall corn state, and Rusty declares he is from upper New York State, where they have apples. Rusty survives the events of the film, but he, like MacArthur, declares he will be back in the South Pacific to fight again.] AFI. *NYT* 21 Dec. 1945, 25; *V* 21 Nov. 1945, 10.

The Postman Always Rings Twice. [Alternate title: *Bar-B-Q*]. Dir. Tay Garnett. MGM, 1946. 113 min. Principals: Leon Ames, Hume Cronyn, John Garfield, Cecil Kellaway, Lana Turner. Literary source: James M. Cain, *The Postman Always Rings Twice* (New York: Knopf, 1934). [This film features an Iowa femme fatale, Cora Smith (Turner), who has settled down with an older husband to run a diner outside Los Angeles. From the moment when drifter Frank Chambers (Garfield) alights at the diner after hitchhiking with the local District Attorney, he and Cora develop a powerful attraction, possibly love, leading to deliberate murder, betrayal, jealousy, and accidental death perceived as murder. By the time Frank arrives, Cora is desperate to make a success of the rundown diner and rid herself of her boozing, cheapskate, bossy husband who later, after surviving a planned "accident," threatens to move her to northern Canada to take care of his paralyzed sister. At one point Cora returns home to Iowa when her mother has a heart attack. Growing up, Cora's beauty had made her irresistible to predatory men from age 14, which may account for her leaving Iowa and settling down with a steady man who offered a wedding ring. The film noir cinematography, the husband's songs, and the hints of God's providence working its way out suggest that all the frail humans in this love triangle were doomed from the start. Cora is the antithesis of the wholesome Iowa girl-next-door, but her flight to California is a common motif in many Iowa films.] AFI. *NYT* 3 May 1946, 15; *V* 20 Mar. 1946, 8.

A Foreign Affair. [Alternate title: *Operation Candy Bar*]. Dir. Billy Wilder. Paramount, 1948. 115 min. Principals: Jean Arthur, Marlene Dietrich, John Lund, Millard Mitchell. Academy Award nominations: Screenplay, Cinematography. [This comic romance explores moral customs in post-WWII Germany. Congresswoman Phoebe Frost (Arthur) from Iowa investigates the lives of the occupation forces and is shocked by the practices she finds. Her sexual conservatism is juxtaposed against the overt eroticism of war-weary Erika von Schluetow, played by Marlene Dietrich, who is having an affair with one of Frost's constituents in the army. Before the film is over, Phoebe Frost learns some important things about the limits of her own impulse control when she passionately pairs up herself with that same Iowa constituent. A memorable moment is Phoebe's singing of the "We Are from Iowa" song in a German nightclub.] AFI. *NYT* 1 July 1948, 19; *V* 16 June 1948, 8.

Sealed Verdict. [Alternate title: *Dossier*]. Dir. Lewis Allen. Paramount Pictures, 1948. 82 min. Principals: Broderick Crawford, Charles Evans, John Hoyt, Paul Lees, Florence Marley, Ray Milland, John Ridgely. Literary source: Lionel Shapiro, *The Sealed Verdict* (Garden City, NY: Doubleday, 1947). [Major Robert Lawson (Milland) leads the Judge Advocate's Office in Reschweiler, Germany. It seeks to prosecute General Otto Steigman (Hoyt) for war crimes. The assistant to Major Lawson is Private Clay Hockland (Lees) from Iowa, who has a pregnant German girlfriend, Erika, (Jeffrey). Private Hockland is apparently shot in the street and lies near death in the hospital. (He has actually shot himself to protect his fiancée.) General Kirkwood (Evans) decides to exploit the incident for publicity and has the private's parents from Iowa flown to Germany along with a gossip reporter. The young man dies, and his girlfriend Erika is dying in labor before they arrive. Mrs. Hockland wants to save the baby and take it back to Iowa so as to promote kindness in the world. Critics found the plot overly complex and melodramatic, and the film has fallen out of circulation.] NS. AFI. *NYT* 3 Nov. 1948, 36; *V* 8 Sept. 1948, 10.

Go for Broke! Dir. Robert Pirosh. Metro-Goldwyn Mayer, 1951. 92 min. Academy Award nomination: Best Writing, Story, Screenplay. Principals: Warner Anderson, Hugh Beaumont, Gianna Canale, Akira

Fukunaga, Don Haggerty, Harry Hamada, Ken K. Okamoto, George Miki, Henry Nakamura, Lane Nakano, Frank Okada, Henry Oyasato, Tsutomu Paul Nakamura, Walter Reed, Dan Riss, Frank Wilcox. [This is a story of the fighting Nisei of WWII's 442nd Regimental Combat Team and is an early predecessor of *The Tuskegee Airman*. The American-born Japanese, who were otherwise destined for internment under Roosevelt's notorious Executive Order 9066, were allowed to fight on the European front where they earned thousands of Purple Hearts and Medals for Valor. Led by the bigoted Texan Lt. Michael Grayson (Johnson), the Japanese must prove their loyalty and fighting prowess. The film follows the familiar WWII convention of depicting America's harmonious diversity under stress. One of the Japanese-American soldiers worked at an egg operation in Iowa.] AFI. *NYT* 25 May 1951, 31; *V* 28 Mar. 1951, 6.

***Our Miss Brooks*.** Warner Bros., 1956. 85 min. Dir. Al Lewis. Principals: Eve Arden, Richard Crenna, Gale Gordan, Jane Morgan, Don Porter, Robert Rockwell. [*Our Miss Brooks* began on radio, had a four-year run on TV, and then transferred to the big screen. Wisecracking English teacher Miss Constance Brooks (Arden) loves handsome, sincere biology teacher Phillip Boynton (Rockwell), who has an ailing mother he loves and an aunt in Cedar Rapids. In contrast to a rich newspaper editor who aggressively woos Miss Brooks on his yacht, Iowa-connected Boynton romances in slow motion, repeatedly taking Connie to the zoo. She remarks on his sexual naiveté: he keeps his male and female hamsters in separate cages, and he turns away whenever he sees an undressed store window dummy. Miss Brooks will quit teaching when she finally marries Mr. Boynton, as per the customs of the era, and they will begin to fill the picket fenced white house with children. Mom will live across the street.] AFI. *V* 15 Feb. 1956, 6.

***The Tarnished Angels*.** [Alternate title: *Pylon*]. Dir. Douglas Sirk. Universal, 1958. 91 min. Principals: Jack Carson, Rock Hudson, Dorothy Malone, Robert Middleton, Robert Stack. Literary source: William Faulkner adapted the screenplay for this film from his novel *Pylon* (New York: Smith and Haas, 1935). [Sixteen-year-old La Verne (Malone) leaves Iowa to follow Roger Shuman (Stack), a former WWI flying ace now doing air stunts and racing at carnivals. She becomes pregnant, and Roger reluctantly marries her. With their son, they do the carnival circuit during the Depression, La Verne contributing a parachute act that highlights her sexy 1950s style body. Burke Devlin (Hudson), a paternalistic reporter in New Orleans who falls for La Verne, watches the obsessive Roger destroy himself in a risky race. Devlin compels La Verne to return with her son to Iowa. La Verne, a "bad girl" who craved romantic adventure, will give her son a more normal life by returning to Iowa.] *NYT* 7 Jan. 1958, 31; *V* 20 Nov. 1957.

All of Me. Dir. Joel Holt. Joseph Brenner Associates Release, 1963. 73 min. Principals: Brenda DeNaut, Joel Holt, Alice Denham. [Danielle (DeNaut) is a young woman from Iowa who has won a beauty contest. She is attacked in the New City harbor area. A TV producer, Bill (Holt), happens by and listens to her sad story. She has come to New York to get into modeling and encounters a photographer named Terrell. Soon he is working on her to pose for cheesecake style photography, and eventually to remove all her clothes. Then he begins molesting her. When she flees, Bill is the one who can rescue her. Bill convinces her to go to the Sunny Rest Lodge, a nudist camp, where she learns to become more comfortable with herself and with Bill.] NS.

What's the Matter with Helen? [Alternate titles: *The Best of Friends; The Box Step*]. Dir. Curtis Harrington. Filmways/Raymax, 1971. Principals: Debbie Reynolds, Dennis Weaver, Shelley Winters. [Two middle-aged mothers, divorced Adelle (Reynolds) and widowed Helen (Winters), flee notoriety and death threats in their Iowa hometown of Braddock after their sons have been convicted of murdering a local woman. The film opens in 1934 Iowa with the two women fleeing the courthouse together in a taxi and then conversing in Adelle's dance studio. Adelle invites Helen to come with her to Hollywood where she plans to open a song and dance studio to train future Shirley Temples. At first, the two women get along well and make a go of the studio. As Adelle becomes more involved with a rich father of one of the girls (Weaver), Helen shows increasing signs of religiously-based mental instability, finally murdering Adelle when she announces her marriage. Helen has previously murdered: first, her husband back in Iowa (with her son looking on), and then a revenge killer who came to California posing as a lawyer with an inheritance for her, and then her white rabbits. The film shows two Iowa threads common in the movies: the dream to leave Iowa's rural life for Hollywood stardom and characters with strong religious beliefs. The film has a strong lesbian subtext. Helen pushed her husband under a plow when she was tired of sex with him, and she obviously plots to keep "darling" Adelle at her side. The film ends with Helen playing maniacally on the piano with dead Adelle in one of her dance costumes propped up against the wall, while her fiancé looks on aghast.] AFI. *NYT* 1 July 1971, 62; *V* 9 June 1971, 17.

What's Up, Doc? Dir. Peter Bogdanovich. Saticoy Productions, 1972. 90 min. Principals: Madeline Kahn, Ryan O'Neal, Randy Quaid, Barbra Streisand. [This screwball romance features a quirky love triangle: befuddled Professor Howard Bannister (O'Neal), from the Music Conservatory at Ames, Iowa; his conventional and boring Iowa fiancée, Eunice Burns (Kahn); and a fast-talking, street smart local, Judy Maxwell (Streisand). The pedantic, priggish professor and his whiny, frumpish partner have come to San Francisco for a meeting of the American Conference of Musicologists. He is contending for a $20,000 fellowship to study "early man's musical exploitation of igneous rock formations." Judy's urban California sophistication and intellectual brilliance (the result of being kicked out of a series of fine colleges) lead Howard away from his repulsive Eunice. After chaotic mishaps and confusions, Howard and Judy fly back to Ames together for true love, while Eunice remains in San Francisco with an eccentric young philanthropist.] AFI. *NYT* 10 Mar. 1972, 42; *V* 8 Mar. 1972, 20.

The Day of the Locust. Dir. John Schlesinger. Paramount, 1975. 144 min. Principals: William Atherton, Karen Black, Burgess Meredith, Donald Sutherland. [A faithful adaptation of the Nathanael West novel of the same name, the film shows ordinary people caught up in the glamorous dream/sleazy nightmare that was Hollywood of the 1930s: costume dramas, down and out old vaudevillians, studios willing to lie for insurance money, prostitution, religious revivals raking in bucks, blonde wannabe starlets. Two outsiders are Tod Hacket (Atherton), an artist from Yale, and Homer Simpson (Sutherland), a sexually repressed accountant from Waynesville, Iowa, just outside Des Moines (a reference to Winterset, home of John Wayne?). Both men long for Faye Greener (Black), the vain, shallow aspiring actress whose sexy style masks her irresponsibility and vulnerability, and both die in a riot at the opening of Cecil B. DeMille's *The Buccaneers*. Throughout the film, we see a thoroughly emasculated Homer: Faye lives with him because he is generous and sexually undemanding, he wears an apron, a drag performer sits on his lap, his clothes and décor are old-fashioned, he doesn't drink, and he prepares patriotic party food while the men who lust after his "hen" watch a cock fight in his garage. At the novel's end, Homer snaps after an annoying 12-year-old child performer taunts him. Homer jumps up and down on the boy, killing him, and starts the riot that ends with his bloody corpse hoisted in a crucifixion pose by an angry mob —the "locusts." Homer, with all his exaggerated "Iowa" traits, is only one of Hollywood's many victims, like the naked woman who jumped to her death from the "H" in the Hollywood sign, a story told by a tour guide in the film's opening.] AFI. *NYT* 8 May 1975, 48; *V* 30 Apr. 1975, 19.

Hearts of the West. [Alternate title: *Hollywood Cowboy*]. Dir. Howard Zieff. MGM, 1975. 102 min. Principals: Alan Arkin, Jeff Bridges, Blythe Danner, Andy Griffith, Donald Pleasance. [Iowa farm boy Lewis Tater (Bridges) dreams of being a published writer of westerns and takes a course from a phony correspondence school in Nevada. He heads to Nevada and then on to Hollywood, where he gets caught up in the movie industry. Miss Trout (Danner) advises this big, good-looking, naive kid and becomes the romantic interest, though the single-minded Tater is obsessed with writing—not acting or romance. Tater first tells Trout he is from Nevada, but then admits his Iowa origins. When he has a run of bad luck, he remarks that back home he was always the one to get the peppercorn in his soup. Trout asks him at one point if they dance in Iowa. The humor comes mainly from the contrast between farm boy Tater and the more sophisticated, materialistic Hollywood crowd in the early days of talkies. Did the Hollywood scriptwriters get confused and think Iowa was the state with potatoes?] AFI. *NYT* 4 Oct. 1975, 14; *V* 1 Oct. 1975, 26.

For Ladies Only. Dir. Mel Damski. Catalina Production Group/ Viacom, 1981. 94 min. Principals: Patricia Davis, Lee Grant, Gregory Harrison, Steven Keats, Viveca Lindfors, Dinah Manoff, Marc Singer. [This is the quintessential traveling Iowan fable, remade for the age of sexual liberation. John Lawrence Phillips (Harrison) is a University of Iowa theater graduate who aspires to a Broadway acting career. As "Mr. Just-in-from-Iowa," the designation he gets from a secretary in a casting agency, it is apparent that he is too poor, too naive, and too honest to make it in the Big Apple. As his acting aspirations and finances slide away from him, he reluctantly takes a job as a waiter at a male stripper club. He is gradually seduced into becoming the club's most elegant star. For a period he behaves like a gigolo, sleeping with wealthy women and performing at private parties. The suicide of a fellow stripper during a police raid at the club reinforces the message of the good young women in his life. They want him to return to the dream he brought from Iowa. Pleasing them in the end, he acts in a role as a Western Union delivery boy at a community theater.]

Heat and Dust. Dir. James Ivory. Merchant-Ivory Productions, 1983. 130 min. Principals: Christopher Cazenove, Julie Christie, Nikolas Grace, Zakir Hussain, Shashi Kapoor, Charles McCaughan, Greta Scacchi. Literary source: Ruth Prawer Jhabvala, *Heat and Dust* (London: J. Murray, 1975). [This film tells the story of two British women in India. BBC announcer Anne (Christie) travels to India in the 1980s to investigate the life of her great aunt, Olivia Rivers (Scacchi), the bored wife of a British District Collector of Satipur who left her husband for the local Indian prince in 1923. Anne encounters Chid (McCaughan), a spiritual seeker with roots in Iowa who has abandoned his name and claims to have renounced all previous identity. He craves spiritual power in India through yoga. Pathetically ridiculous, he tries to seduce Anne, who sleeps instead with her Indian landlord. Because Indian food has allegedly destroyed his liver, Chid eventually has to return to his Aunt's place in Washington, Iowa. Is this a cultural comment on Iowa's bland food? He also raves about his aunt's clean bathroom and kitchen. Chid's sole function in the film is to represent misguided spiritual pilgrims to modern India. He also establishes clean, green Iowa, as an antithesis to dusty, exotic India.] *NYT* 15 Sept. 1983, III, 18; *V* 19 Jan. 1983, 21.

Fraternity Vacation. Dir. James Frawley. New World Pictures, 1985. 93 min. Principals: Cameron Dye, Stephen Geoffreys, Leigh McCloskey, Tim Robbins, Sheree J. Wilson. [Two sets of rival fraternity members from Iowa State University leave an Iowa blizzard for vacation in Palm Beach, where bikini-clad young women, eager to party, line the streets and beaches. Joe and Mother are saddled with Wendall Tvedt (pun on vet), the ultimate nerd, whose parents "own one of the largest pig farms in central Iowa." Wendall (Geoffreys) is the epitome of Iowa clumsiness, lack of sophistication, sexual naiveté, and niceness. While Joe (Tucker) and Mother (Robbins) compete with rivals Charles and J. C. to see who can first bed blonde beauty Ashley (Wilson), Wendall's honesty and sweetness win over a California girl, two prostitutes, and, ultimately, the coveted Ashley. All the boys return to Iowa reunited through partying and with a new respect for Iowa "niceness" as a ploy to score with girls.] *NYT* 12 Apr. 1985, 5; *V* 27 Feb. 1985, 14.

Out of Bounds. Dir. Richard Tuggle. Fries Entertainment, 1986. 93 min. Principals: Raymond J. Barry, Anthony Michael Hall, Jeff Kober, Meatloaf, Glynn Turman, Jenny Wright. [This film highlights the cultural contrasts between rural DeWitt, Iowa, and central Los Angeles. A naive and depressed Daryl Cage (Hall) leaves his parents, who are separating because of pressures on the farm, to visit his successful brother in LA. A bag mixup at the airport leaves Daryl holding a supply of heroin. After his brother's murder, he links up with a street-smart punk waitress to thwart both hostile police and drug dealers. Initially calling him "Iowa" and "Farm Boy," the waitress transforms Daryl's look, and he instantly picks up lethal urban skills. In the final showdown, he hurls a knife into the heart of the drug dealer, using a skill honed on the side of an Iowa barn. Like so many departing Iowans, he settles in LA. Iowa niceness has won romance, and his toughness and integrity have allowed him to survive.] AFIs. *NYT* 25 July 1986, 18; *V* 23 July 1986, 16.

Star Trek IV: The Voyage Home. Dir. Leonard Nimoy. Paramount, 1986. 119 min. Principals: James Doohan, Catherine Hicks, DeForest Kelley, Walter Koenig, Nichelle Nichols, Leonard Nimoy, William Shatner. Source: based on the *Star Trek* television series by Gene Roddenberry (NBC, 8 Sept. 1966-2 Sept. 1969). [In this save the world installment of the film series, *Star Trek's* crew must ward off an alien force that is evaporating the oceans. The task requires time travel back to 1986 San Francisco to retrieve a particular species of whale from that era. In the course of introducing himself to whale expert Gillian (Hicks), Captain Kirk (Shatner) mentions that he's from Iowa. She calls him "Farm Boy." In this situation, the "from Iowa" designation helps Kirk gain the trust of a skeptical earthling.] AFIs. *NYT* 26 Nov. 1986, C14; *V* 19 Nov. 1986, 16.

Fort Figueroa. Dir. Luis Valdez. CBS Summer Playhouse, 1988. 60 min. Principals: Anne E. Curry, Charles Haid, Anne Haney, Holly Fields. [This was a pilot for a proposed television sitcom series. The Perrys, a family from Iowa that has just lost its farm, inherits a very multicultural apartment complex in Los Angeles. Because of the large number of Mexican immigrants, their complex is given the name "Fort Figueroa." They are steadily confronted with things they find strange, such as a Korean congregation within their Methodist Church.] NS. *NYT* 2 Aug. 1988, C18; *V* 24 Aug. 1988, 97.

Your Mother Wears Combat Boots. Dir. Anson Williams. Kushner-Locke Company, 1989. 105 min. Principals: Barbara Eden, Hector Elizondo, David Kaufman. [A Davenport mother (Eden) lost her husband when he died in a parachute jump during the Vietnam War, leaving her to raise her son, Jimmy (Kaufman), on her own. Jimmy ditches college for the army, not letting his mother know until he begins airborne training. This feminine, overprotective, acrophobic, but fit mom (thanks to aerobics and jogging) goes to Fort Benning and takes the place of an AWOL soldier to find her son and beg him to return to college and forget jumping out of planes. After a number of *Private Benjamin*-type scenes, Jimmy agrees to bail out of the program if she can complete it. With the help of two female soldiers, she trains hard. Eventually she learns her son needs to pursue this interest of the father he never knew, and her sergeant (Elizondo) convinces her she needs to jump for her own sake. This is army training light, with an oversupply of remarks about women looking for husbands. The film ostensibly opens in Davenport, but without distinguishing landmarks.]

Quick Change. Dir. Howard Franklin and Bill Murray. Devoted Productions, 1990. 89 min. Principals: Geena Davis, Bill Murray, Randy Quaid, Jason Robards. Literary source: based on the novel *Quick Change* by Jay Cronley (Garden City, NY: Doubleday, 1981). [City planner Grimm (Murray), his friend Loomis (Quaid), and his girlfriend, Phyllis (Davis), brilliantly pull off a bank robbery in NYC. Murray robs the bank dressed as a clown. They escape the crime scene, but they are thwarted by a series of comic disasters. They just can't find the exit from New York. Trying to find the Brooklyn Expressway, they ask for directions from a pleasant, well-dressed man standing outside a pale yellow convertible. Until he saw the plates were from Iowa, Grimm had feared the man might be a felon or a homicidal killer. The man gets out his map. "Is everyone so nice in Iowa?" Grimm remarks. The man tells them the car was stolen and robs them of their loot. "Dubuque?" Loomis asks after the robbery. "Des Moines," Grimm snaps.] AFIs. *NYT* 13 July 1990, 12; *V* 11 July 1990, 30-31.

Lunatics: A Love Story. Dir. Josh Becker. Sam Raimi-Robert Tapert, 1991. 87 min. Principals: George Aguilar, Bruce Campbell, Deborah Foreman, Brian McCree, Theodore Raimi. [This offbeat romance, set in Los Angeles, highlights big city dangers that bring together Nancy (Foreman) from Iowa and Hank (Raimi) from Michigan. He came West after more than three years of hospitalization for delusions and suicidal threats back home. Fear of the streets has kept him barricaded behind foil-covered walls for more than six months. Nancy, who shares with Hank an impulse for poetry, came West with an exploitative man who steals from her and abandons her. She fears a gang that stalks her, threatening to rape and kill her. Learning of her grandmother's death, she develops the guilty delusion that her departure from Iowa killed Grandma. Yet she remains resolute: "I'm not going back to Iowa. I'm gone." The two depressed, delusional refugees from the Midwest eventually defend and console one another and take a trip back to his Michigan home.] AFIs. *V* 16 Sept. 1991, 88.

Soapdish. Dir. Michael Hoffman. Paramount, 1991. 97 min. Principals: Robert Downey, Jr., Sally Field, Carrie Fisher, Whoopi Goldberg, Teri Hatcher, Kevin Kline, Cathy Moriarty, Kathy Najimy, Elisabeth Shue. [In this very funny burlesque of soap operas, Sally Field plays aging actress Celeste Talbert, whose Maggie—"America's Sweetheart," "the queen of misery"—has been beloved by fans since Celeste took the part soon after leaving Des Moines at age 16 for New York City. The film satirizes the soaps' outrageous plots and exposes the ratings game and competition among actors for prominent storylines. The main plot, however, deals with the reuniting of Celeste with her illegitimate daughter (raised by "grandma" in Des Moines as Celeste's "niece") and the girl's father, ham actor Jeffery Anderson (Kline). Celeste's Iowa background is marked by her references to God, her objection to swearing, her "niceness," and her guilt over being a bad mother. Celeste had dreams of big city fame like many Iowa youth in film and life. She discovers, in the end, that family matters most— but playing out her crazy family drama on the air also leads to more awards and terrific ratings. At the end she achieves both family and success, while her scheming nemesis (Moriarty) is doing dinner theater in the sticks.] AFIs. *NYT* 31 May 1991, 10; *V* 3 June 1991, 50.

Married to It. Dir. Arthur Hiller. Three Pair/Orion, 1993. (Release of this 1991 completed film was delayed for two years.) 110 min. Principals: Beau Bridges, Stockard Channing, Robert Sean Leonard, Mary Stuart Masterson, Cybill Shepherd, Ron Silver. [Set in Manhattan, this film features three couples—one pair from Iowa—who become friends. Childhood sweethearts who met through 4-H, Nina (Masterson) and Chuck (Leonard) are now young professionals who discover that their Iowa naiveté, trust, and optimism do not serve them well in the Big Apple. They must recommit to one another after absorbing their

bruising experiences. The film highlights the Iowa couple's embarrass-
ment when they try to describe for urban skeptics the featureless Iowa
culture that they have sought to escape in coming from the Corn Belt to
the Big Apple.] AFIs. *NYT* 26 Mar. 1993, 8; *V* 23 Sept. 1991, 78.

Operation Dumbo Drop. [Alternate titles: *The Dumbo Drop*; *Dumbo
Drop*]. Dir. Simon Wincer. Walt Disney Pictures, 1995. 108 min.
Principals: Doug E. Doug, Danny Glover, Dinh Thienh Le, Dennis
Leary, Ray Liotta, Corin Nemec. Literary source: Jim Morris, "Operation
Barroom," *Fighting Men* (New York: Dell, 1993). [This comic caper
within the Vietnam War story recounts a secret Green Beret operation
in 1968 to move an adult elephant over hundreds of miles of canyons,
rivers, and mountains. The destination is a friendly Montagnard village near the Ho Chi Minh Trail that needs the elephant for labor and
religious ritual. Thus the project is an act of cultural reconciliation. Led
by feuding Captains Cahill (Glover) and Doyle (Liotta), the small task
group includes Iowan Lawrence Harley (Nemac) who is supposed to
handle the elephant because of his "cornpone" background on a dairy
farm. He claims that animals don't like him. His characterization as
an Iowan is thin and afflicted by a Deep South accent. The project succeeds despite squabbling, danger, and higher authorities' official decision to terminate the operation.] AFIs. *NYT* 28 July 1995, C12; *V* 31 July
1995, 36.

Joe's Apartment. Dir. John Payson. Roachco, 1996. 80 min. Principals:
Don Ho, Jerry O'Connell, Robert Vaughn, Megan Ward. [Based on a
popular MTV short film by John Payson with the same title, the plot
turns on a naive, uncool Iowan's adventures in filthy, crime-infested
New York City. When he arrives by bus, Joe (O'Connell), wearing Iowa
Hawkeye duds, is mugged three times in rapid succession and ends
up in a roach-controlled apartment. Thrilled by his slobbish habits, the
hip roaches harmonize as they dance through dirty clothes and rot-
ting food. At first, the roaches sabotage Joe's menial jobs and his bud-
ding romance with idealistic Lily (Ward), daughter of a mob-connected
Senator. Joe is ready to return to Iowa after a string of misadventures
with jobs. He finds himself out of work with a fellow Iowan whose uri-
nal cake company has just suffered a hostile takeover. The roaches rally
to help Joe, creating a garden for Lily where her father had planned a
federal pen. They also bring the lovers together in her sanitary apartment. Full of toilet humor and funky roach music, this film suggests
that roaches, allied with a decent Iowan, would rule the world more

benevolently than native New Yorkers.] AFIs. *NYT* 27 July 1996, 18; *V* 29 July 1996, 59, 61.

The Man Who Knew Too Little. Dir. Jon Amiel. Regency Enterprises. 1997. 94 min. Principals: Peter Gallagher, Geraldine James, Alfred Molina, Bill Murray, Joanne Whalley-Kilmer, Richard Wilson. Literary source: unpublished Robert Farrar novel *Watch That Man.* [The hero Wallace Ritchie (Murray) travels to London from his hometown of Des Moines, where he works for Blockbuster Video. His brother in London, a successful international banker, buys a ticket for Wally to participate in an interactive theater experience. Naive Wally bumbles his way into a Russian and British conspiracy. The agents of both countries are planning a bombing that will revive the Cold War—and their funding. Wally is an Iowa version of *The Pink Panther*'s Inspector Clouseau—clumsy, likeable, trusting, and naively enthusiastic about everything. He is also fearless because he thinks it is all theater, impressing the inevitable sexy female spy and the worldwide espionage community. In the end the CIA recruits him.] AFIs. *NYT* 14 Nov. 1997, 22; *V* 10 Nov. 1997, 40.

Murder at 1600. Dir. Dwight H. Little. Warner Brothers, 1997. 107 min. Principals: Alan Alda, Daniel Benzali, Diane Lane, Dennis Miller, Wesley Snipes. [This action-adventure film features the murder of a young woman in the White House. DC Detective Harlan Regis (Snipes) refuses to collaborate with the presidential staff's desire to suppress a thorough investigation. He creates an alliance of integrity with Secret Service Agent Nina Chance (Lane). She is a sharp shooter from Iowa with Olympic gold medal credentials and too much of a straight arrow for office romance. They eventually sneak into the White House through a tunnel and, after gun battles and other obstacles, they reach the president and unveil the truth about the crime.] AFIs. *NYT* 18 Apr. 1997, 23; *V* 14 Apr. 1997, 91.

Titanic. Dir. James Cameron. Lightstorm Entertainment and Twentieth-Century Fox, 1997. 194 min. Principals: Kathy Bates, Leonardo DiCaprio, Frances Fisher, Bill Paxton, Kate Winslet. Academy Awards: Best Picture, Director, Cinematography, Art Direction, Song, Film Editing, Original Dramatic Score, Visual Effects, Sound Effects Editing, Sound, Costume Design; Nominations: Actress, Supporting Actress, Makeup. [The disaster tale is told through the eyes of elderly Rose Dawson (Stuart) of Cedar Rapids. Because she tells a credible story of the missing Heart of the Ocean diamond, she finally gets the attention of fortune hunters who are dismissive about her age and residence in Iowa. Rose DeWitt Bukater (Winslet) is a young woman whose mother, Ruth (Fisher), would like to marry her into wealth; but she is restless with its conventions and restraints and with an obnoxious fiancé. On board the Titanic, she meets the poor boy Jack Dawson (DiCaprio), who gives her new reasons to live and to rebel. After his death at sea, she adopts his name, renounces the pretentious lifestyle to which she is entitled, and lives out a quiet life in Cedar Rapids.] AFIs. *NYT* 19 Dec. 1997; *V* 3 Nov. 1997, 7.

Saving Private Ryan. Dir. Steven Spielberg. Dreamworks Pictures and Paramount Pictures, 1998. 160 min. Principals: Edward Burns, Matt Damon, Tom Hanks, Tom Sizemore. Academy Awards: Director, Cinematography, Film Editing, Sound, Sound Effects; Nominations: Picture, Actor, Original Screen play, Art Direction. Novelization: Max Allan Collins, *Saving Private Ryan* (New York: Bantam, 1998). [This film about the D-Day invasion and its aftermath consciously evokes the memory of Iowa's Sullivan brothers. A squad is assigned the task of retrieving a Private Ryan (Damon) whose home is in fictional Peyton, Iowa. His brothers have all been killed in various WWII theatres. Once found in contested German territory, he refuses to be saved. In the spirit of self-sacrifice, he has come to recognize as brothers those who fight as warrior comrades. Iowa scenes include childhood reminiscences of seducing a girl in the barn and another scene at the farm where the mother receives word about the death of one of her sons.] AFIs. *NYT* 24 July 1998, E14; *V* 20 July 1998, 45.

Bamboozled. Dir. Spike Lee. Forty Acres and A Mule Filmworks, 2000. 135 min. Principals: Tommy Davidson, Savion Glover, Michael Rapaport, Jada Pinkett Smith, Damon Wayons. [This satire of media racism centers on a frustrated, well-educated African-American writer, Pierre Delacroix (Wayans), who creates an outrageous variety show set in a watermelon patch, featuring black performers, in blackface, as Mantan (Glover) and Sleep 'n' Eat (Davidson). He presents the concept to a large table full of young, white TV writers. One announces, laughing nervously, that he is from Iowa and his first experience with "black people from Africa" was George and "Weezie" on *The Jeffersons*. When Delacroix challenges the liberal writers "to tap into their white angst" by thinking about their reaction to the O. J. Simpson verdict, the Iowa writer begins to express his dissatisfaction with the verdict before the sound fades. Iowa is presented by Spike Lee as a state with little or no knowledge of African-Americans, where racism lies underneath the "niceness" of Iowa people.] AFIs. *NYT* 6 Oct. 2000, E 14; *V* 2 Oct. 2000, 20, 30.

Happy Accidents. Dir. Brad Anderson. Accidental Productions, 2000. 110 min. Principals: Tovah Feldshuh, Anthony Michael Hall, Vincent D'Onofrio, Holland Taylor, Marisa Tomei. [This romantic comedy features two odd characters, Ruby (Tomei) and Sam (D'Onofrio), in a 1999 screwball relationship. At the time of their accidental meeting, she is in distress and in psychiatric therapy about her unsatisfactory, co-dependent relationships with men. Sam presents himself as a bizarre character from Dubuque with a tattooed barcode and a fear of dogs. He claims to be a "back-traveler" from "the Dubuque of the future"—2470 to be precise—and a descendant from an "anachronist" family that asserted "nostalgia rights" to traditional methods of human reproduction. Despite the weirdness of it all—and a call back to Sam's living father in Dubuque that confirms her doubt about his outlandish claims—Sam and Ruby bond forever.] AFIs. *NYT* 24 Aug. 2001, 23; *V* 7 Feb. 2000, 55.

Running Mates. Dir. Ron Lagomarsino. TNT, 2000. 90 min. Principals: Adria Dawn, Faye Dunaway, Bob Gunton, Teri Hatcher, Laura Linney, Bruce McGill, Tom Selleck, Nancy Travis. [Principled Gov. James Reynolds Pryce (Selleck) is a sure thing to be the Democrat's nominee for president. His success is due in large part to the support of a group of women he has slept with, including his wife (Nancy Travis), ambitious campaign manager (Linney), an alcoholic senator's wife (Faye Dunaway), and his media coordinator and Hollywood liaison (Hatcher). A media celebrity at the convention is the youngest delegate, red-haired Katie (Dawn) from Cedar Rapids, a true believer in Pryce and the democratic system. Katie is a bit gawky—no teen queen—but she has a sense of fun. She shows the reporters her new tattoo. Though tempted by a $100 million bribe from special interests, the "princes of privilege," who want their man as VP, Pryce ultimately rejects their offer and asserts, "American is not for sale," largely because of the influence of the women in his life and the image of the Katies everywhere who trust him to do the right thing.] *V* 7 Aug. 2000.

I Spy. Dir. Betty Thomas. Columbia, 2002. 96 min. Principals: Gary Cole, Famke Janssen, Malcolm McDowell, Eddie Murphy, Owen

Wilson. [Bumbling spy Alex Scott (Wilson) resents being upstaged by Carlos (Cole), with his high tech gadgets, his flamboyant heroism, and his seductive charm with women. "The guy is from Iowa," Scott remarks, incredulous. This spy spoof, very loosely based on the 1960s TV series, takes Scott to Budapest with hotshot middleweight boxing champ Kelly Robinson (Murphy). The two bond, but neither is a Bond. They do manage, however, to foil the enemy and retrieve a stealth aircraft. But, as usual, Carlos steals the glory.] AFIs. *NYT* 1 Nov. 2002, 1; 14 Oct. 2002, 27, 32.

Team America: World Police. Dir. Trey Parker. Paramount, 2004. 93 min. Principals: Kristen Miller, Trey Parker, Matt Stone. [The starring marionette in this action satire from the *South Park* creators is Gary Johnson, a summa cum laude graduate of University of Iowa with double majors in theatre and world languages. Red-white-and-blue Team America, headquartered in Mount Rushmore, recruits the wholesome Gary, who wowed Broadway with his sensitive acting in *Lease*, where he moved the audience to tears singing that everyone has AIDS, AIDS, AIDS. Another member of the team is a former Nebraska Cornhuskers quarterback who dreams of romantic scenarios in the cornfields. Gary goes through the stereotypical romantic and action hero plot arcs, which include spying in Egypt with the worst makeup job ever, obscene marionette sex with his blonde girlfriend, and spewing gallons of vomit during the requisite "down and out" angst scene. Ultimately, Gary saves the world from the lonely terrorist Kim Jong Il and a group of left-wing Hollywood actors by out-acting his hero, Alex Baldwin. The film's satire and musical score appear at first to skewer all targets, but ultimately affirm "dicks over pansies and assholes"— in other words, reckless, patriotic, stupid conservative Americans over leftists/internationalists and non-Americans who act with violence. The Washington, DC, montage epitomizes the "Mr. Smith" political beliefs of Gary, the *right* kind of actor (despite his connections with left-wing Iowa City) in contrast to the beliefs of the leftist actors, who babble about hybrid cars, peace, and evil corporations—and who all die violently. Gary's patriotism, if not his sexual predilections, put him squarely in the tradition of Iowa war heroes in the movies.] AFIs. *NYT* Oct. 2004, 1; *V* 18 Oct. 2004, 32, 39.

Hollywood Dreams. Dir. Henry Jaglom. Rainbow Films, 2007. 100 min. Principals: Karen Black, Tanna Frederick, Justin Kirk, Melissa Leo, Zack Norman, David Proval. [Margie Chizek (Frederick), from a large family in Mason City, goes to Hollywood to become a star, but in her first audition we see her burst out crying and forget her lines. Later we learn that quirky Margie, obsessed with old movies, is both more fragile and more manipulative than she first seems. Ultimately, she must choose between love with a straight actor who has made a name in gay roles (while pretending to be gay)—or a chance at a lead in a play, with a movie option. Margie wears an Iowa sweatshirt and proudly tells new friends all about Iowa's celebrities and notable accomplishments: e.g., Meredith Willson, John Wayne, Donna Reed, Glenn Miller, the Gallup Poll, and the first hamburger. Her Aunt Bee (Leo) comes to visit from Iowa, and we expect a Mayberry clone—but it turns out Bee once had a lesbian fling and tells Margie's boyfriend, Robin (Kirk), that Margie is in denial that her brother Frankie died at age 18, wearing Margie's clothes. Their "dramatic" grandmother had encouraged both of their Hollywood dreams as well as cross-dressing, but their mother later forced the boy to "be a man." The actor boyfriend seems ready to love and protect Margie for life, even knowing her past, but for Margie that would mean facing up to the fact that she will never be a star and that her brother is dead. Margie herself is a complex person, not the usual naive innocent, and the picture presented of Iowa is both realistic and surprising. The film focuses on gay marriage, both open-mindedness and homophobia in the heartland, and Hollywood's gender expectations.] AFIs. *NYT* 25 May 2007, 22; *V* 20 Nov. 2006, 50-51.

Burlesque. Dir. Steve Antin. Screen Gems, 2010. 119 min. Principals: Christina Aguilera, Cher, Eric Dane, Cam Gigandet, Stanley Tucci. [A singing waitress, Ali (Aguilera), from rundown Dwight's Bar in Iowa, takes the pay owed her to buy a Greyhound Bus ticket to Los Angeles, where she finds work waiting tables at a burlesque lounge run by Tess (Cher). Not surprisingly, Ali eventually becomes the star act, finds love with the bartender from Kentucky, and saves the place from financial ruin. The bartender, Jack (Gigandet), calls her Iowa when he meets her. They agree that back home there is "not one person whose life I wanted to lead." A rival, Nikki, insults Ali's farm rearing. Ali retorts that at least she "knows a cow when she sees one." Iowa is portrayed as a bleak place where Ali, who lost her mother at a young age, was lonely and unloved—with no future. In the past, Iowa usually represented family values; in this film, Ali finds love and family at the urban club, where, despite some conflicts, people are loyal to each other. Tess and her gay assistant, Sean (Tucci), become the parent figures Ali lacked back home. The film is a performance vehicle for Aguilera and Cher.] AFIs. *NYT* 24 Nov. 2010, 11.

Promised Land. Dir. Gus Van Sant. Focus Features, 2012. 106 min. Principals: Matt Damon, Hal Holbrook, John Krasinski, Frances McDormand. [Steve Butler (Damon) grew up in Eldridge, Iowa, where he helped his grandfather paint the barn. He continues to wear the grandfather's boots and mourns the economic devastation of his hometown when the Caterpillar plant closed in nearby Davenport. Steve and his partner, Sue (McDormand), are a successful sales teams for Global, a natural gas company that aggressively pressures people to allow fracking on their land, minimizing the risks. Steve feels that the rural areas of the country are futureless, and he is helping by offering them big money so they can leave. The sales campaign stalls in a small Pennsylvania town when the local science teacher turns out to have MIT and Cornell credentials. Then an environmental activist shows up with a horror story about fracking that ruined his family's Nebraska farm. Steve encounters locals who care more for their land than the big bucks. Several revelations lead Steve to a change of heart by the film's end, and he betrays his own company to join cause with the people of Pennsylvania. In an early scene Steve describes life in a rural Iowa small town, including the rituals of Friday night football and cow tipping. It is because he knows small rural towns that he is a convincing spokesman for Global, even though he has developed a certain cynicism and thinks he knows the game. Interestingly, Richard Corliss, in a *Time* magazine review, argues the film is a retelling of *The Music Man* in which a con man gets converted by a community and voluntarily exposes his con.] *NYT* 21 Dec. 2012; *V* 5 Dec. 2012.

IV. Iowa Documentaries

The Mormon Battalion. Edward Finney Productions, 1950. 6 reels. Principals: Edward Finney, Narrator. [The visuals of this film depict the Mormon Battalion's wagon party making its way from Council Bluffs to California in 1846. Another strand shows a contemporary bus-based re-enactment of the trip. The Mormon Battalion was recruited by California to invade Northern Mexico. After the trek and the service, the Mormons returned to their homes in Iowa and Utah. The film was never copyrighted and no intact copy is currently available.] NS. AFI.

The Home Economics Story. Iowa State Univ. Productions, 1951. 25 min. *Why Study Home Economics?* Centron Corp., 1955. 10 min. [Available at the Iowa State University Library archives and online at the Prelinger Collection/Moving Image Archives, these short films portray the home economics field and college education for women in the early 1950s. *The Home Economics Story*—set and filmed on the Iowa State College (now University) campus in Ames—is aimed at prospective students and their parents. The film follows four female friends who study home economics in college. The amateurish production values and the typically 1950s emphasis on marriage and motherhood as sacred social roles for women led Mystery Science Theatre 3000 to satirize the film in episode 317 ("Viking Women and the Sea Serpent"). Yet the film stresses professions for women (e.g., hospital dietician, industrial research, clothing buyer, teacher) and the importance of women studying science. Only one woman—and not one of the four—gets engaged at the end. The four head off for their new professions. The film further shows how, for Kay, who dreams of more in life, home economics is the "acceptable" route that allows her to go to college. Details of 1950s college life include formal dances, meeting at the malt shop, gabbing among the girls in the dorm, and wearing bobby sox, saddle shoes, sweaters, and pearls. *Why Study Home Economics?,* also made in Iowa, begins with two high school girls debating whether studying home economics is a waste of time. Naturally, when one of the girls consults the home economics teacher, Miss Jenkins, for supportive arguments, the girl learns that home economics is the gateway to many careers including social services, extension services, journalism, industrial research, and managing a restaurant. And, of course, a housewife/mother needs to operate her home and raise her children according to scientific and democratic principles. To contemporary eyes, this cheesy film seems to uphold 1950s stereotypes of women as domestic goddesses, but it also provides arguments for women's education in an era in which enrollments of women in college took a nosedive.]

Small Town, USA. Information Service/Pathescope Company of America/Eurovision, 1957. 30 min. Principals: Anamosa, Iowa, residents. [This documentary, intended for foreign audiences during the Cold War and housed at the Iowa State University archives, presents a pastoral view of a small town in the America's heartland, Anamosa, Iowa, which depends on agriculture for its existence. The film is pure *Our Town,* Iowa-style. We meet boys fishing, a storekeeper, the dedicated doctor, the newspaper editor, the county agricultural agent, farm families passing on a way of life from one generation to the next, a congregation with voices lifted in song, and residents celebrating July 4th with a parade and fireworks. The commentary emphasizes the diversity of ethnicities, churches, and the abundant choices of consumer goods at the grocery and hardware stores. Though rooted in reality, the film idealizes a rural Iowa way of life shown in numerous fictional films, even those made in much later decades when agriculture dominated the Iowa experience to a lesser degree. Anyone who knows Anamosa will realize that there is no reference to one of the town's most important institutions—the State Penitentiary. This film can be viewed on YouTube.]

The Last American Hobo. [Alternate title: *The Last of the American Hoboes*]. Dir. Titus Moede. Micah Productions, 1975. 80 min. [In this documentary, with a soundtrack of songs about hobo life ("Christmas in Hoboville," "Big Rock Candy Mountain"), a young man whose grandfather told him hobo stories hits the road for three weeks to film interviews with hobos. They talk about living as transients during the Great Depression and since—riding in boxcars, following symbols left by other 'bos, and making money by temporary labor or collecting recyclable trash. Their stories link with the songs to show both the romance and realism of hobo life. The film mentions historical events such as the 1929 Stock Market crash, a march by the homeless on Washington, the death of a famous hobo who once was a leader of the International Workers of the World, and homeless Vietnam vets. The film ends in Britt, Iowa, which has, since 1900, hosted an annual Hobo Convention, where thousands of hobos and tourists congregate to watch a parade, eat Mulligan Stew, crown a Hobo King and Queen, and pay tribute to the lives and culture of hobos.]

Bix: Ain't None of Them Play Like Him Yet. Dir. Brigitte Berman. Bridge Films, 1981. 112 min. Principals: Louis Armstrong, Richard Basehart (narrator), Hoagy Carmichael, Bill Challis, Doc Cheatham, Charlie Davis, Jack Fulton, Matty Malneck, Artie Shaw, Spiegle Willcox. [This documentary on the life and influence of Davenport native Bix Beiderbecke features his best recorded music, photos, news clippings, handwritten letters, interviews with musicians and Davenport friends and family, and beautiful Middle West landscapes. Obviously an influence on Pupi Avati's *Bix: An Interpretation of a Legend*, this film, while noting his family's disapproval of his career and life, posits other explanations for Bix's early death. The grueling pace of touring and the relentless demands of fans who wouldn't let the celebrity stop playing or drinking broke down Bix's health. Bix has the typical Iowa traits of quietness and generosity, but the film stresses his natural musical genius and influence on other musicians who admired his unique style that no one could imitate. Davenport hosts a Bix Beiderbecke Jazz Festival every summer, along the Mississippi River, that attracts thousands of Quad Cities residents and jazz enthusiasts. As with other celebrities who died young, his legend lives on.]

Harry Hopkins . . . At FDR's Side. Dir. Frank Nesbitt. PBS, 1989. 88 min. Principals: Walter Cronkite (narrator), Claude Pepper, Arthur Schlesinger. [Researched and produced by Verne Newton, this documentary takes us through the life of FDR's closest aide Harry Hopkins, starting with his birth in Sioux City to a harness making father and a Methodist mother, a teacher who insisted that "actions mean more than words." This phrase defines Hopkins' life. After graduating from Grinnell College, he became a social worker in the Lower East Side of Manhattan, where he saw desperate poverty. He went on to partner with FDR as Governor of NY and then as President. A blunt man, a controversial man uninterested in playing politics, and a man in ill health most of his life, Hopkins was the results-oriented administrator and unofficial diplomat extraordinaire who worked alongside FDR to feed the starving and employ the unemployed during the Great Depression, earned the trust and respect of Churchill and Stalin as an unofficial envoy for FDR during WWII, and rapidly mobilized war production before and after Pearl Harbor. More than once, he risked his life for his country: flying to Russia to meet with Stalin early in WWII and leaving a sickbed to orchestrate the Yalta Conference later in the war. Having left behind him a legacy of action and few words, an address he gave at Grinnell College defines the principles of public service that he abided by. This documentary, with vivid historical footage and first-hand testimony, earned an Emmy nomination and is available through Filmakers Library.]

Incident at Oglala. Dir. Michael Apted. Spanish Fork Motion Picture Company, 1992. 86 min. Principals: Leonard Peltier, Robert Redford (narrator). [This documentary tells the story of the deaths of two FBI agents on June 26, 1975, at the poverty-stricken and fearful Pine Ridge Indian Reservation in South Dakota—and of the trials that followed. The first trial of two AIM members in Cedar Rapids resulted in acquittal, even though the defense feared that white, working class jury members from Iowa would be prejudiced against militant Indians with long hair. The second trial, of Leonard Peltier, held in North Dakota, led to a conviction for both murders. The film argues that that the government was determined that the FBI agents be avenged in court, even if it meant legal chicanery, intimidation of witnesses, and evidence tampering. The film concludes that Peltier is one more victim in a long series of injustices perpetrated by the government against Native Americans.] AFIs. *NYT* 8 May 1992, B8; *V* 3 Feb. 1992, 80.

Troublesome Creek: A Midwestern. Dir. Jeanne Jordan and Steve Ascher. West City Films, 1995. 88 min. Academy Award nomination: Documentary. [This is the story of Russel and Mary Jane Jordan of Wiota, Iowa, and their farm family, present and past. It focuses on a 1990s family economic crisis that results when bankers become aggressive about forcing the payback of delinquent loans. In creating a "Midwestern" (contrasted with the adventure-filled Western movies the Jordans watch on TV), daughter Jeanne Jordan and her husband have scripted and shot a film with the eyes of loving insiders. The story presents with poignancy and humor the familiar pastoral images of Iowa landscape as well as interiorscapes of working farm places and the gritty realities of a farm liquidation sale. This film won the Audience Award and Grand Jury Prize at the Sundance Film Festival in 1995.] AFIs. *NYT* 6 Feb. 1997, C6; 16; *V* 5 Feb. 1996, 61.

Donna Reed. Dir. Patty Ivins. A&E, 1996. 50 min. Principals: Steve Allen, Shelley Fabares, Mary Owen, Penny Owen, Paul Petersen. [This *Biography* series feature "I'll Take the Moon" presents rural Denison native Donna Reed (born Donna Belle Mullenger) as a strong professional woman and peace activist as well as an Academy Award-winning film actress and beloved wife and mother (like the television role she played on the successful *The Donna Reed Show*). Growing up in the 1920s and 1930s in a hard-working rural Iowa family who liked reading, singing, and going to the movies, shy Donna read Dale Carnegie's *How to Win Friends and Influence People* in high school, leading her to take part in drama and debate at Denison HS. After graduation, Donna moved to live with her Aunt Mildred in Los Angeles and attend City College. She got her start as an actress after winning a local beauty pageant. The documentary stresses Donna's continual fight to rise above supporting roles in B movies, even after she fought her way into the cast of the huge hit film *From Here to Eternity*, where she played against type. Today Donna's most famous film role is as Mary

Hatch in *It's a Wonderful Life*. The WWII film *They Were Expendable* paired Reed with another Iowa native, John Wayne. Besides her leadership in the Another Mother for Peace organization during the Vietnam War era, Donna's legacy includes The Donna Reed Foundation for the Performing Arts in Denison, which has since her death in 1985 held workshops for young performers and film technicians.]

Iowa: An American Portrait. Dir. Tom Hedges. An Iowa Public Television-Stamats Production, 1996. 60 min. Writer: Hugh Sidey. Narrator: Tom Brokaw. Readers: Simon Estes, Cloris Leachman, Sada Thompson. [Funded by corporations and foundations for Iowa's Sesquicentennial in 1996 and repeatedly broadcast on Iowa Public Television, this film is bucolic, with fewer than a half dozen images taken in the larger cities. Commentary within the documentary suggests that small town Iowa life is a model for democracy.]

The Big One. Dir. Michael Moore. Dog Eat Dog Productions, 1998. 96 min. Principals: Garrison Keillor, Phil Knight, Michael Moore, Rick Nielsen, Studs Terkel. [This humorous and heart-breaking documentary by corporation foe Michael Moore tells the story of his 47-city book promotion tour for *Downsize This* (New York: Crown, 1996). In his journey across America Moore meets workers underpaid or fired by companies that are making record profits. Moore stops at a cafe in Iowa to talk with a woman who has to work two jobs to provide her family with food—and, as a result, seldom sees them. In West Des Moines, Moore attends a secret meeting of Borders employees upset that they are required to pay for an HMO plan that has no listed doctors for Des Moines. When Moore revisits Borders at the film's end, the employees have unionized. An example of realism about Iowa, Moore's film shows that some Iowans can't afford food in a state that produces so much of it. In a typical Moore polemic, he also suggests that Iowans, like other Americans, suffer from the effects of corporate greed.] AFIs. *NYT* 10 Apr. 98, 1; *V* 15 Sept. 1997, 75.

Dreamfield. Dir. Kris Ostrowski and Tim Crescenti. Crescenti Moon Productions, 1998. 45 min. Host: James Earl Jones. [This made-for-ESPN documentary explores the fan culture and popular religion that have grown up around the *Field of Dreams* movie and the tourist sites at Dyersville. We see interviews with persons who have come to Iowa, seen as heaven on earth, to renew marriage vows, reconcile familes, and celebrate baseball as it used to be played, just for the love of it. We also see a Sunday sermon from a minister extolling the childlike faith of the film's mantras—"If you build it, he will come" and "If you build it, they will come." On-screen presences include Lou Brock and Maury Wills, notable baseball players, as well as William Kinsella, author of the *Shoeless Joe* novel that was the basis for the screenplay.]

Streetcars of Omaha and Council Bluffs. Dir. Richard Orr. Orr, 1998. 107 min. [This documentary, available at the Omaha Public Library, traces the history and routes of streetcars, mainly in Omaha, but with footage of the inter-city streetcar line that ran from Omaha through Council Bluffs and back. The color and black and white film footage was shot between 1947 and 1955, when the last streetcar ran. Following various streetcar routes allows viewers to see stores, schools, billboard advertisements, fashions, and city landmarks of the post-WWII era.]

Yidl in the Middle: Growing Up Jewish in Iowa. Dir. Marlene Booth. New Day Films, 1998. 57 min. Principals: Marlene Booth and family members. [Currently residing in Cambridge, Massachusetts, Marlene Booth found herself irritated at explaining to skeptical acquaintances that—no kidding—she was actually a Jewish Iowan. She also wanted to understand better her roots in Des Moines during the 1950s and 1960s. Her film is a compilation of snapshots, home movies, and interviews that reflect her happy childhood in Iowa but also her family's status as outsiders in culturally homogenous Iowa. She tells no tales of horror, but sadly recounts tales of slights, exclusions, and unwelcome ham served to Jewish women at a luncheon. Several controversies arose in Des Moines about whether the film was fair and whether it should be hosted by particular groups.]

Alert 3: The Crash of UA 232, Sioux City Iowa, July 19, 1989. G. R. Lindblade and Co., 1999 (revised version of 1989 video). 58 min. [Actual footage of the United 232 DC-9 plane crash in Sioux City and the rescue/ response operation is combined with interviews of city leaders to show how advance planning and cooperation saved 184 lives. This video has been used worldwide to train communities for handling disaster.]

Alert 3: Lessons Learned from the Crash of UA 232, Sioux City, Iowa, July 19, 1989. G. R. Lindblade and Co., 1999. 58 min. [Responding to questions about the aftermath of the United 232 DC-9 crash in Sioux City, this video focuses on how the community handled post-traumatic stress, communicated with families of victims, housed unexpected visitors, and learned from the experience to create an even better system of disaster preparedness. It has also been used for training purposes in many communities in the US and abroad.]

Le cerveau en emoi (English title: *The Brain in Turmoil*). Dir. Anne Georget. Canal Vie, 1998. 62 min. Principals: Antonio Damasio, Hanna Damasio, Maria João Pires. [The Damasios are well-known researchers at the University of Iowa who explore connections between brain structures and consciousness, particularly in cases where strokes and traumatic injuries lead to impairments in rational decision making and capacity for normal emotions. This film reviews some of their cases and introduces comments by associates of the Damasios and one of their emotionally deficient patients (Pires). Antonio Damasio uses these cases to restate his widely-known challenge to Cartesian mind-body dualism. The body as physical brain decidedly affects the mind—as so clearly demonstrated by the cases of physically damaged brains. The film is shot with French commentary in Iowa City at the University Hospital.]

Ann Landers: America's Confidante. A&E Biography Series, 1999. 60 min. Principals: Walter Cronkite, Henry Ginsburg, Margo Howard, Ann Landers, Barbara Walters. [Abe and Becky Friedman came to the United States from Russia and settled in Sioux City, Iowa, where, on July 4, 1915, Becky gave birth to twins Esther Pauline (Eppie) and Pauline Esther (Popo). This biography of Eppie Lederer, advice columnist Ann Landers, tells us about the twins' lives in Sioux City: their father sold chickens from a horse-drawn cart before opening a grocery store and later buying several movie theatres; the lively twins dressed alike and were virtually inseparable as they went through grade school, Central High School, and two years at Morningside College in Sioux City. The beginning of a lifetime separation began at Sioux City's Martin's department store where Eppie met and then married a poor shoe salesman, Jules Lederer, sending her life into a different trajectory from Abby's. Though Eppie and Popo had a double wedding (Abby marrying a rich man), Eppie struck off on her own with her husband and daughter, helping her husband sell pots and pans and working for the Democratic Party before becoming Ann Landers, advice columnist for the *Chicago Sun Times*. Throughout the cinematic biography, a former Sioux City boyfriend of Eppie, Henry Ginsburg, offers commentary on Ann and Abby's lives, including their long-time estrangement.]

Donna Reed: Intimate Portrait. No dir. listed. Greif Company, 1999. 60 min. Principals: Steve Allen, Grover Asmus, Norma Connolly, Shelley Fabares, Robert Osborne, Mary Owen, Tony Owen, Mickey Rooney. [This Lifetime Channel biography about "an Iowa farm girl who lived a Hollywood dream" makes frequent mention of Donna Reed's upbringing in rural Denison as Donna Belle Mullenger. An aspiring actress, Donna traveled to Los Angeles at 17 to live with an aunt and attend LA City College, cleaning rooms and ironing to support herself. "Discovered" after she won a City College beauty contest but cast in B movies at first, Donna eventually broke out with *They Were Expendable*, *It's a Wonderful Life* (at first a flop for which she was blamed), and *From Here to Eternity* (which won her an Oscar). The biography details her three marriages and family life, her hit TV comedy *The Donna Reed Show*, activism against the Vietnam War, two-year stint on *Dallas*, and death from cancer at 64. Early on, Donna's rural Iowa wholesomeness was the image MGM sold. She was a hard worker, kind person, and family-oriented wife and mother, all stereotypically Iowan female traits, but Donna was also a smart and assertive professional woman who took charge of her career, fighting for close-ups in *From Here to Eternity*, controlling with her producer husband Tony Owen every aspect of *The Donna Reed Show*, eventually winning a lawsuit against the producers of *Dallas* when they dropped her from the show. The biography also shows clips from the Donna Reed Performing Arts Festival in Denison that was held after her death from 1986 to 2010.]

Freestyle: The Victories of Dan Gable. [Alternate title: *Gable*]. Dir. Kevin Kelley. University of Iowa/Shadow Bird Productions, 1999. 105 min. [This HBO documentary, produced by the University of Iowa Video Center, suggests that Waterloo native Dan Gable is to wrestling what Babe Ruth was to baseball and Michael Jordan has been to basketball. Gable racked up 182 consecutive victories in high school and college competition, narrowly losing a championship match his senior year. In 1972 he won an Olympic Gold Medal; his six opponents failed to earn a single point. As coach at University of Iowa, his Hawkeyes dominated college wrestling for 20 years until he retired in 1997, with a .932 winning record. An image that opens and ends the film is the older Gable sweating as he does one pull-up after another in an empty gym, creating the illusion he has worked out through the entire length of the film. This is the message about Gable: he is a personification of Iowa-stubborn work ethic and single-minded, successful pursuit of a goal.]

It's Yesterday Once More! Dir. Jon Chambdidis. Mason City Foundations, 1999. 80 min. [This documentary begins and ends with Iowa movie references. Hartzell Spence's description of Mason City from his filmed book *One Foot in Heaven* starts the video, and it ends with Meredith Willson, the creator of *The Music Man*. The video traces Mason City's development from the first settlement in the 1850s to the early 1960s, including famous residents such as Bill Baird, Carrie Chapman Catt, and Willson. The video also discusses Iowa's settlement and puts the growth of Mason City within the context of Iowa's growth. The videotape shows the challenges the first European settlers faced as they moved into the land of the Sioux and the Winnebago Indians. It further shows the impact of the Homestead Act, trains, immigration, agriculture, industrialization, wars, and the growth of banking and business. Finally, it shows features of cultural life in Iowa: schools and libraries, opera houses and vaudeville, arts and architecture. This video is available for sale at Music Man Square in Mason City.]

The Surf Ballroom. Produced by Nelson Breen, Debra Lass, and Iowa Public Television, 1999. 57 min. [This documentary profiles the saga of a notable ballroom in Clear Lake, Iowa, long a source of regional enjoyment and pride. It shows us a mix of urban and rural Iowans in settings where they share common tastes. Most famous as the last venue for Buddy Holly, Ritchie Valens, and J. P. Robertson in 1957 before their fatal plane crash, it had earlier hosted leading groups from the big band era including Count Basie, Cab Calloway, Woody Herman, Tommy Dorsey, and Glenn Miller. The Surf's history also illustrates a valiant struggle to maintain live, local music in the age of mega-shows by superstars—despite bankruptcies, fires, and wrecking balls.]

Trekkies. Dir. Roger Nygard. Neo Art and Logic, 1999. Principals: Denise Crosby and various *Star Trek* actors and fans. [Crosby, who played Tasha Yar in 34 episodes of *Star Trek: The Next Generation* (1987-1994), interviews enthusiastic fans about their costumes, collectibles, fan groups, convention experiences, favorite stars, and lives. We see a dentist's office, Starbase Dental in Orlando, decorated with memorabilia and staffed by professionals in *Star Trek* uniforms. We visit a Klingon language school in Minnesota and the Little Rock copy shop where the *Star Trek*-costumed juror at the Whitewater trial, Barbara Adams, works. Several minutes of the film focus on Riverside, Iowa, which has a sign announcing the "FUTURE BIRTHPLACE OF CAPTAIN KIRK:

175

2287 A.D.!" Riverside has hosted regular *Star Trek* celebrations.] AFIs. *V* 27 Oct. 1997, 48.

Dvorak and America. Dir. Lucille Carra. Travelfilm Company, Czech Television, and AVRO, 2000. 56 mins. [This documentary film tells of the period in the 1890s when composer and conductor Antonin Dvorak traveled to the United States. He taught at the National Conservatory of Music in New York City, founded by Jeanette Thurber, but also spent a very happy summer in Spillville, Iowa, a Czech colony that felt to him like his home in rural Bohemia. The film notes that Dvorak appreciated the beauty of Iowa's hills and woods but also recognized the hard lives of the Czechs who settled in this "huge, lonely land" with its harsh winters. Dvorak helped shape a distinctively American music, based on Negro spirituals and other indigenous musical forms. While in the United States, he wrote his "From the New World" symphony and conducted it at Carnegie Hall.]

"Thirty Year Cold Turkey *Reunion in Greenfield." Living in Iowa.* Iowa Public Television. Broadcast 16 Jan. 2000. 30 min. Produced by Nancy Heather, hosted by Morgan Hallgren, and narrated by Mike Cornelison. [Greenfield, one of three shooting sites for *Cold Turkey*, had the imagination to stage a reunion featuring the cast and the extras. Director Norman Lear and actors Mike Cornelison, Dick Van Dyke, and Jean Stapleton all appear. The narrative thread of this documentary is organized aroun Norman Lear's views of the local Iowans—characterized by by him as "self-deprecating" people who "think that they're hicks"—and they get really excited by the reappearance of Hollywood celebrities. He also reports that the experience of Iowans in Greenfield became important when he produced his *All in the Family* TV series. Whenever network execs would object that something "would not play in Des Moines," he would reply, "Yes it will. I've been there. I'm an Iowa kid." The residents of Greenfield, many of whom had acted as extras, feel inspired once again to go "cold turkey" and finish the festival with a bonfire of cigarette packages.]

The True Story of the Fighting Sullivans. Dir. Arthur Drodker. A&E Television Networks, 2000. 50 min. [This military-focused documentary, which appeared in the *History's Mysteries* format of A&E's History Channel, reconstructs the circumstances under which the Sullivan brothers died in 1942 during their service on the USS *Juneau*. It is based on interviews with Frank Holmgren (a rescued *Juneau* crew member), surviving family members, and authors Dan Kurzman (*Left to Die*, 1994) and Jack Satterfield (*We Band of Brothers*, 1995). It includes scenes from Waterloo and footage of the Sullivan brothers' parents in press conferences and other public settings.]

Hybrid. Dir. Monteith McCollum. Latent Films and Picture Entertainment, 2000. 92 min. [*Hybrid* is a beautifully made biographical presentation of the filmmaker's grandfather, Milford Beeghly, a farmer from Pierson, Iowa, who devoted his life to developing hybrid seed corn and growing Iowa's famous tall corn. At age 99 during most of the filming, Beeghly makes the sex life of corn fascinating, pointing out that corn on the cob is "a mouthful of ripened ovaries." His relatives point out his failure to establish intimacy with them, preferring silence to talk—leaving his first wife bitter and driving a daughter into therapy. Later in life, however, Beeghly remarried and loosened up. The documentary intersperses film footage of the very old Beeghly in overalls and seed corn cap with interviews of relatives. We also see Beeghley Best Seed Corn television ads from the 1950s and artistic shots of corn and Iowa rural landscape. The film is full of quirky details: Beeghly was dressed as a girl and called "Mildred" by his mother until he attended school; in his 90s he and his second wife Alice read Shakespeare together outdoors; he demonstrates his prowess with a toothpick that saved his own teeth. The film reminds us that during and after WWII the Corn Belt was praised for growing "seeds of peace" by relieving world hunger. Perhaps the images remain longest: Beeghly's hand closing and unclosing on seeds of corn, kittens lapping up milk from cows fed with corn, tassels floating over an ear of corn, engaging in conjugal relations.] AFIs. *NYT* 3 Apr. 2001, 5; *V* 13 Nov. 2000, 30-31.

Forgotten Journey: The Stephens-Townsend-Murphy Saga. Dir. John Krizek, Kit Tyler, and Miles Saunders. Forgotten Journey Productions, 2001. 57 min. [Funded in part by the city of Council Bluffs and Humanities Iowa, this documentary tells the story of the successful 1844 trek of 50 people, including women and children, from Council Bluffs ("the great crossroads to the American West") to Sutter's Fort in California. Led by Stephens, the group walked alongside wagons pulled by oxen across the Great Plains, the Rockies, deserts, and the Sierra Nevada range, often in severe weather. All survived the trip through the largely unknown wilderness, and two babies who were born en route survived. The success of the expedition, despite incredible obstacles, was the result of strong leadership and commitment to each other—which allowed the group to separate several times to take different routes and then go back for each other. One member spent months alone high in the snowy Sierras, hoping but never certain he would be rescued. This was the first group to take wagons through California's high country.]

The Formula. Dir. Chris Hanel and L. P. Stephen Phelan. TFN Fan Films, 2002. 53 min. Principals: Chris Hanel, Abe Peterka, Justin Wheelock, Rebecca Peterka. [This is a *Star Wars* fan-made film based on "the formula"—namely, always have a laser sword fight. It is also about the experience of making that film by the four youthful friends who spend their time at the Excalibur game store (featuring *Star Wars* merchandise) where two of them are clerks and the others hang out. Thomas Harrison, aka "Servo" (Chris Hanel), has a vision of "a fully crafted plot and storyline" for the film, which amounts to a sword fight in the woods between a Sith and a bearer of "The Force." He has angry confrontations with his friends about the quality of their video, but they calm him and help him create a satisfying short, which they quickly watch six times at the store. IMDb lists the shooting location as Cedar Rapids.]

The People in the Pictures. Dir. Laura Bower Burgmaier. Iowa Public Television, 2002. 59 min. [A. M. "Pete" Wettach (1901-1976) was a young man from the East who wanted to be a farmer, attending Iowa State University for a degree in agriculture. His efforts to farm were defeated by weather and depression era economics, so he became an employee of Roosevelt's FSA (Farm Security Administration). A hobbyist photographer, he carried a large format (5x7 inch) Graflex and took intimate, artful pictures of families to whom his agency offered assistance. Over a period of 40 years, he made some 50,000 negatives. Using those images to identify persons to interview—many subjects had been small children at the time—this program reveals a Depression era subsistence economy sustained by family and communal labor. In addition to documenting the look of fieldwork, the film describes children's tasks (wood gathering, milking cows, fetching water, and delivering meals to workers) and women's labor (vegetable gardens, chicken management, vegetable canning, cooking). We see outhouses, children's dresses made of chicken sacks, and communal work events. Wettach had an uncanny and loving eye for the significant details defining a way of life that would disappear after rural electrification, indoor toilets, and cars that would reliably run in winter. Discussions of commodity price collapse and bank failures offer important parallels to the farm crisis of the 1980s.]

Crank: Made in America. Dir. Eames Yates. HBO, 2003. 54 min. [This documentary on crank (methamphetamine) addiction destroying lives is "filmed in the place you'd least expect—Iowa" (mainly in the Des Moines area). The film's opening and closing shots of pastoral Iowa (green landscape, birds, clouds) provide a contrast to the three featured families whose addictions lead to nightmare lives, of which filthy houses, disappearing teeth, and loss of weight and jobs are the least of the damaging effects. The documentary focuses on how a crank high feels, the drug's history, and its powerful addictive properties. The drug, which can be manufactured in anyone's kitchen, is presented as almost instantly addictive, and only 6% of users have managed to kick the addiction, the lowest rate of any drug. A sad personal example is the father who swears he will stop crank when his baby is born. Thirty-six hours later he is using crank "for one last time." Crank is the #1 drug problem in rural Iowa, the documentary claims. "It's the devil's drug. It takes everyone prisoner," one of the users declares.]

Discovering Dominga. Dir. Patricia Flynn. Jaguar House Film/ University of California Extension Center for Media and Independent Learning, 2003. 57 min. [The film documents the journey of Denese Becker. She was the sole survivor in her immediate family after a 1982 massacre in her Guatemalan Maya community. In 1985 she came to Iowa as the twelve-year-old adoptee child into a minister's family in Algona. There she does not feel that her peers are willing to accept her account of what happened to her family. She grows into adulthood, marries Blaine Becker, and has two children, but she continues to be haunted by her memories of slaughter. Blaine and supportive friends in Algona help her unravel the mystery of the Rio Negro massacre, in which 177 were killed by military and paramilitary forces and buried in a pit. They also travel with her to Guatemala for emotional support. The film alternates between Iowa scenes of growing awareness and anger about foreign policy in Central America and Denese/Dominga's growing activism in Guatemala as a person demanding to exhume the bodies and enlisting as a witness in the possible prosecution of those responsible. The film shows her conflicted identity, her desire to be in both places to play different roles. Her marriage is the victim of these conflicts over where her loyalties belong. The film ends without any

179

resolution of the emotional, legal, or political issues that hang over the massacre.]

Puttin' on the Glitz. G. R. Lindblade and Company, 2003. 23 min. [Sioux City has restored the Orpheum theatre palace and vaudeville venue to its former glitz and glory. By the time it closed in 1992, it had become a twinplex movie theatre. The restoration is a triumph of fundraising by the Orpheum Theatre Preservation Project committee ($12 million was raised in a year) and craftsmanship by restoration specialists and local contractors under the direction of Ray Shepardson. The miracle of the Orpheum is the extent to which the original architectural features—including marvelous chandeliers—survived the renovations over the years. In restoring the Orpheum, fidelity to the original architectural style was a priority. Modern amenities were added: a spacious green room, deluxe restrooms, and bars for patrons. The new Orpheum has attracted Broadway touring shows and individual performers such as Willie Nelson and Bill Cosby. The Sioux City Symphony and other local performing groups also use the Orpheum facility.]

A Century of Iowa Architecture. Dir. not listed. Iowa Public Television, 2004. 126 min. Principals: Bob Broshar, Kate Schwennsen, Bob McCoy, John Rice, David Kruidenier, Paul Mankins. [This documentary reflects a centennial celebration project of the Iowa Chapter of the American Institute of Architects. It polled its members "to select what they deemed the 50 most significant Iowa buildings of the 20th century." The results reveal a list of accomplishments in a wide array of small towns and cities in the state including Mason City, Sioux City, Grinnell, Davenport, and Burlington. Architects, architectural historians, and journalists guide the viewer through the fifty monuments, some of which were designed by Frank Lloyd Wright, Louis Sullivan, I. M. Pei, Eero Saarinen, Richard Meyer, Frank Gehry, and Mies van der Rohe. A companion book for the centennial is Jason Alread's *A Century of Iowa Architecture* (Des Moines: AIA Iowa, 2004)].

Villisca: Living with a Mystery. Dir. Kelly Rundle. Fourth Wall films, 2005. 115 min. Principals: Edgar V. Epperly, Robert K. Ressler, Bruce Stillians. [In 1912, before the brutal, still unsolved axe murders of eight residents asleep in one house, Villisca, in southwest Iowa, was regarded as a rural Eden because it had become an economically prosperous and culturally progressive railroad town. Curious, horrified citizens demolished any evidence at the original crime scene and later divided the community with their opposing theories of the crime. The Presbyterians blamed a jealous local politician and businessman while the Methodists targeted a visiting minister with a history of insanity. The documentary suggests a stranger traveling by train may have carried out this murder and others. For years the community buried the unforgotten mystery in silence while they watched their town fall victim to economic woes. In the last decade Villisca, with ambivalence, has created a small tourism industry around its famous "unsolved mystery."]

America's Lost Landscape: The Tallgrass Prairie. Dir. David O'Shields. New Light Media, 2005. 60 min. Principals: Nina Leopold Bradley, Annabeth Gish (narrator). [With beautiful cinematography of the tallgrass prairie, this documentary presents the history of this now almost lost landscape and argues for its preservation. Iowa is mentioned often in the narrative. If Iowa is a 1,000 piece puzzle, only 1 piece remains of prairie and that one is not intact. The 1832 defeat of Chief Black Hawk and his followers and the treaty that followed opened up the Sauk and Fox lands in Iowa to settlement, the beginning of the end of the prairie as settlers plowed the land for crops and grazing livestock. A Black Hawk County farmer traces his ancestry back to a Prussian immigrant who came to Iowa to farm in the 1860s, one of many immigrant settlers. Aldo Leopold, of Burlington, author of *A Sand County Almanac* (1949), is heralded as inspiring the conservation movement in the 1930s and beginning efforts to preserve the prairie. The Neal Smith National Wildlife Refuge near Prairie City is an example of a current prairie preservation project. Another is in the Loess Hills of western Iowa. The Practical Farmers of Iowa aim to show that prairie restoration and agriculture can co-exist. Throughout the film Native American and conservation experts share their stories and views, interposed with the voices of the dead such as Black Hawk and Leopold.]

Bonnie and Clyde: The Story of Love and Death. [Alternate title: *Love and Death: The Story of Bonnie and Clyde*]. Dir. not listed. A&E Biography Series, 2005. Approx. 60 min. [This biography of the famous Depression gangster-lovers on the lam tells their individual stories as well as their paired history after waitress Bonnie Parker met ex-con Clyde Barrow, both of them having grown up in poverty-afflicted Texas. One scene shows Bonnie and Clyde with Clyde's older brother Buck and his wife, along with gang member W. D. Jones, hiding out in Dexter, Iowa, near an amusement park, in late July of 1933. Mortally wounded Buck and his wife were left behind and surrendered. Bonnie and Clyde escaped in yet another stolen car. On May 23, 1934, near Gebsland, Louisiana, officers with Browning automatic rifles, Clyde's own weapon of choice, sprayed the pair's car with bullets, ending their legendary story. The documentary presents interviews with scholars and family members of the pair as well as the gang's own photographs and Bonnie's poetry left behind during one of their fast escapes.]

Caveman: V. T. Hamlin and Alley Oop. Dir. Max Allan Collins. VCI Entertainment Distributors, 2005. 53 min. Principals: Jack and Carol Bender, Teddy Dewalt, Will Eisner, Dave Graue. [The creator of the long-running comic strip *Alley Oop*, V. T. Hamlin, grew up in Perry, Iowa. Even though he moved around the country in later life, he always considered himself and his wife as "two kids from Iowa." The comic strip built on a strong interest in dinosaurs early in the century. The addition of time travel allowed Alley to travel to Shakespearean England, Troy, and other places and eras. Hamlin worked for the *Des Moines Register* more than once. Dave Graue assisted Hamlin regularly from 1950 and then took over the strip. Now the Benders are continuing the legacy. The versatile Max Allan Collins wrote the *Dick Tracy* strip for more than a decade.]

Going to Tromadance. Dir. Insane Mike Sanders. Prescribed Films, 2006. 96 min. Principals: Jason Bolinger, Insane Mike Sanders, Lloyd Kaufman. [Prescribed Films of Ottumwa takes a modest approach to its script and production values in this self-effacing documentary. A narrative is generated as viewers travel along on the self-recorded 2005 road journey of Bolinger and Sanders, who are making a film about driving from Ottumwa to Park City, Utah, and then returning. Their objective is to have their road trip film accepted at the following year's Tromadance Festival 2006. (Prescribed Film's entries for previous Tromadance festivals had been rejected.) Cinematography is handheld. At the festival they schmooze with Lloyd Kaufman, festival founder, trying to ingratiate themselves by promising to include a short take of him in a film—a promise fulfilled in *The Bag Man* (2005). Everywhere the pair goes, they mention their long road trip all the way from Iowa. This droll film was not accepted at Tromadance 2006, but it does stream at Amazon.com.]

Iowa's World War II Stories. Dir. Not listed. Iowa Public Television, *Iowa Stories*, 2006. 58 min. Principals: More than 20 women and men who entered military service. [Released around the time of Ken Burns's *The War* (2007) this documentary brings a strong focus on Iowans as part of the WWII effort. 276,000 served in the war, 8,398 not returning. IPTV located surviving vets who had served in all the theaters in Europe, North Africa, and the Pacific, many of them in historically significant episodes such as the bombing of Pearl Harbor, the Bataan Death March, the Tuskegee Airmen bomber escort group, the Battle of the Bulge, D-Day at Omaha Beach, and the liberation of the Dachau concentration camp. As well as survivor accounts of combat, women described their service as war technicians, nurses, military police work. The transformation of industry is shown, with the large munitions factory at Ankeny and the conversion of Maytag's appliance manufacture to war materiel. These survivors remain articulate and sometimes still shaken by their experiences.]

Paul Conrad: Drawing Fire. Dir. Barbara Multer-Wellin. Multer Media/Parallax Productions, 2006. 54 min. Principals: Tom Brokaw (narrator), Paul Conrad. [Political cartoonist for the *Denver Post* and the *LA Times,* Paul Conrad won three Pulitzer Prizes for his fearless work "drawing and quartering" eleven Presidents and his fierce, haunting artwork. A staunch advocate of social justice and free speech as the cornerstones of democracy, Conrad began his career in Iowa, where he was born in Cedar Rapids to a Catholic, Republican family. He drew on Catholicism's commitment to social justice all his life but rejected his father's conservatism. He attended a parochial school in Des Moines, where he practiced his art on the walls in the form of graffiti. Later, he attended the University of Iowa to study art and was recruited to cartoon for the Daily Iowan. In his work and with his family, he advocated wide reading and uncensored expression of ideas. He took pride in the threatening letters his newspapers received and his presence on Nixon's enemies list. The documentary traces 50 years of presidential history via Conrad's cartoons. His favorite targets were Nixon, Reagan, and G. W. Bush. The documentary argues that challenging government through political cartoons and editorials is the function of a democratic nation's newspapers, something that is being eroded by corporate ownership.]

Bill's Big Pumpkins. Dir. Ryan Foss and William R. Nagel. Quantum Petshop Productions, 2007. 87 min. Principals: Bill Foss, Linda Foss.

[Bill Foss of Buffalo, Minnesota, dreams of growing the biggest pumpkin in Minnesota history. The film takes us through a growing season, which ends in a first prize for Bill at the Stillwater competition for a 1020.5-pound pumpkin, but not the record. (The following year he beats the Minnesota record.) Competitive pumpkin growing requires research, good seeds, daily care, careful records, good luck with the weather, and networking with other pumpkin growers. Bill enters several competitions during the late summer and fall, including the Minnesota State Fair and the Pumpkin Fest in Anamosa, Iowa, named after Ryan Norlin, an eight-year old who was killed in a Mississippi River accident. The Anamosa festival, which includes a parade as well as the pumpkin weighing, attracts 15,000-20,000 people each year and has earned the town the official title of Pumpkin Capital of the State of Iowa. Saving his biggest pumpkin for Stillwater, Bill comes in Fourth place in Anamosa with a 992-pound pumpkin. The documentary includes a scene at the Wapsi Country Club in Anamosa, where the good-natured, determined Bill meets and greets other members of the pumpkin subculture. At one point, Bill is interviewed by *Successful Farming* magazine, based in Des Moines.]

King Corn. Dir. Aaron Woolf. Mosaic Films, 2007. 88 min. Principals: Earl Butz, Ian Cheney, Curt Ellis. [In this documentary filmed mainly in Greene, Iowa, Bostonites Cheney and Ellis, with family roots in Greene, return to plant an acre of corn and follow their corn through planting, growing, harvesting, cattle feeding, corn syrup processing, and creating the products that fuel our fast food industry and line the supermarket shelves. The filmmakers avoid stereotyping Iowans as hicks and present food issues in their complexity. An aged Earl Butz discusses why, in 1973, the government maximized corn subsidies that resulted in higher yields, industrialized farming practices, cheaper food for all of us—and a junky, high fat, high sugar diet leading to obesity and diabetes. The film's musical track, interviews, and Iowa scenes are respectful of Iowa farmers such as Chuck Pyatt and show the beauty of the Iowa rural landscape and the look of an actual Iowa small town with its Dairy Queens, bakeries, summer celebrations, trains, and elevators. The film includes expert interviews, statistics on food production, and powerful visuals (cows in feedlots, mountains of corn). In the end the guys lose $19.92 on their corn crop, offset by government subsidies, and decide to turn their cropland into grassland.] AFIs. *NYT* 10 Oct. 2007.

The King of Kong. [Alternate title: *The King of Kong: A Fistful of Quarters*]. Dir: Seth Gordon. Large Lab, 2007. 79 min. Principals: Walter Day, Bill Mitchell, Steve Wiebe. [Presiding over the subculture of 1980s arcade game competition is Fairfield resident Walter Day, who practices transcendental meditation and plays the guitar when he is not heading the Twin Galaxies team responsible for verifying results, ensuring fair play, and determining the world champions of Donkey Kong and other arcade games. The documentary narrates Seattle family man Steve Wiebe's final dethroning of 25-year Donkey Kong champion and icon Billy Mitchell, a bizarre, arrogant man with his own cadre of spies and groupies. In truth Billy is afraid to confront Wiebe in a public competition. With the support of fair-minded Walter Day, Wiebe earns the respect of the gaming community that Billy once held. Besides upholding ethical standards in good Iowa tradition, Walter Day reminds viewers of Fairfield's significant transcendental meditation presence in the state.]

A Little Salsa in the Prairie. Dir. Kent Newman. Full Spectrum Productions, 2007. 55 min. [A town long known for its railroads and meat-packing industry, Perry was populated mainly by immigrants from various northern European countries. In 1990 Perry had 47 Latinos, but by 2000 they had increased to 1837, nearly one-quarter of the town's population. Most of the new immigrants were recruited from Mexico and Central America by IBP, later Tyson. Perry's story is also the story of Storm Lake, Marshalltown, and other Iowa small towns communities whose rapid demographic changes affected schools, housing, businesses, city governments, and interpersonal relations. To deal positively with the challenges of the language barrier and cultural friction, the community set up forums that helped air feelings, identify issues, and create action plans. Not all problems are solved, but Perry has moved toward a community that is pulling together.]

Lost Nation: The Ioway. Dir. Kelly Rundle. Fourth Wall Films, 2007. 56 min. [The Ioway tribe once lived in the area from Pipestone, Minnesota, in the north to St. Louis, Missouri, in the south before they were removed to Nebraska and Kansas. The more traditional Ioway eventually moved farther south to Oklahoma. These Native Americans are now a lost part of Iowa history, victims of the government policy of restricting and then removing Indian tribes, a policy that had completed its aim by 1846 when Iowa became a state. Place names in Iowa are a reminder of this lost culture. Historians, anthropologists, and remaining Ioway tell the story of the tribe, past and present, including the roles played by two conflicted men, White Cloud, an assimilationist who in the 1820s and 1830s agreed to treaties with the government to the tribe's detriment, and Great Walker, who regretted the loss of ancestral lands. Contemporary Ioway take pride in their heritage and wish to know more about their history and culture.]

A Promise Called Iowa. Prod. Sara Frasher. IPTV, 2007. 60 min. Principals: Michael Gartner, Wayne Johnson, Martin Miller (narrator), Walter Mondale, Kenneth Quinn, Robert Ray, David Yepsen. [This 2007 Emmy-winning documentary pays tribute to former Republican Governor Robert Ray and to Iowa individuals, businesses, churches, government agencies, and newspaper editors who stepped up to make Iowa a leading state in the resettlement of Southeast Asians after the end of the Vietnam War. The documentary focuses on several waves of refugees from Vietnam, Laos, and Cambodia, especially the Thai Dam who were allowed, as an exception to government policy, to settle as a group in Iowa during the 1970s and the Boat People who came to Iowa in the early 1980s. Later, Iowa raised money to aid Cambodian victims of Pol Pot's killing fields. Besides interviews with Ray and other state-level leaders in the resettlement project, the documentary highlights the stories of the Walker family who took in a number of grateful Tai Dam refugees, and of Ted Tran, who was welcomed by a family near Cedar Rapids when he was nine years old, having left Vietnam with two siblings and no parents on a boat. Tran later became an assistant to Representative Leonard Boswell (Dem.) of Iowa. Walter Mondale remarks that Iowans should be proud of their leadership in the resettlement of refugees, a humanitarian act that helped heal the wounds of the Vietnam War.]

Being Lincoln: Men with Hats. Dir. Elvis Wilson. Elvis Wilson and Victoria Radford, 2008. 80 min. Principals: Dennis Boggs, John Mansfield. [This documentary film explores the world of "Lincoln presenters," men with physical resemblance to Lincoln who study his life and offer staged presentations. A narrative thread here is that Dennis Boggs, an experienced presenter of 15 years, is providing training for the novice Mansfield. We see Mansfield in his first Lincoln competition. Beyond the focus on Mansfield's learning, we are introduced to the entire culture of presenters, some 180 men in 38 states. They gather for the 2007 Association of Lincoln Presenters at a hotel in Mt. Pleasant, IA. Many documentaries explore quirky subcultures in the United

States, and this film might be seen in that way. But it also testifies to the kind of emotionally moving civil religion in which Lincoln remains a central figure.]

Epic Surge: Eastern Iowa's Unstoppable Flood of 2008. Ed. Paul Jensen and Rollin Banderab. KCRG News, 2008. 108 min. Principals: Bruce Aune, Beth Malicki. [KCRG compiled a coffee table book and this DVD to chronicle the June 2008 once-in-500-years flood that devastated Cedar Rapids, Iowa City, and smaller communities such as Palo. The Cedar River waters rose over 30 feet. The film follows the reporting of KCRG anchors Bruce Aune and Beth Malicki and their news team on a day-to-day basis. Flood photography and interviews with victims, disaster officials, and volunteers showed emotions surging from fear to a sense of urgency to depression to anger to faith and gratitude. Memorable moments include the downtown area with rushing water that reaches the bottom of street signs, sandbaggers struggling to save University of Iowa buildings and Cedar Rapid's Mercy Medical Center, the 100% evacuation of tiny Palo, the four-plus hour detour via Des Moines and Waterloo for an Iowa City to Cedar Rapids trip, and people perilously staying in their houses to avoid separation from beloved pets. The film is a tribute to the heroism of the afflicted communities as well as to its local news media.]

Expelled: No Intelligence Allowed. Dir. Nathan Frankowski. Premise Media/Rampant Films, 2008. 95 min. Principals: Ben Stein. [Ben Stein's controversial documentary claims science in the USA has built walls to keep out ideas that challenge the theory of evolution and serve to support religious belief—specifically, the idea of intelligent design. Besides interviewing scientists and others, he intercuts his argument with images that provide emotional persuasion (e.g., linking the scientific establishment with Hitler and Stalin and his own views with Jefferson and the American flag). He interviews a Professor Gonzalez from Iowa State University whose writing about intelligent design led to denial of tenure, which the administration of ISU acknowledges later in the film. These segments were filmed at ISU in Ames.]

Freakin' Records Freakin' Movie. Dir. Insane Mike Sanders. Prescribed Films, 2008. 86 min. Principals: The Matthew Clay Band, The Nick Sorak Band, and She Swings, She Sways. [This concert film of three bands was recorded at Evans Middle School in Ottumwa on 6 November 2006. The musical groups are local. The audio commentary indicates that the film was shot in a single evening. Special features on the DVD include interviews with the bands. Jason Bolinger, of Prescribed Films, drums for two of them.]

A Friend Indeed: The Bill Sackter Story. Dir. Lane Wyrick. Xap Interactive/Extend the Dream Foundation, 2008. 90 min. Principals: Jack Doepke, Barry Morrow, Beverly Morrow, Jeffrey Portman, Bill Sackter, Thomas Walz. [This documentary dramatizes the later life of Bill Sackter, previously portrayed by Mickey Rooney in the popular TV films *Bill* and *Bill: On His Own*. Sackter, a Minnesota Jewish man, was institutionalized because of his retardation for 44 years. Then Barry Morrow, a media specialist for the University of Iowa's School of Social Work, and Tom Walz, the Director, hired Bill as a consultant with 44 years of experience in disabilities. They also helped him to create a rich, new life in the outside world until 1983 when he died in Iowa City. Happy, warm-hearted Bill with his bad wigs and harmonica became a grandfather figure in the Morrow family, a friend indeed to many in the Iowa City community, and a nationally admired figure with a powerful story about living well with disabilities. The film uses more than a decade's worth of photos and film footage taken by Morrow. Soon Bill became the proprietor of Wild Bill's Coffee Shop at the School of Social Work, dispensing coffee and friendship to everyone who passed his way, including children from a nearby pre-school. With the usual two lane road through the cornfields, lots of recognizable Iowa City scenes, and a Des Moines scene with Governor Ray, the movie is a touching and inspirational tribute to Bill and to those who cared for Bill, both by providing love and security and by helping him become increasingly independent.]

Ready, Set, Bag! Dir. Alex D. da Silva and Justine Jacob. Ensemble Pictures, 2008. 80 min. Principals: Brian Bay, Roger Chen, Ryan Hamilton, James Hunter, Jacob Richardson, Jon Sandell, Kim Weaver, Brenda Wygle. [We follow eight grocery store employees from different parts of the country as they prepare for and then compete in Las Vegas for the title of Best Bagger in America. Brenda Wygle from New Hampton, Iowa, has worked 15 years at Fareway. She lives with her husband, an avid hunter/fisherman, her son, and her daughter, who shares her love of shopping and will follow her mom's footsteps into this competition. Brenda does not make it into the final round of the competition, won by Brian Bay of Utah, but she has some luck gambling in Las Vegas. The film builds suspense as competitors and their friends and families are interviewed before, during, and after the competition. These competitors are normal, hard-working Americans dedicated to customer service.]

A Ride along the Lincoln Highway. Prod. Rick Sebak. WQED Pittsburgh, 2008. 60 min. [This PBS documentary celebrates the Lincoln Highway past and present from the Eastern terminus at 42nd and Broadway in New York City to the western terminus in San Francisco's Lincoln Park. In 1913 entrepreneurs from automobile-related businesses promoted a cross-country highway to encourage driving. In 1992 the Lincoln Highway Association revived to research and promote the highway. The documentary looks at businesses, landmarks, and people along the route today. The film shows a gourmet Lincoln Café in Mt. Vernon, Iowa, and a statue of Abraham Lincoln erected by a Scranton farmer whose land runs along Iowa's Highway 30. The DVD Special Features include stops in Woodbine and Belle Plaine.]

Wild Combination: A Portrait of Arthur Russell. Dir. Matt Wolf. Polari Pictures/IMO Films, 2008. 71 min. [Iowan Arthur Russell—cellist, singer, composer—was probably a musical genius, though not widely acknowledged before his death from AIDS in the early 1990s. Throughout the documentary, images of cornfields, childhood photos, and interviews with his parents (his father an insurance salesman and his mother a cellist) are juxtaposed with his few years in San Francisco in the 1960s and the years following in Manhattan where he associated with avant-garde musicians and poets and performed at The Kitchen and in discos. His sensible, loving parents from Oskaloosa never totally understood or appreciated his music—his dad remarks that it is hard to tap your feet to Arthur's music—but they accepted their son when they learned he was gay and took into their family Arthur's long-time partner, Tom Lee. Arthur made music compulsively, continually experimenting with sounds. Recordings of some of the many tapes he left have found him a new audience. As a child in Iowa, Arthur, who grew up with several siblings, was a big reader and a loner, his face scarred all his life from adolescent acne. Despite his reserve and perfectionism, he had the ability to encourage other musicians and to make friends with experimental artists such as Allen Ginsberg. Just as Arthur Russell's music mixed popular, classical, and experimental forms, he himself was a product of the Iowa cornfields and the bicoastal waters.]

By the People: The Election of Barack Obama. Dir. Amy Rice and Alicia Sams. HBO Documentary, 2009. 116 min. Principals: Barack Obama, Michelle Obama, David Axelrod, Robert Gibbs, Ronnie Cho. [This admiring, insider-style documentary of Obama's 2008 campaign treats the Iowa caucus battleground as central to his eventual victory. There are plenty of scenes familiar to Iowans—the State Fair photo ops, the call center, interviews with skeptical customers in a café, and the Democratic Party caucus process with its "viability threshold" and delegates moving from group to group. The film conveys the grinding drudgery, thrills, crises, and fatigue of the primary process. Iowa filming took place in Des Moines and Iowa City. One sees events in Washington, DC, Minnesota, New Hampshire, New Mexico, and other states. Also included are video clips from news programs, pundits, and moments from Hillary Clinton's campaign as well as that of John McCain and Sarah Palin. The film ends with Obama seated in the Oval Office.]

Food, Inc. Dir. Robert Kenner. River Road Entertainment/Participant Media, 2009. 94 min. Principals: Michael Pollan, Eric Schlosser, Gary Hirshberg, Joel Salatin, Barbara Kowalcyk. [This documentary explores industrialized meat production from activist standpoints that emphasize food safety, nutrition, and animal cruelty. The narrative framework is embellished by the onscreen presences of Michael Pollan (*The Omnivore's Dilemma*, 2006) and Eric Schlosser (*Fast Food Nation*, 2001). Notable examples of animal abuse, state "ag gag" and "veggie libel" laws, bacterial contamination of hamburger (*e coli*), and dietary effects are covered. There are scenes of corn, probably shot in Iowa, and two Iowa State University scientists speak briefly on camera—Alan Trenkle, a ruminant nutrition expert, and Lawrence Johnson, who researches crop utilization. Johnson, who did not understand that he was appearing in a strongly anti-corporate film with heavy editing of his statements, disavowed his role and warned others about food activists. This film has been broadcast by PBS in its *POV* series.] AFIs. *NYT* 12 June 2009, C8; *V* 11 Sept. 2008.

Landslide: A Portrait of Herbert Hoover. Dir. Chip Duncan. The Duncan Entertainment Group, 2009. 58 min. Principals: Jonathan Alter, Timothy Egan, Margaret Hoover, George Nash, David Kennedy, Robert Reich, Amity Shlaes, Timothy Walch. [Born at West Branch to Quaker parents in 1874, Hoover lived his first decade in Iowa. Orphaned at 10, he was sent to Oregon to be raised by a maternal uncle. The film develops a picture of Hoover, the mining engineer after a Stanford education, as one of the richest and most competent men of his era. He became internationally famous when he organized food relief for Belgium during WWI. Serving two terms as Secretary of Commerce under Harding and Coolidge, he successfully organized a massive volunteer relief effort for the Mississippi River Flood of 1927. After a decisive victory for the presidency in 1928, the limited public policy knowledge in his time, coupled with his conservative instincts, led him to make numerous mistakes in dealing with the Great Depression. Vintage film and talking heads, including Timothy Walch, who directs the Hoover Presidential Library at West Branch, provide context for Hoover's successes and failure. This film makes no attempt to develop a connection between his early life in Iowa and later experiences as an adult.]

Picture Perfect: Iowa in the 1940s. Dir. Laura Bower Burgmaier. IPTV *Iowa Stories* 2009. 40 mins. [From 1939-1942, Everett Kuntz, a young man in Ridgeway, documented the small community's life. With an inexpensive Argus snapshooter, he shot rolls that were developed but not printed at the time. As a man of 80 with a fatal cancer, he decided in 2002 to have the negatives printed so that the history embedded in his negatives could be recovered. He had made spontaneous and admiring images of children at play, farm machinery, buildings, and adults at work and in civic or religious settings. Many voices from that era are heard in the interviews, which contain unapologetic expressions of nostalgia. This was "a time of perfect innocence" and "life was simple but not easy." People "accepted their responsibilities" and acted for the welfare of the tightly knit rural community.]

AbUSed: The Postville Raid. Dir. Luis Argueta. New Day Films, 2010. 96 min. [The worst kept secret in Iowa was the employment of undocumented aliens from Mexico, Guatemala, Russia, Bosnia, and other countries at the large Agriprocessors kosher meat-packing plant in the small town of Postville in rural northeast Iowa. On May 12, 2008, the Immigration and Customs Enforcement (ICE) agency raided and arrested 389 alien workers, attempting to process them all within four days. In the rush to prosecute, the workers' rights were violated, and they were treated inhumanely. The resulting investigations revealed that the plant was guilty not only of knowingly employing undocumented workers but of violations of child labor laws, low wages, not paying workers what they were owed, sexual harassment, health and

191

safety violations, and cruel policies such as not allowing bathroom breaks for nearly 12 hours. Because the plant was in such a small town and its residents were devastated by the raid, the Postville raid became a rallying point for oversight of the meat-packing industry, immigration policies, and enforcement practice. The film opens with the usual Iowa icons (crops, barns, windmills) but then intercuts images of a happy multi-cultural community working together prior to the raid. The documentary includes interviews with lawyers, judges, teachers, clergy, and the workers and their families, including children.]

Brent Houzenga: Hybrid Pioneer. Dir. Kristian Day. Modern American Cinema, 2010. Approx. 60 min. Principals: Josh Boyd, Brent Houzenga, Van Holmgren, Chris Roberts. [A farm kid fascinated with comic books and punk music has become a moving force for Des Moines' young artists scene—through passion, networking, and a strong work ethic. His artistic style was inspired by finding two 1890-era photo albums in someone's trash. His old style photos, overlaid with contemporary graffiti designs, decorate recycled windows; his tools are mainly a spray paint can and razor blade. The hybrid style, he says, represents himself: with his rural roots and punk sensibilities. Declared to be the first in Modern American Cinema's Made in Iowa documentary series, the film also shows us Brett as a musician and arts entrepreneur. He has established studios and performance spaces in Des Moines for himself and other young artists, musicians, and performance artists who appreciate his talent, generosity of spirit, and philosophy of "do it yourself" when it comes to promoting art. Brent acknowledges that his farming parents wish he had a regular job and don't understand his art but supported his interests as a child and continue to do so now. We see Des Moines scenes in the movie and get a brief look at the Fort Dodge Permanent Collection Gallery.]

Country School: One Room, One Nation. Dirs. Kelly and Tammy Rundle. Fourth Wall Films. 2010. 72 min. [This film explores the history of the one-room school in the Midwest states of Iowa, Kansas, and Wisconsin. Onscreen interviews are recorded with Living History Farms curators in Des Moines, Professor Dorothy Schwieder of Iowa State, other Iowa historians, and Iowa residents who attended a one-room school. We see glimpses of restored schools in Marshalltown and New Hampton. Twenty-four different Iowa schools are identified in the credits. The documentary relates both fond recollections of lessons learned as well as terrible discipline problems that resulted in confrontations, vicious whippings, and a teacher's demonstration of brutal power to compel obedience. (She bashed a student desk to splinters with a two-by-four in the classroom.) It also addresses a number of issues that remain challenges to education, such as ineffective teachers, poor attendance, health problems, student bullying, poor libraries and textbooks, and the need for bilingual instruction. The film received partial funding from the Humanities Iowa and Preservation Iowa.]

Fat, Sick and Nearly Dead. Dir. Joe Cross. Reboot Media, 2010. 97 min. Principals: Joe Cross, Siong Norte, Phil Staples. [At 310 pounds accumulated through eating unhealthy foods and with a serious autoimmune disease, Australian Joe Cross decides to carry out a 60-day juice fast in the United States, with the supervision of health professionals. He spends 30 days in New York City and 30 days driving across the country to San Diego, interviewing Americans along the way about their weight, health, and eating habits. While Joe's weight loss and health improvement is dramatic, the most compelling story belongs to Phil Staples, a truck driver from Sheldon, Iowa, who at 430 pounds lives in shame-filled despair. After visiting the Sanford medical clinic in Sheldon with Joe, Phil begins his juice diet at a Spirit Lake resort and eventually drops to 202 pounds. He can now walk, swim, and lift weights—and he has shed all his medications. He reconnects with his children and helps his brother lose weight after a heart attack. Another success story belongs to Siong Norte of Waterloo who struggles with the juice fast for 10 days but persists—and gets rid of serious migraine headaches. The documentary contains informational segments and presents the argument that we have a choice about what we eat and how we live: we can resist the fast food culture that is an early death sentence.] *NYT* 1 Apr. 2011, C8.

Ghost Player. Dir. Joe Scherman. DreamCatcher Productions, 2010. 55 min. Principals: Keith Rahe and other Ghost Players. [From 1990 to 2007, a group of former baseball players from the Dyersville area, led by Keith Rahe, formed the Ghost Players, who came out of the cornfields in uniform at the *Field of Dreams* site to celebrate baseball, family, and good Iowa values. Over the years they performed regularly at the Dyersville field, combining ball playing with comedy and audience interaction. They also held baseball clinics for children and traveled to Japan and overseas military bases to share their love of baseball. Crowds responded enthusiastically to the Ghost Players, long after the release of the original film. The players themselves were transformed by this largely volunteer service, touched by the effect of their shows on audience members. The film skims over the conflicts between the two families who owned different halves of the field, simply stating that the performing players became the Left and Center Ghost Players.]

Go-Bama: Between Hope and Dreams. Dir. A. Rahman Satti. IndieFlix/Realeyz, 2010. 80 min. [Resonating to the 2008 Obama presidential theme of hoping for change were many Americans and the East German-Sudanese filmmaker who created this documentary. Already shooting the campaign before the Iowa primary, he reports the battle between cynicism and hope in his own heart. Satti injects his own Afro-German background of growing up in East Germany with a German mother and a Sudanese father. Two generations of his family had experienced disillusionment resulting from Nazi and later communist dictatorship, compounded by racism. Satti interviews voters and tracks two Obama staffers. Satti wants to share the hopes, but remains uneasy until the country—with its terrible history of slavery and racism—elects a president who, like himself, had an African father. The documentary presents several scenes in Des Moines, including the primary caucuses in below zero weather and the celebration of the crucial Iowa victory. His interviews in Iowa are primarily with young people from other states who left their homes for unknown areas of the country to work for Obama.]

High Times on Lower Fourth Street. G. R. Lindblade and Company, 2010. 63 min. [This documentary compiles oral histories and images, from the late 19th century to the present, of Sioux City's famous and infamous Fourth Street. Those who worked, policed, and witnessed the street tell their stories. At one end of the street was Main Street, where Sioux City went to shop at Younker-Martins, buy shoes or jewelry, get a soda at a drugstore, or purchase specialty meats and ethnic baked goods. On Lower Fourth, the east end of the street, people congregated in droves for illicit fun. In 1886 an angry "wet" shot and killed the Methodist temperance minister George C. Haddock. Before liquor by the drink was legalized in the late 1960s, the bars competed to provide citizens, both rich and poor, with alcohol—and local police were paid to ignore all but the most blatant criminal activity. During the WWII years, soldiers in the area frequented the bars, brothels, and restaurants. Farmers who brought their pigs and cattle to the famous Sioux City Stockyards stopped by 4th Street before returning home. Chicago criminals hid out in Sioux City. The Gospel Mission and the

Salvation Army attempted to save souls. On a given night in its heyday, police might make 100 arrests on Lower Fourth. Now the area is an upscale entertainment/restaurant destination. The documentary ends with the song "Fourth Street Boogie."]

Iowa's Radio Homemakers: Up a Country Lane. Dir. not listed. Iowa Public Television, 2010. 58 min. Principals: Evelyn Birkby, Chuck Offenburger, Tom Morain. [From the 1920s forward, homemaker shows on the radio provided family chat, advice, and recipes to women, many of whom were isolated on farms or in their homes. Shows like KMA's *Kitchen Klatter* (broadcast from Shenandoah) were like a "community bottle of glue," uniting neighbors. The film provides a social history of Iowa rural life—showing, for example, the effects of rural electrification and the development of new homemaking technologies and convenience items in the 1950s. Evelyn Birkby from rural southwest Iowa is featured in the documentary. Since the early 1950s, she has written a weekly homemaker column and shared her life (and always recipes) with her neighbors who have, in turn, shared their lives and recipes with her, sometimes even showing up, unannounced, on her doorstep. Evelyn's commentary shows an understanding of and empathy with farm women—how selling eggs and cream gave farm women a sense of economic partnership in their marriages, how neighbors helped neighbors in a crisis (as they did when her daughter died), and how too many homemakers felt a lack of self-esteem and belittled their amazing accomplishments. These shows are an important part of the history of Iowa rural life.]

A Million Spokes. Dir. Varda Hardy. Streetropical Media/Rrell Entertainment, 2010. 100 min. Principals: Chau Nguyen-Johnson, Erik Kondo. [RAGBRAI—the *Register*'s Annual Great Bike Ride Across Iowa, the 1973 brainchild of Donald Kaul and John Karras—takes place each year in late July. About 20,000 bicyclists from every state and around the world ride across the state from river to river as individuals or team members. The documentary follows the 2009 RAGBRAI from Council Bluffs to Burlington, with cinematography capturing Iowa's beautiful rural landscape, its hospitable small towns, and the colorful riders (a woman with her dog along for the ride, a unicyclist, a rider with a cow costume complete with udders). RAGBRAI traditions and culture are part of the film—dipping the wheels in the rivers, nighttime entertainment, beer drinking, sleeping in tents, and caring for aching knees, abrasions, and ailing bikes. The film follows particular individuals and teams: a breast cancer survivor, an Australian who loves his beer, a grieving husband honoring his wife who committed suicide due to depression, a fighting couple, an Iraq veteran, a paraplegic man supported by his family, a Dream Team of high risk teens with their mentors. The film not only shows one of Iowa's most distinctive events but captures the generosity of spirit that is Iowa.]

Roll Out, Cowboy. Dir. Elizabeth Lawrence. Rollout Cowboy, LLC, 2010. Principals: Chris Sand, Jonah Carpenter, Shawn Parke. [This documentary film addresses rural poverty in the upper Midwest. The subject is presented through the experiences of Chris Sand, a.k.a. Sandman, the Rapping Cowboy, who resides in Dunn Center, North Dakota (pop. 146). His group, the Mustaches, sets off on a tour that takes them to tiny venues like bars, pizzerias, and outdoor meetings of rural advocacy groups. The Mustaches convey populist messages through ballads, raps, and dancing. Sand, the little band's front man, compares himself to Woody Guthrie and Hank Williams—while aspiring to become a world-uniting Will Rogers. We see his financial struggle in several incidents: buying a mice-infested house in Dunn Center for $1000 and taking a job as a truck driver to earn more money but then wrecking the truck. The Mustaches' tour takes them briefly to a small outdoor gathering at someone's home in the vicinity of Des Moines. Back at home in Dunn Center, the quixotic Sand aches to do something that will keep his small town from dying and works to reopen an abandoned community center. The film exposes us to people in the Midwest who are deeply unhappy and alienated from the economic system.]

Train to Nowhere. Dir. Paul Kakert. Storytellers International, 2010. 58 min. [In 2002, eleven decomposed bodies of Guatemalans and Mexicans were found inside a locked freight train in Denison, Iowa. This documentary explores this tragedy by interviewing relatives, immigration and law enforcement officials, medical examiners, a psychologist, and a physiologist—many from Iowa. Already across the border in Texas, the eleven undocumented immigrants entered the grain car to be transported farther into the country to escape detection. Their locked car was undetected and traveled on to Oklahoma, where it sat for four months before moving on to Denison. The smugglers did not tip off the officials about the eleven people, who spent 24-36 hours in a hell with no hope before slipping into comas and dying. The documentary focuses primarily on a long-time Mexican-American immigration agent from Omaha, a Guatemalan victim's brother from New York City (who himself entered the illegally in the 1970s and is now a citizen), and a train conductor who aided the smugglers and was imprisoned for his crime. Humanities Iowa helped fund the film.]

Winnebago Man. Dir. Ben Steinbauer. Bear Media/Field Guide Media, 2010. 87 min. Principals: Keith Gordon, Jack Rebney, Ben Steinbauer. [During two weeks of a hot, humid Iowa summer of 1988 Jack Rebney performed in an industrial video for Winnebago RVs. The outtakes of Jack's increasing frustration and vociferous swearing went viral via videos (and later on YouTube), earning Jack the title of the "angriest man in the world." Twenty years later, filmmaker Ben Steinbauer became obsessed with finding out what happened to Jack, even hiring a private detective to find him. The documentary, Ben hopes, will give Jack, now living like a hermit in northern California, a chance to have his say. At first, Jack wants to present himself as "Mary Poppins"—until he defiantly turns "Genghis Khan." Soon after, he contacts Ben to say he was, in fact, humiliated and angry about the outtakes and unwanted celebrity. Jack, who goes blind during the shooting of the film, is still an angry man—but his anger is now channeled primarily at Dick Cheney. Ben would rather hear Jack's personal story of his childhood, marriage, and CBS broadcasting career, but Jack will not cooperate. The film ends with Jack attending a Found Footage Film Festival, where a sold-out San Francisco audience loves him, finding a kind heart as well as the expected crankiness. The Winnebago corporate headquarters in Forest City did not know where Jack was, when contacted, and did not want to be associated with the infamous video. They fired Jack after the video incident. Jack feelingly describes Iowa summer: 100 degree heat, 97% humidity, and flies everywhere. Some interviewees seemed to think being in Iowa was plenty to be angry about, and Jack makes fun of Iowa pronunciation.] AFIs. *NYT* 9 July 2010, 8; *V* 16 June, 2009.

Bully [Alternate title: *The Bully Project*]. Dir. Lee Hirsch. Where We Live Films and The Bully Project, 2011. 98 min. Principals: Ja'Meya Jackson, Kelby Johnson, Alex Libby, Jackie Libby, David Long. [Bullied as a child, Lee Hirsch created this first feature documentary to "speak for the silent" victims of school bullying. Alex Libby of Sioux City and his family provide a major storyline, along with students and families from Oklahoma, Georgia, and Texas. Alex, with Asperger's, has a loving family, but endures, mostly in silence, harassment at East Middle School and on the school bus, where he is punched, threatened, and called "Fishface," making him feel he would like to become a bully. In a moving scene with his mother, they both realize he has no friends. For a time unaware of the severity of the bullying, Alex's parents come to blame themselves and the school, which has neither listened to them nor kept its students safe. The film highlights other bullied children in Sioux City and shows ineffective administrative response. This sad film has inspired both activism and controversy. The Sioux City scenes show Alex, with his haunting face, in his world: his working-class home and neighborhood, the school, the interstate in winter, and trains rumbling through Sioux City. After the film was released, the family moved to Oklahoma, at the invitation of another family in the film, and Alex is reportedly thriving. The Executive Producer, Cindy Waitt, has Siouxland connections.] *NYT* 29 Mar. 2012, C10; *V* 25 Apr. 1 2011.

Capone's Whiskey: The Story of Templeton Rye. Dir. Kristian Day. Modern American Cinema, 2011. Principals: Scott Bush, Mike Ironside, Keith Kerkhoff, Merle Kerkhoff. [During the Depression, despite Prohibition, farmers in south Carroll County began cooking whiskey to survive, even creating their own innovative technology they couldn't patent. The townspeople kept the existence of the stills "hush hush," and the community, even the local priest, justified the criminal activity as necessary for keeping farms, families, and towns intact. Templeton Rye, named after the tiny town of Templeton, became a highly coveted commodity. It was Capone's favorite whiskey, and he and other bootleggers ran the whiskey from Iowa to Chicago. Trucks full of sheep or milk often hid the contraband liquor. Today Templeton Rye is produced legally. Part of the Made in Iowa documentary series, the film was shot in Des Moines, Dubuque, Iowa Falls, Manning, Sioux City, Templeton, and Wall Lake.]

Chasing Hollywood. Dir. Tony Passarella and Bartolomeo Tumbarello. Westbridge Entertainment, 2011. 67 min. Principals: Reggie Bannister, Dominic Capone, Joe Estevez, Antonio Fargas, David Faustino, Larry Thomas, James Vallo. [This hybrid could be called a mockumentary promo film for the director James Vallo, who helmed and acted in the screwball sci-fi *Spaced Daze* (2005). Vallo shows us real and earnest kids while he often makes fun of himself and his enterprises. Known actors and directors, being themselves on screen, give platitudinous but sage advice to aspirants for a place in the screen industry. "Believe in yourself." "Don't try if you can think of anything else to make a living." "Be willing to start in a minor role and just observe." "Consider a part of the business that doesn't require you to be on screen." "Dedicate yourself to the craft." "Don't give up." The Iowa aspect of this film consists of five young acting hopefuls from Des Moines who pool their resources to drive to and overnight in Chicago for a casting interview with James Vallo. Speaking of their motivations and hopes, they allow us to see the very modest resources supporting their yet undeveloped careers. The outcome of the audition for these traveling Iowans is unknown, except that James Vallo offers them free pizza from one of his side businesses. (He works pizza for health insurance.) Though Vallo solicits extravagant praise from colleagues, he undercuts it by presenting several deflating facts about himself.]

Gospel without Borders. Dir. Cliff Vaughn. EthicsDaily.com, 2011. 53 min. [The DVD jacket describes this film well: it "brings more light and less heat to the issue of immigration. It separates myth from fact, examines what the Bible says about treatment of the 'stranger,' shows the experiences of documented and undocumented immigrants, and provides handles for Christians to advance the common good." The four chapters take us to Arizona, Arkansas, North Carolina, Alabama, and finally to Des Moines where the Hispanic migrant population has transformed Trinity United Methodist Church both spiritually and physically. The Church embraces a Las Americas congregation that has found help and acceptance at Trinity and, in turn, helped rebuild the old church into a beautiful building for worship. The film tells individual stories and shows various forms of ministry (including Baptist and Catholic) that respond to a higher law than the current US laws on immigration.]

Green Fire: Aldo Leopold and a Land Ethic for Our Time. Dir. Ann Dunsky, Steve Dunsky, and Dave Steinke. US Forest Service/Aldo Leopold Foundation, 2011. 73 min. (director's cut), 57 min. (public television version). Principals: Peter Coyote (voice), Curt Meine (narrator). [This Emmy-winning documentary presents the life, philosophy, and legacy of Burlington-born conservationist Aldo Leopold (1887-1948), a man ahead of his time. He worked in the newly created the US Forest Service, was one of the first ecology professors (at University of Wisconsin) and a practicing environmentalist (in Wisconsin's Baraboo area), created the University of Wisconsin Arboretum, and influenced US Government wilderness preservation projects. He is best known today as a lyrical science writer (especially for writing *Sand County Almanac*). With the support of his wife and five children, Leopold created "a land ethic for our time." In Iowa Leopold developed a life-long habit of keeping records on the natural environments in which he lived and worked. As a young man Leopold shot a deer and saw a "green fire" in its dying eyes, causing him to realize the deer and the mountain had a more comprehensive environmental truth to tell. This truth—that humans, land, and all animals and plants are part of a complex ecosystem—is the basis for contemporary ecology. As a result, Leopold took on the preservation of cranes in Sand County. His followers are now restoring wolves to habitats in the Southwest United States. His children and other contemporary environmentalists pay tribute to his influence.]

Haunted Iowa. Dir. Jesse Alne and Seth Alne. Alne Enterprises Entertainment, 2011. 135 min. Principals: Seth Alne, Jesse Alne, D. J. Erkenbrack, Dan Gehrt, Johnny Houser, Kole Knipfel, Meegan Robinson. [With a nod to *The Blair Witch Project* and *Paranormal Activity*, a group of college-age students, who have named themselves the Calhoun County Paranormal Investigators (CCPI), became fascinated with ghosts and decided to make a documentary about their confrontations with ghosts haunting Iowa buildings: a theatre in Cherokee, an old opera house in Dubuque, an abandoned school in tiny Farrar, and the state's most famous haunted house, the site of the 1912 axe murders in Villisca. The group, sometimes joined by Villisca expert Johnny Houser, take their camera and various other pieces of equipment to these locales with reputations for ghosts and find increasing evidence of paranormal presence: doors opening, eerie voices, sudden cold drafts, knockings, and bumps in the dark, accompanied by the investigators' startled comments: "Oh, my God!" "Dude, what was that?" "My hands are shaking." Their aim seems to be making contact rather than ghost busting. In the Farrar school they think they have seen and communicated with a dead-but-not-gone child-molesting principal. In Villisca, during a reenactment of the original murders, Johnny is possessed by the original murderer who urges him to "Do it, do it, do it!" The CCPI asserts that Iowa, to the surprise of many, is actually a haunted locale.]

Henry Wallace: An Uncommon Man. Dir. Joan Murray. VideoTakes, Inc., Productions, 2011. 57 min. [Henry A. Wallace of Adair County came from a well-educated family dedicated to public service and was mentored by George Washington Carver at Iowa State University. This documentary shows Wallace as environmentalist, statesman, internationalist, and intellectual. At a young age, he founded Pioneer Hi-Bred, which increased corn yield. During the Great Depression, as Secretary of Agriculture under FDR, Wallace tackled problems of grain surpluses, low prices, and soil erosion, and he created the food stamp, school lunch, and rural electrification programs. FDR later tapped him as his vice president in 1940 and put him in charge of industrial mobilization for the war. Despite his successes as an administrator, Wallace was an uncommon politician who didn't smoke and drink and disliked political game-playing. An articulate, straightforward progressive on the environment, civil rights, women's rights, international cooperation, and peace, Wallace won the hearts of common people and alienated Democratic Party bosses, leading to his loss of the vice presidency in 1944. He served Truman as Secretary of Commerce, but Truman was forced by the party to disassociate himself from Wallace's critiques of the defense industry, segregation, and Cold War. Wallace went on to edit *The New Republic* briefly and continued to write books. The end of the film stresses Wallace's ideas from the 1930s and 1940s that have become public policy from the Kennedy era to the present. Wallace's personal style and habits were typically Iowan, and, cosmopolitan internationalist and intellectual that he was, he was known for his ability to connect with "plain people" around the world who lived close to the land.]

New York Says Thank You. Dir. Scott Rettberg. Individual Entertainment Company/Walnut Hill Media, 2011. 86 min. Principals: Jamal Braithwaite, Brian Fitzpatrick, Evan Parness. [It began with a five-year-old boy from New York City. He conceived the idea of helping other disaster victims across the United States—just as Americans stepped up to help New Yorkers after 9-11. Firefighters from NYC and others have, each year, gathered to help a family or community in need somewhere in the United States. The number of NYC participants has snowballed through word of mouth, and beneficiaries in one year have become volunteers for coming years. All have found that helping others is a way to heal and a symbol of our national good will to others. The film opens with the aftermath of a deadly tornado in Little Sioux that killed four Boy Scouts. Throughout the film we see scenes from Little Sioux and other devastated communities helped by the New York Says Thank You project. The project built a chapel at the Scout Camp near Little Sioux where the shelter once stood. The parents of the dead boys see the communal building of the chapel as a sign of God's goodness and a wonderful memorial to their boys. Other

201

communities—devastated by fire, hurricanes, or tornadoes—have had similar transformative experiences. The message of the film is "pay it forward."]

America's Darling: The Story of Jay N. "Ding" Darling. Dir. Samuel Koltinsky. Marvo Entertainment Group, 2012. 75 min. Principals: Chris Steffen. [This well-researched documentary tells the story of two-time Pulitzer Prize-winning political cartoonist, artist, and hugely influential conservationist Ding Darling (1876-1962). Darling's family moved to Sioux City when he was ten. After graduating from Beloit College in 1910, Darling got his start as a journalist, sketch artist, and reporter for the *Sioux City Journal*. By 1913 he began a long career at the *Des Moines Register*. Hosted by his great-great grandson Chris Steffen, the film stresses Darling's results-oriented leadership style, lifelong passion for nature, and ability to motivate that led to the establishment of the Fish and Wildlife Commission, creation of the Duck Stamp (which has created funding for wetland conservation), development of a coordinated system of natural wildlife refuges, and establishment of programs at land-grant universities to train environmental scientists. Besides beautiful natural photography and shots of Ding's cartoons, we see his unusual homes in Des Moines and on Sanibel Island, Florida. A figure of national and international importance, Ding was a friend of Herbert Hoover, worked for FDR, and traveled to Russia at Stalin's invitation. His legacy includes the Ding Darling National Wildlife Refuge on Sanibel, protected natural environments throughout the U. S., and the Duck Stamp artist competitions.]

City of Literature. Dir. Ben Hill. University of Iowa, 2012. 58 mins. Principals: Paul Engle, Loren Glass, Marvin Bell, Samantha Chang, Paul Ingram, Nicholas Meyer, Mary Bennett, Ethan Canin, Laurel Fantauzzo. [Iowa City is one of three cities in the world designated by UNESCO as a City of Literature. Through still photographs from the University of Iowa's distant past, historical film clips, and contemporary voices, this film characterizes a unique literary culture. Early in its nineteenth-century history, student literary societies laid the foundations for a university curriculum in which artistic creation could claim a legitimate place. Iowa was the first university to offer a degree program in creative writing and has been widely emulated. The program is frank about literary politics on campus and the results. Paul Engle, "a cornfield kid crazy for English words," was the catalyst for the Iowa Writers Workshop and then the International Writing Center after he was forced out of the Workshop by English Department resentments over his international travel and absences from the campus. Interviews with faculty members, students, and the Prairie Lights Bookstore owner elucidate the unique factors that have produced alumni who have won forty Pulitzer prizes.]

Great Plains: America's Lingering Wild. Dir. Michael Farrell with Michael Forsberg. NET Television and Michael Forsberg Photography, 2012. 120 min. [This PBS broadcast documentary is a two-part exploration of the territory that includes several Midwestern states. Intensive land use and persistent drought have transformed the Great Plains. The filming celebrates the surviving natural landscape beauty and the fragile wildlife, which have awakened natural compassion and dedicated ecological advocates. The first hour, "A Long, Hard Struggle" travels to Nebraska, the Dakotas, New Mexico's Weaver Ranch, and Kansas's Flint Hills riverine area. Everywhere Forsberg goes, he documents threatened species like the prairie dog and ferret. The second segment, "We Live with the Land," takes the exploration to Montana's Missouri Breaks and South Dakota's Cheyenne River Ranch, where herds of buffalo have been restored. Iowa's Broken Kettle Grassland Preserve in Plymouth County is visited as a rare "less than 1%" survival of native prairie in a state that has been almost entirely plowed for agricultural production. At Broken Kettle burning has been reinstated as a grassland management practice; the grass can now sustain a small herd of buffalo. Scott Moates, the Director, who is accompanied by his young daughter, speaks eloquently in expressing the hopes he feels for the experiences that she will be allowed to have in the future.]

The Grey Area. Dir. Noga Ashkenazi. Musical Chairs Productions, 2012. 65 min. [This documentary grew out of a feminism class conducted by two Grinnell professors at the Iowa Correctional Facility for Women in Mitchellville. The statistics presented and the interviews with psychologists, corrections officials, lawyers, parole officers, the Mitchellville staff, and the co-director of the Center for Gender and Justice tell a story about intractable social problems and inequities in the justice system that perpetuate the victimization of women. We see the inmates in the prison classroom analyzing the meaning of "the personal is political" and "privilege" in their own lives. In the classroom and personal interviews, we hear the women talk of unbelievable neglect, abuse, and traumas—which social service agencies and law enforcement were unable to alleviate. For many, prison is the only safe place they have ever known. The end of the documentary—two years later—shows two severely abused women denied hope of a commutation of their sentences for yet another 10 years. As the camera follows the professors driving past houses on the roads to and from Mitchellville, we know that in too many of those homes, girls and women are living lives of pain that head them toward incarceration.]

The Hope and the Change. Dir. Stephen K. Bannon. Amigo Media, Citizens United Productions, Victory Film Group, 2012. 68 min. [This documentary is actually a campaign film, produced by several conservative foundations, that uses blatant propaganda techniques to condemn Obama's leadership in his first term. Its aim is to convince Democrats and independents to vote against him in the 2012 election. The main technique is to interview ordinary people, including several Iowans, who ostensibly believed in Obama as almost a Messiah in 2008 and now feel he has brought the country to division and disaster. Rather than addressing issues such as the bailouts and health care with any factual information, the film shows Obama hanging out with celebrities, playing basketball, and going on frequent vacations while bailing out corporations, raising taxes and the deficit, and forcing a communist-style health care system on the country—while ordinary people are working hard, but not getting by. Among the disappointed talking heads, eight are identified as citizens of Iowa.]

Janeane from Des Moines. Dir. Grace Lee. Wilsilu Pictures, 2012. Principals: Jane Edith Wilson, Michael Oosterom. [Call it "fakeumentary," this hybrid documentary on the 2012 Iowa Republican presidential primary combines a fictional Janeane (Wilson) and her ensemble of supporting actors in roles as husband Fred (Oosterom), work colleagues, and health care providers. The people who play themselves— to the extent that they actually disclose themselves—are the trusting and sympathetic Republican presidential candidates of 2012 and the news organizations who came to Iowa and accepted Janeane's fictional identity. Janeane claims to be a home health care aide who is about to lose her job, her marriage (Fred has started hanging out in a Des Moines gay bar), and her own health to breast cancer. She is a Tea Party-type Republican who thinks that Planned Parenthood is "just murderers," hates gay marriage, attends Bible study groups, and opposes Obamacare. She is filmed interacting with the candidates one-on-one, pleading with them to tell her what to do about her family income problems (the house is being foreclosed), and no doctor will touch her medical problems except providers at Planned Parenthood. The candidates are moved by her tears but very uncomfortable regarding specifics and only assure her that they will grow the economy or end Obamacare. The Iowa scenes include conservative Christian rallies and the state fair. The ethics of this film have been debated and compared to those of the prankster Borat (Sacha Baron Cohen).] *NYT* 12 Oct. 2012, C5; *V* 29 Sept. 2012.

The Matchmaker. Dir. Seth Camillo and Dustin Morrow. Stanley 9 Films, 2012. 73 min. Principals: Seth Camillo, Willie Daly, Dustin Morrow. [Lacking romantic confidence, two single Iowa City filmmakers determine to make a documentary about Willie Daly, from the tiny rural village of Lisdoonvarna, Ireland, who comes from a family of matchmakers and is part of an annual September singles festival there. Seth and Dustin hope they will find love as well as make a movie. Amid Irish scenes, music, drinking Guinness, and dancing, the filmmakers interview people with ages from 15 to 90 about their romantic or pragmatic hopes, crushes, effective dating moves, and the challenge of finding someone to love. Though the guys get some good advice, they mostly strike out until they meet two young women from Germany and have some fun with them. The Iowa City scenes start the movie as they interview friends and family at a wedding about their romantic prospects and film themselves in their University of Iowa dorm room filling out Willie's questionnaire. In Ireland, they describe Iowa as having cows, corn, pigs, and soybeans, stressing their rural roots in a rural area of Ireland, where many of the single females come to try to find a rich farmer to marry.]

American Meat. Dir. Graham Meriwether. Multiple Partners including MacArthur Foundation, 2013. Approx. 70 min. Principals: Joel Salatin, Chuck Wirtz. [West Bend farmer Chuck Wirtz shows his commodity operation, producing hogs at a high overhead cost to himself, for a corporation that can curtail production at any time and that uses a great deal of fossil fuel in transportation costs. Dave Struthers of Collins faces losing his hog operation due to massive debt and a decreased market for hogs. Industrialized farming has led to ghost farms and ghost towns, Larry Ruppert of Curlew testifies. Joel Salatin's famous farm operation in Virginia, however, shows that grass-feeding chickens, pork, and beef can be efficient and profitable as well as producing much better-tasting meat. The documentary presents statistics and discusses economic realities (e.g., farm subsidies go to the industrialized farm operations; humane and organic meat production costs more) but presents practical alternatives for producing better tasting meat under more humane circumstances and for selling the meat locally, cutting down on fuel use. Farmers like Chuck Wirtz are experimenting with more humane and organic livestock production and distribution through farmers' markets, cooperatives, and direct sale to chefs. A final section shows the health benefits of eating organic foods.]

Caucus. Dir. A. J. Schnack. Bonfire Films of America and Rival Pictures/Om Films, 2013. 144 min. Principals: Michele Bachman, Herman Cain, Newt Gingrich, Ron Paul, Tim Pawlenty, Rick Perry, Mitt Romney, Rick Santorum. [The filmmakers patiently track numerous candidates from August 2011 to Caucus Day 2012. We see the usual scenes at the State Fair where Romney graciously chomps a vegetarian corn dog thrust toward him. On the campaign trail, we witness the usual chitchats, arm waving, glad-handing, and hugging. One glimpses the charming qualities of candidates and their flashes of clever response. A conservative presidential run in Iowa is not an easy trip. Candidates face rude accusations of hatefulness or indifference. Hecklers at the University of Iowa shout down Gingrich to prevent him speaking, but he waits them out. Intense focus goes to Michele Bachman, who campaigned the longest and fell the farthest, and to Rick Santorum, who ultimately beat Romney by 34 votes in the recount. This is a necessary film for students of electoral politics and for aspiring candidates. Others will enjoy the experience with thanks to the filmmakers who drove thousands of miles.] *NYT* 7 Nov. 2013; *V* 5 Nov. 2013.

Dear Ann Landers. S'More Entertainment, 2013. 55 min. Principals: Eppie Lederer (Ann Landers), David Susskind. [Not a documentary but a television interview, this 2013 DVD preserves a conversation between Susskind and Sioux City native and widely syndicated advice columnist Ann Landers a year or two after her divorce from her husband of 36 years in 1975. Eppie clarifies her attitude about her divorce and living single (she doesn't blame herself, respects her ex, and enjoys her freedom) and about her relationship with her sister Popo (they are competitive as advice columnists but get along well). Then the conversation turns more generally to relations between the sexes in the early days of women's liberation, the effects of unemployment, and the Vietnam War (which Ann opposed in her column). When asked what advice she would give David Susskind's TV audience, Eppie makes an appeal for people to practice kindness toward each other. The interview brings out an anecdote about Eppie's Sioux City mother and her Yiddish sense of humor. Included on the DVD is a Susskind interview with Dr. Eugene Kennedy, a Loyola psychologist whom Ann Landers often consulted.]

The Farm Crisis. Dir. Laura Bower Burgmaier. Iowa Public Television, 2013. 90 min. Principals: Gov. Terry Branstad, Sen. Charles Grassley, Sen. Tom Harkin, former Rep. Jim Leach, the late Mark Pearson, former Sen. Tom Daschle, Neil Harl, and Willie Nelson. [This film is a moving and painful retrospective on Iowa farmers during the late 1970s through the 1980s. It lays out the unique convergence of commodity price fluctuations, droughts, Carter's Soviet grain embargo, and leveraged debt that produced massive foreclosures, sheriff's auctions, personal bankruptcies, suicides, the murder of a banker, and the failure of small town businesses. The widow of one suicide quotes his succinct note: "The farm killed me." Narrated by NBC News reporter Harry Smith, the film mixes historical footage and contemporary interviews with political leaders and representatives from rural advocacy organizations. It includes cautionary perspectives about current land and commodity prices—which may be two more bubbles waiting to be pricked.]

Lost Nation: The Ioway 2 and 3. Dir. Kelly Rundle. Fourth Wall Films, 2013. 112 min. [This DVD contains two documentaries about the Ioway tribe from its ancestral settlements in Wisconsin and Iowa to later nineteenth- and twentieth-century removals to Nebraska, Kansas, and Oklahoma. The two films are sequels to the earlier documentary *The Ioway*, also directed by Kelly Rundle, written by Kelly and Tammy Rundle, and produced by Fourth Wall Films. Like the first, these two films combine beautiful images, interviews with Ioway experts, photographs and commentary that chronicle the detailed history of the tribe, discussion of archaeological digs (including the Iowaville site near Selma, Iowa, and the Blood Run site near Granite, Iowa), and moving commentary by Ioway tribe members about their lived experience. In segments 2 and 3, we see how the Ioway's experience reflects that of all tribes as the government, with the assistance of Christian missionary groups, has for over 200 years aimed to eradicate Native Americans, their culture, their language, and their land. While celebrating the survival of the Ioway and recent victories (preserving eagles, winning settlements from lawsuits against the government for treaty violations, carrying on traditions with the younger generation), the films portray precisely how the official policy of genocide and ethnic cleansing has been implemented. The films show the coercion of the Ioway into boarding schools and into accepting individual land allotments. At the close of the documentary sequence, we hear a South Dakota man talk eloquently about his struggle to overcome the hate and violence in his heart so that he can embrace life and forgiveness while never forgetting the past. We also see a young Ioway girl with tears streaming down her face describing a visit to the Ioway exhibit at the Milwaukee Historical Museum. Her fear is that cultural experiences that are part of her life, traditions such as sweat lodges, will one day be museum exhibits only. All three documentaries use Iowa locations and experts.]

Married and Counting. Dir. Alan Piper. Speakeasy Productions, 2013. 93 min. Principals: Stephen Mosher, Pat Dwyer, George Takei (voice over narrator). [In 2010 two men—Dwyer and Mosher—contemplate their 25th anniversary as a same-sex couple. They decide to celebrate by having weddings in every jurisdiction of the United States that recognizes same-sex marriage. In a mood they describe as "aggressively joyful," they intend "to be married as fully as the law allows." They arrange for, and allow documentary cinematography to follow, their marriage ceremonies in Vermont, New Hampshire, Iowa, Massachusetts, California, Washington, DC, and finally New York City. They rush toward the wedding arranged in Iowa with fears that the recall election for the judges who approved of same-sex marriage will rapidly end their opportunity. Because a Jewish friend in Des Moines offered to host the wedding, they observe Jewish wedding ritual. While in Des Moines, their car breaks down by an evangelical church, one of whose members rescues them and while driving informs them of his former gay life that his church managed to cure. Takei's narration, along with subtitles, provides information about the history of civil and same sex unions.] *NYT* 25 Apr. 2013; *V* 13 June 2013.

More Than a Game: 6-on-6 Basketball in Iowa. Dir. not identified. IPTV, 2013. 59 min. [High school girls have played basketball for over a century in Iowa. From 1934 to 1993 they played 6-on-6, half court, two dribble basketball. Decades before Title 9, girls' basketball was the most popular sport in Iowa, especially in small towns where everyone went to the twice weekly games and emptied out when their team went to the state tournament in Des Moines to play in front of sell-out crowds. Male administrators fought for and promoted girls' basketball. Superstars like Denise Long and Jeanette Olson were statewide celebrities, and all the players were stars in their hometowns.

The documentary provides a history of the sport and interviews with players, coaches, long-time head of the Iowa Girls High School Athletic Union Wayne Cooley, and sports reporters. Girls' basketball, so often mocked by *Des Moines Register* columnist Donald Kaul, is an important part of the history of small town Iowa and led to a state-wide respect for girls' athleticism and for the girls themselves.]

Movie Star: The Secret Lives of Jean Seberg. Dirs. Gary McGee and Kelly Rundle. Fourth Wall Films, 2013. 92min. Principals: Elaine Brown, Carol Hollingsworth, Richard Ness, Mary Ann Seberg, Mark Westin. [This documentary reprises the life of Seberg, born at Marshalltown in 1938. She achieved instant celebrity when selected by Otto Preminger for *Saint Joan* (1957). Journalists tagged her as being from "a little place in the middle of nowhere" and called her Cinderella. Learning to act as a young star, she achieved significant artistic recognition for *Breathless* (1960) and other films of the French New Wave. Interviews with Iowa friends and relatives reveal details about her Iowa roots, aspirations, and early feats. Seberg had been a civil rights activist early on, joining the NAACP at the age of 14. In the late 1960s she attracted FBI attention because she financially supported the Black Panthers and a Montessori School of Malcolm X. J. Edgar Hoover personally ordered that she be "neutralized," and she felt tormented by the resulting lies spread by the FBI, one of them that she was pregnant by a Black Panther leader. She had a stressful miscarriage and brought the baby to Marshalltown for burial. Shortly afterward she committed suicide.]

Spinning Plates. Dir. Joseph Levy. Chaos Theory Entertainment 2013. 93 min. Principals: Grant Achatz, Cindy Breitbach, Mike Breitbach, Annie Breitbach, Mikie Breitbach, Gabby Martinez, Francisco Martinez, Thomas Keller. [This film narrates through intercutting the styles and stresses of three different types of restaurant. At the top of the food chain is Alinea in Chicago with three Michelin stars, elite prices, and tiny, artful dishes. In the middle tier is Breitbach's Country Dining of Balltown (near Dubuque), which serves country comfort food from modestly priced, all-you-can-eat menus with plenty of pota-toes, gravy, fried meats, and pies. La Cocina de Gabby offers Mexican food in Tucson and teeters at the edge of foreclosure for both home and restaurant. Breitbach's unique challenge is two fires within a ten-month period; the first destroys their 150-year-old restaurant, and the second burns down the replacement that was built with community support and donations. The Breitbach's segment displays a remarkable community role for a restaurant that is literally the center of life in its town of less than seventy citizens.] *NYT* 24 Oct. 2013, C8; *V* 4 Feb. 2013.

V. Films Made in Iowa without Iowa Fictional Settings

This listing reflects the information of the Iowa Film Office (1984-2009), and shooting location information provided by the American Film Institute Catalog of Feature Films, and IMDb, which for more recent films receives its technical information from the companies that produce the films.

Penitentiary. Dir. John Brahm. Columbia, 1938. 79 min. Principals: Robert Barrat, Walter Connolly, John Howard, Jean Parker. Literary source: Martin Flavin's *The Criminal Code* (New York: H. Liveright, 1929). [Filmed in Anamosa, Iowa, this drama follows the mishaps of William Jordan, who is arrested at his 21st birthday celebration for hitting and accidentally killing a man who has acted improperly toward a female friend. The victim's father gets the inept legal counsel to plead manslaughter, and Jordan lands in jail. He falls in love with the warden's daughter while working as a chauffeur for her. On the verge of parole, he is pressured to inform on a fellow prisoner, but he upholds "the criminal code" and remains silent. The film provides a happy ending the original play did not: the other prisoner confesses so that Jordan can go free. The film presents a legal system in which punishments do not fit the crimes.] NS. AFI. *NYT* 7 Mar. 1938, 13; *V* 26 Jan. 1938, 15.

Gaily, Gaily. [Alternate title *Chicago, Chicago*]. Dir. Norman Jewison. Mirisch Productions, 1969. 107 min. Principals: Beau Bridges, Hume Cronyn, Brian Keith, George Kennedy, Melina Mercouri. [Based on Ben Hecht's autobiographical novel *Gaily, Gaily* (New York: Signet, 1963), this comedy, partly filmed in Dubuque, tells of naive Ben Harvey's adventures when he leaves hometown Galena, Illinois, for Chicago. He mistakes a bordello for a boarding house and later teams up with a hard drinking reporter to investigate government corruption. The film was nominated for Oscars for Art Direction, Costume Design, and Sound.] NS. AFIs. *NYT* 17 Dec. 1969; *V* 31 Dec. 1968.

Huckleberry Finn. Dir. Robert Totten. ABC Circle Films, 1975. 78 min. Principals: Royal Dano, Jack Elam, Antonio Fargas, Merle Haggard, Ron Howard, Don Most. [This bland version of Twain's *Huckelberry Finn* with actors from *Happy Days* was filmed along the Mississippi River in

Iowa, but the setting is not distinctively Iowan. The original story takes place in and on the Mississippi in Missouri and Arkansas.]

F.I.S.T. [Alternate title: *FIST, Federation of Interstate Truckers*]. Dir. Norman Jewison. Huron Productions, 1978. 145 min. Principals: Peter Boyle, Melinda Dillon, Tony Lo Bianco, Sylvester Stallone, Rod Steiger. [This film portrays a Jimmy Hoffa-type labor leader. The action portrayed is in Cleveland and Washington, DC, but the filming took place in Dubuque.] AFIs. *NYT* 26 Apr. 1978, 15; *V* 19 Apr. 1978, 26.

All the King's Horses. Dir. Donald W. Thompson. Mark IV Pictures, 1977. 80 min. Principals: Grant Goodeve, Dee Wallace. [Based on a true story, the film focuses on a Christian young woman, Sandy, who meets and marries Jack, a motocross racer who at first accepts Christ only superficially. From the start, their marriage is troubled with resentment, criticism, jealousy, and violence, leading Sandy to abuse prescription drugs and Jack to drink too much. Christ is the "King," mentioned in the title, who puts the pieces of this broken marriage together again. Filming in Des Moines is indicated in a radio broadcast that announces it as the location for a Christian lecture on "Where Have All the Fathers Gone?"]

Home Safe. Dir. Donald W. Thompson. Mark IV Pictures, 1981. 74 min. Principals: Newell Alexander, Anita Jesse, Howard Culver, Michael Hornaday. [Three generations of men have lived their lives without Christ. Thus they fail at learning discipline and responsibility, create an unsafe home, and jeopardize an ultimate "safe home" in Heaven. Based on a true story, the Disney-style narrative features an unruly dog, a tiger freed from a zoo, and a python escaped from a cage in a school science room. The mother and older son, both Christians, with their pastor, bring the three men to accept Christ and the Bible's authority. The opening credits thank the Des Moines Police Department, the City of West Des Moines, the Iowa Highway Patrol, and the Urbandale Little League—but references in the film are to East Aurora and Springfield.]

Pennies from Heaven. Dir. Herbert Ross. 1981. MGM, 107 min. Principals: Steve Martin, Bernadette Peters, Christopher Walken. Literary source: Dennis Potter, *Pennies from Heaven* (New York: Quartet, 1981) and the TV series of the same name, BBC Mar. 1978-Apr. 1978. Academy Award nominations: Costume, Sound, Screenplay adaptation.

[This is a musical about a sheet music salesman in Chicago during the Depression. Dubuque was the site for the filming.] AFIs. *NYT* 11 Dec. 1981, C16; *V* 9 Dec. 1981, 18-20.

Children of the Corn. Dir. Fritz Kiersch. New World Pictures, 1984. 93 min. Principals: R. G. Armstrong, Peter Horton, Courtney Gains, Linda Hamilton, John Franklin, Robby Kiger. [Based on a Stephen King short story, in his collection *Night Shift* (New York: Doubleday, 1978), this film is about cult killings by spirit-possessed teens. Filmed near Whiting, this film gave extra roles to residents of Woodbury County. Its fictional setting is Gatlin, Nebraska. King wrote the screenplay, which was not followed by the producer, so he asked that his name be removed from the screen credits.] AFIs. *NYT* 16 Mar. 1984, C7; *V*, 14 Mar. 1984, 22, 26.

Starman. Dir. John Carpenter. Columbia, 1984. 115 min. Principals: Karen Allen, Jeff Bridges, Richard Jaeckel, Charles Martin Smith. Academy Award nomination: Actor. [This film about an alien includes an opening scene at a truck stop in Cedar Rapids. Fictional setting is Wisconsin.] AFIs. *NYT* 14 Dec. 1984, 18; *V* 5 Dec. 1984, 17.

Brother Enemy. Dir. Russell S. Doughten, Jr. Mark IV Pictures, 1987. 76 min. Principals: Marv Emery, Debbie LePorte, Paul Schwink, Robert Shook, William Wellman, Jr., and Dan Wood. [David Wiemer, a puppeteer with a popular children's program, returns to his hometown to work on a puppet show to raise money for a community center. Angry that basketball practice will be suspended for two months, a group of teens demolish Wiemer's workshop and are caught. Wiemer convinces the judge to sentence them to work with him to create a puppet show based on a Bible story. The film's credits establish that the film was made in central Iowa.]

Luther the Geek. Dir. Carlton J. Albright. Troma Entertainment, 1990. 80 min. Principals: Jerry Clarke, Stacy Haiduk, Thomas Mills, Joan Roth, Edward Terry. [Young Luther from rural Illinois, grows up obsessed by a carnival geek who bites off the heads of chickens and drinks their blood in exchange for alcohol. After 20 years in prison for murders, Luther, with his metal teeth, is paroled and terrorizes a rural Sterling, Illinois widow, her daughter, and her daughter's boyfriend. Luther makes chicken noises when he stalks his prey. The movie was filmed, in part, in various Iowa locations.]

The Indian Runner. Dir. Sean Penn. Westmount Communications, 1991. 126 min. Principals: Patricia Arquette, Charles Bronson, Sandy Dennis, Dennis Hopper, David Morse, Viggo Mortenson. [Penn's film presents a contemporary, non-pastoral Midwest as the setting for a series of family tragedies. Council Bluffs was the shooting location. Penn credits a song ("Highway Patrolman") from Bruce Springsteen's album *Nebraska* (Columbia, 1982) as inspiration for a tale of two estranged brothers. Joe (Morse) is a dispossessed farmer married to a Mexican immigrant. Farming economics has forced him to accept an unwelcome job with law enforcement in Cass County (between Lincoln and Omaha, in Nebraska). His brother Frank (Mortenson) is a sociopathic veteran of the Vietnam War, a physically and emotionally violent abuser of alcohol and of the people close to him.] AFIs. *NYT* 20 Sept. 1991, C6; *V* 27 May 1991, 79-80.

Omaha. Dir. Dan Mirvish. Bugeater Films, 1995. 85 min. Principals: Hughston Walkinshaw, Jill Anderson, Frankie Bee. [This low-budget comedy with scenes shot south of Council Bluffs, Iowa, features Simon (Walkinshaw) just returning from travels to Nepal and other countries where he went for spiritual enlightenment. The prayer stones he brings home are actually emeralds, leading crooks, a TV news team, and some Iowa kickboxers (who wear Iowa State and Harkin for Senate tee-shirts) to chase him. The film's climax takes place at Carhenge in Alliance, Nebraska. The director is a former speechwriter for Senator Harkin.] AFIs.

Citizen Ruth. Dir. Alexander Payne. Independent Pictures, 1996. Principals: Laura Dern, Swoosie Kurtz, Mary Kay Place, Burt Reynolds, Kurtwood Smith. [This satiric movie, filmed in Omaha and Council Bluffs, puts in the middle of a fierce pro- and anti-abortion struggle an indigent, drug-addicted pregnant woman, Ruth (Dern), whose interests get lost in the ideological struggle over the fate of the fetus. Ruth has an eye to the main chance, but no more so than her "protectors" on both sides of the debate. The bleak setting is not identified as Iowa-Nebraska, but there are strong Midwest signifiers. Gail (Place) serves corn, potato salad, and steak. Her husband Norm (Smith), a reformed sinner, works at a hardware store and wears an orange vest and a button that says, "Ask me!" Ruth's huffing habit (inhalant abuse) reveals a truth seldom portrayed in Iowa films of the era: drug problems exist in Iowa.] AFIs. *NYT* 13 Dec. 1996, 16; *V* 5 Feb. 1996, 61.

Twister. Dir. Jan de Bont. Warner Bros. and Universal Pictures, 1996. 114 min. Principals: Cary Elwes, Jami Gertz, Helen Hunt, Bill Paxton, Lois Smith. [This blockbuster film of spectacle and disaster was made in Iowa with a staging area and farmhouse near Eldora. It certainly looks like Iowa, but its fictional setting is identified as Oklahoma.] AFIs. *NYT* 10 May 19961; *V* 13 May 1996, 65, 69.

Crimes of Passion: Nobody Lives Forever. [Alternate title: *Crimes of Passion: Edna Buchanan's Nobody Lives Forever*]. Dir. Paul Wendkos. O'Hara-Horowitz Productions, 1998. 100 min. Brenda Bakke, Greg Evigan. [Based on an Edna Buchanan novel, this suspenseful police drama was filmed in Davenport, Kalona, and Vancouver, British Columbia. Detective Rick Barrish (Evigan) gets caught up in a dangerous love affair between his partner and a childhood friend while trying to catch the instigator of a million dollar heroin deal.] NS.

Election. Dir. Alexander Payne. Bona Fide Productions/MTV Films, 1999. 103 min. Principals: Matthew Broderick, Jessica Campbell, Chris Klein, Reese Witherspoon. [Relentlessly determined Tracy Flick (Witherspoon) will do anything to be student council president. She makes more than 400 decorated cupcakes for election day and lies about vandalizing posters. Her story is told by student council advisor and history teacher Jim McAllister (Broderick), who encourages a rival to run against her and throws away two ballots so that Tracy will lose. His cheating is exposed, and, like a teacher-friend who had an affair with Tracy her junior year, Jim loses his job and his wife. The dark comedy was filmed in and around Omaha, including Carter Lake, Iowa.] AFIs. *NYT* 23 Apr. 1999, 21; *V* 19 Apr. 1999, 46, 50.

Silverwings. Prod. Dan Nannen. Silverwings Productions, 2000. 123 min. Principals: J. P. Richardson, Lisa Todd, Sandy Grillet. [This is a *Star Trek*-modeled fantasy, in which two F-16 military pilots patrolling in an anomalous storm are transported into another land and time where they find warring people. The Luxars are being victimized by an Overlord. In this strange land, the discovered people are dressed as if for a renaissance fair (the Glastonbury Revelers of Des Moines) and fight with swords and arrows. Tracer (Richardson) develops a new romance (in the manner of Captain Kirk) with Crystal (Todd) and retrieves enough rockets and dynamite from his F-16 to breach the fortress in which Prince Jaznar is held. The film is populated with a large number of energetic amateur actors for crowd and battle scenes. Much of the action occurs around Des Moines' Salisbury House, Saylorville Lake Park, and Living History Farms. In the end the pilots decide that they must take advantage of a similarly strange storm to fly back to their world, but the love-smitten Tracer decides to stay while Berek (Grillet) returns alone.]

The Road to Perdition. Dir. Sam Mendes. Twentieth Century Fox/ Dream Works, 2002. Principals: Tom Hanks, Tyler Hoechlin, Jennifer Jason Leigh, Jude Law, Paul Newman, Stanley Tucci. Literary source: Max Allan Collins, with Richard Pier Raynes, *The Road to Perdition* (New York: Pocket Books, 2002), a graphic novel. [The narrative derives from a Midwestern, fact-based story by Iowa creator Max Alan Collins of Muscatine. Its character focus falls on a Depression-era hit man, Michael Sullivan (Hanks), whose 12-year-old son, Michael, Jr. (Hoechlin), witnesses a murder Dad commits for his boss, Tom Rooney (Newman). The morally agonizing, murderous fallout of the son's unwelcome knowledge drives the film. Settings in Chicago and a generic Midwest include the Quad Cities area, which occasioned some filming near Davenport, Iowa.] AFIs. *NYT* 12 July 2002, E1; V 1 July 2002, 25, 29.

Tully. [Alternate title: *The Truth about Tully*]. Dir. Hilary Birmingham. Telltale Films, 2002. Principals: Bob Burrus, Glenn Fitzgerald, Anson Mount, Julianne Nicholson. [Based on an O'Henry Prize-winning story by Tom McNeal ("What happened to Tully," *Atlantic Monthly* July 1991), this affecting heartland drama is set in Nebraska but was partly filmed in Iowa. A father and his two sons, Earl (Fitzgerald) and Tully (Mount), who is a local heartthrob, live on a farm. All work hard to make a go of it. The slow pacing, skillful acting, and literate screenplay contribute to the film's poignancy. Secrets emerge from the past that threaten the present and future just as the boys are finding love and learning about love from their father. The film makes reference to Nebraska locales such as Hastings and Highway 20 and includes scenes seldom shown in Midwest films—such as Earl eating popcorn at a Hitchcock Film Festival at the local theatre.] AFIs. *NYT* 1 Nov. 2002, 14; *V* 24 Apr. 2002, 33.

Death to Mental Slaves. Pagan Flames Productions, 2004. [Black metal bands perform in this video compilation, accompanied by a CD compilation. The credits proclaim the black metal philosophy, which is strong on individualism, anti-conformity, and shock effects, as suggested by titles like "Bloodthirst and Misanthropy" and "Genocide in the Name of Satan." The filming location is listed as Cedar Rapids.]

Sigma Die! Dir. Michael Hoffman, Jr. Production Magic, Inc./ Raymond L. Blagmon Productions, 2007. 90 min. Principals: Reggie Bannister, Joe Estevez, Aly Hartman, Brinke Stevens. [Five sorority girls rent a cabin for the summer of 2005. It doesn't take long for them and their fraternity boyfriends to send the girls' chaperone to a faked convention so they can have a wild party with a keg, pot, sex, and horror stories around the campfire. The film includes every fraternity/ sorority cinematic cliché, including togas and bare-breasted coeds. What's most unusual is that the film starts with the bloody climax, moves to one day earlier, flashes back to a 1985 panty raid that ended in tragedy for a young man caught enjoying wearing female lingerie, and finally replays the action up to the climax with alterations and a surprise revelation of the killer's identity. The film does not identify the Midwestern town or the college (sometimes referred to as the university), but Dubuque was one of several locations.]

The Thickness of Delirium. Dir. Brian James McGuire. Bartoli Filmworks, 2007. 82 min. Principals: Brian James McGuire, James E. McGuire, Leann Slaby. [A father (J. McGuire) abandoned his son when the boy was eight, forcing the mother to leave Utah abruptly for Michigan. Judging from the disorderly state of her house, she does not seem to have been happy there. The grown up son, Shawn (B. McGuire), is traumatized when his father doesn't even show up for his mother's funeral. He gets in his car and heads for Ogden, Utah, taking a gun with him. En route he meets Ronnie (Slaby), a wannabe country-western singer from Hazard, Nebraska, a town of under 100 people. She claims to have loving parents and shows lots of confidence and optimism, but her desperate clinging to Shawn belies her positive talk. When Shawn and Ronnie reach Ogden, they tour Shawn's remembered spots, and Shawn's depression lifts a little. Will Ronnie "save" Shawn? Will he ever confront his father? What about that gun? These questions are in the viewer's head as the movie approaches its climax. The screenplay does not refer to Iowa, and the film does not have identifiable Iowa scenes, but the Bartoli Filmworks "Production Notes" indicate Iowa, and the Iowa Film Office listed Des Moines as a shooting location.]

Eliot Ness: An Untouchable Life. Dir. Max Allan Collins. MACPhilms, 2005. 104 min. Principals: Michael Cornelison. [In a one-man play written by Collins (of Muscatine) and staged at the Des Moines Playhouse, Cornelison's Eliot Ness talks to the audience about his whole life, not just his years in Chicago going after Al Capone and Frank Nitti. We hear about his efforts to clean up corruption in the police force and city of Cleveland and his exploits with southern bootleggers, as well as his upright upbringing on Chicago's South Side as the son of a successful Norwegian baker and a doting mother. According to Collins' well-researched, clever script, Ness began practices now standard in law enforcement: rigorous training, profiling of serial killers, and decreasing juvenile delinquency by setting up boys' clubs. In the Capone section, Ness talks about Des Moines as a cooling off place, with lots of corn and welcome peace and quiet. Both he and Capone frequented the Hotel Fort Des Moines, Ness even going there for a honeymoon with his first wife.]

Spring Break Massacre. Dir. Michael Hoffman, Jr. Disruptive Media, Inc., 2008. 81 min. Principals: Reggie Bannister, Sarah Minnick. [Sexy college women at a slumber party at a remote house outside Mapleton, Illinois, during Spring Break, their frustrated boyfriends out on the town, a creepy neighbor, a stern father away at a tool convention, an escaped convict—those are the elements of this slasher flick/murder mystery filmed partly in Dubuque.]

Children of the Corn. Dir. Donald Borchers. Twentieth Century Fox, 2009. 92 min. [Using the same director, this is a remake of the 1984 film. This time, the director worked with Stephen King to achieve more character-based evil children and thus was able to display the author's name among the screen credits. Again, it is killer children of adults egged on by biblically sounding babble. Set fictionally in Gatlin, Nebraska, the film was shot at Princeton, Tipton, and Davenport in the Quad Cities area. This is but one of many remakes for the *Corn* franchise, the others having been shot in California and Texas.]

Megafault. Dir. David Michael Latt. The Asylum, 2009. 90 min. Principals: Bruce Davidson, Eriq LaSalle, Brittany Murphy. [This earthquake disaster movie was filmed in Davenport. TNT explosions in the West Virginia mountains set off earthquakes from there to Colorado and Wyoming. Iowa is shown on a map, but the path of the earthquake lies south of Iowa. This highly unbelievable script focuses on a young seismologist (Murphy). Getting her back to her small family seems to be the main aim of the military and FEMA, despite the destruction of much of the central United States and a huge threat to the West Coast.]

Dog Jack. Dir. Edward T. McDougal. Screen Media Films, 2010. 113 min. Principals: Kenneth Craig, Benjamin Gardner, Eddie Huchro, Kevin Holman, Louis Gossett, Jr., Frank Kasy. [Based on a novel by Florence Biros about a real-life heroic dog, this Civil War film is narrated by elderly Jed (Louis Gossett, Jr.), a former slave who as a teenager (Gardner) left his plantation with dog Jack to join the Pennsylvania 102 regiment. The film shows death and bloodshed (in PG-13 fashion) but stresses the moral complexities of war and relationships between fathers and sons. This family movie, filmed partially in Mt. Pleasant, Iowa, ultimately teaches a Christian message about love, even in times of war.]

Driver's Ed Mutiny. Dir. Brad Hansen. Collateral Damage Productions, 2010. 94 min. Principals: Hunter Johnson, Kyle Miller, Jillian Riley, John Snipes. [Filmed partly in Iowa, with an old Volvo supplied to the Iowa filmmakers, and with Iowa displayed on a map at the end of the film, this teen road trip movie unites a greaser, Nick (Hunter Johnson), a princess, Cole (Riley), and a nerd, Peter (Miller)—all from the Chicago suburbs. They steal their driver's ed car from an obnoxious teacher to head for LA. Their route does not take them through Iowa, though they are driven back on I-80. The film starts off like hundreds of other teen comedies but becomes more authentically human and nuanced as the trio drives across the country on Route 66. The teens all leave with crippling family issues, but they learn en route about friendship and sacrifice, gaining perspective on their lives. The film captures scenery along the way, including colorful Route 66 landmarks.]

Peacock. Dir. Michael Lander. Cornfield Productions, 2010. 90 min. Principals: Cillian Murphy, Ellen Page, Bill Pullman, Susan Sarandon. [Filmed in Odebolt, Greenfield, and Boone, Iowa, while set in Nebraska, *Peacock* tells the story of a troubled bank employee John Skillpa (Murphy) who leads an unknown multiple identity life as John and "Emma." Disclosure is threatened when a train caboose smashes into his yard and calls attention to the two differently gendered people who enter and exit the house. The community assumes John is married to Emma. John is forced to confront the childhood traumas that led to his dual life. Various local extras appeared in the film.]

Fertile Ground. Dir. Adam Gierasch. After Dark Films, 2011. Principals: Leisha Haley, Gale Harrold. [The fictional setting for this haunted house film is New York City and a town within driving distance. A young married couple, Emily Weaver (Haley) and Nate Weaver (Harrold), are respectively a clothes designer and a painter in NYC. At film's beginning she is pregnant and has a miscarriage. Seeking a more tranquil environment for her recovery, they buy a rural home linked to Nate's family lineage back to 1813. It is haunted by popping light bulbs, slamming doors, murmuring voices, and a 150-year-old skeleton—an earlier Weaver wife murdered by her husband—which causes a backup in their septic line. The emotional stress of the hauntings, and her suspicions about her husband's disappointment when she becomes pregnant again, lead to a finale in which she stabs her husband to death and ends up in psychiatric detention. Des Moines and Perry are identified as the shooting locations.]

Molly's Girl. Dir. Scott R. Thompson. My Town Pictures/Aries Entertainment, 2012. 125 min. Principals: Andre Davis, Emily Schweitz, Kristina Valada-Viars, Sondra Ward. [Dumped by her female fiancée who accuses her of fighting the wrong enemy, gay marriage activist Mercedes gets drunk and takes home the exotically dressed, eccentric, lying, clingy Molly (Valada-Viars), a Senator's daughter. Filmed in Des Moines, Ottumwa, and Fairfield but set in Illinois, the film has comic moments but poignantly shows how both abuse and idealization can harm people, leading to lies, isolation, misguided anger, and deep unhappiness. There are shots of the Iowa State Capitol building.]

VI. Films with Iowa Mentions

The Iowa references in these films are listed in Chapter 1.

The Covered Wagon (1923)

A Harp in Hock (1927)

Design for Living (1933)

King of the Underworld (1939)

Made for Each Other (1939)

Lillian Russell (1940)

High Sierra (1941)

Gung Ho (1943)

The Hard Way (1943)

Buffalo Bill (1944)

Double Indemnity (1944)

Hollywood Canteen (1944)

Sioux City Sue (1946)

Angel and the Badman (1947)

It Happened on Fifth Avenue (1947)

You're in the Navy Now (1951)

Mister Roberts (1955)

Detective Story (1951)

The Spirit of St. Louis (1957)

The Apartment (1960)

Elmer Gantry (1960)

Kisses for My President (1964)

In Cold Blood (1967)

The Rain People (1969)

Sidelong Glances of a Pigeon Kicker (1970)

Bad News Bears (1976)

The Goodbye Girl (1977)

Telefon (1977)

Hardcore (1979)

Airplane II: The Sequel (1982)

Mass Appeal (1984)

This Is Spinal Tap (1984)

The Secret Government: The Constitution in Crisis (1987)

Married to the Mob (1988)

The Civil War (1990)

The Bodyguard (1992)

Dave (1993)

The Program (1993)

Tommy Boy (1995)

Mystery Science Theatre 3000: The Movie (1996)

Orgazmo (1997)

A Civil Action (1998)

Mercury Rising (1998)

The Truman Show (1998)

Galaxy Quest (1999)

About Schmidt (2002)

Legally Blonde 2 (2003)

Bad Girls from Valley High (2005)

Michael Clayton (2007)

Slacker Uprising (2007)

Louis Sullivan: The Struggle for American Architecture (2010)

Chapter 3: Challenges in the Study of Iowa Films

Definitions

In 1996, when we first considered research on Iowa films, definitional questions quickly presented themselves. Are Iowa films limited just to those filmed in Iowa and with fictional Iowa settings? Films that have Iowa characters—wherever they happen to find themselves—seemed important, since they are meant to carry their state characteristics. But what about films set and filmed outside Iowa with "pretend Iowa" physical settings? (*Butter's* Iowa State Fair was filmed at the Louisiana State Fair.) Should we include films that had a quick mention of Iowa, such as a Dubuque joke or a reference to a character's second cousin in Sioux City? We initially concentrated on films about Iowa life and Iowans. In our most recent updating, we have included every category of Iowa film, aiming to be as comprehensive as possible.

Identification

In speaking with audiences and individuals over the past 18 years, we have often encountered curiosity about how we compiled our list. In 1996 we began with our own personal recollections of Iowa-related films. Then we told others of our interest. Memories, including our own, were occasionally misleading. We were told a few times, for example, that *The Glenn Miller Story* was an Iowa film. Glenn Miller was born at Clarinda in 1904 and lived there there until his family moved to Nebraska in 1907 and then to Missouri in 1915. On the basis of that brief Iowa association as infant and toddler, there is a Glenn Miller Birthplace Society Museum and restored home in Clarinda.[1] *The Glenn Miller Story*, starring Jimmy Stewart as Miller, locates the Miller family in Colorado. The Glenn Miller film *Orchestra Wives* (1942) does contain a scene in an Iowa City hotel. Besides being misled by Iowa celebrities, we also found that any generic rural or small town Midwestern setting was sometimes assumed to be Iowa. We were sometimes told that the Bedford Falls of Frank Capra's *It's A Wonderful Life* is an Iowa town. But there is no identifiable Iowa marker within the film, part of its genius consisting of its creation of a universal small-town icon. Seneca Falls,

New York has staked its claim to the true model and has developed movie-themed tourism.

We picked up leads from several listserv groups of H-Net: H-PCAACA (Popular Culture and American Culture Associations), H-Film, and H-Iowa. These sources were quickly supplemented by Internet resources, the most comprehensive being the Internet Movie Database (IMDb), whose production information includes shooting locations, plot summaries, and linked reviews. *The American Film Institute Catalog of Feature Films, 1893-1975*, had more detailed synopses, production histories, and review citations. But it is slow in moving its listings toward the present and often contains summaries that ignore very apparent Iowa connections.

Colleagues at Morningside College and members of the Humanities Iowa staff and board provided titles to us, often of films made in their hometowns or films they had watched on TV, as a video rental, or at the local cinemaplex. Video catalogs such as *Critics Choice* led to "finds," as did articles on Iowa films in production in the *Des Moines Register*. A *Register* article led us to Bob Ford, who ran an Iowa Film Festival in southern California for more than a decade.[2] His list included films with references to Iowa. Some films we unearthed through communication with Iowa tourist sites such as the *Field of Dreams* site in Dyersville, Music Man Square in Mason City, the National Sprint Car Museum at Knoxville, and the Hobo Museum in Britt. In short, serendipity, outreach, and persistence with databases, and opportunism in buying films all characterize our method.

After the first annotated filmography was published in 2003, we waited ten years to update the list. (We did slip into a folder any suggested titles we received during that decade.) By 2013, we could use more extensive online resources, including an expanded and steadily updated IMDb database, which now includes nearly every film made, even films with tiny budgets and ones still in pre-production. We used the IMDb's Iowa film list and an updated list from the Iowa Film Office, complete through 2011. We also found and made use of Tim Lostetter's *Iowa in the Movies* (Flatbridge Media, 2013), especially helpful in its listing of "Iowa mention" films, and a helpful but incomplete list of films made in Iowa posted on the Internet by the *Des Moines Register*. [3] Our continued ties with the Humanities Iowa Office helped us find films funded by its board. The Iowa Public Television website and Iowa Film Festival websites (Chapter 4) provided more titles. In 2013 Marty joined the Advisory Board for the Iowa Historical Museum's "Hollywood in the Heartland" exhibit, opening June, 2014. This group of Iowa film experts—and in particular the new head of Produce Iowa, Liz Gilman—suggested titles. The informal network of film directors accessed via websites, email, or Facebook after finding the names listed on IMDb provided invaluable information on new or retitled films.

Identifying films in the era of independent production is complicated when titles often change several times from earliest conception through festivals and distribution via DVD or streaming. We searched unsuccessfully for the 1985 *Echoes of War* until director Donald W. Thompson told us this was an early title for *Life Flight*—a film already on our list. *Arnolds Park*, the theatrical release, became the *Carousel of Revenge* DVD. *Easton's Article* became *Router* and then *Black Web*. We are convinced some of the "lost films" we still look for have been retitled.

Dates

Dating films is tricky since they can have differing copyright dates, preview dates (for example, at a film festival or a local theatre showing), initial theatrical release date, video release date, TV debut date, and sometimes even re-release date. We list the initial release year to the general public, generally relying on reviews in the *New York Times* and *Variety*, scholarly databases such as the *American Film Institute Catalog*, and IMDb. For some titles that never achieved public visibility, we were compelled to use dates on the videotape or DVD container. Discrepancies in film dating among various sources are common.

An excellent example of date ambiguity is *A Place for Heroes*, copyrighted in 2013 by Scott Thompson's My Town Pictures. Yet, as this book is being written, the film awaits distribution. In an email to John Lawrence dated 9 July 2014, Thompson said that his film had "sneak previews in May 2013." We could not screen *A Place for Heroes*, or characterize it in our film listings. We could obtain the image used for the film's poster. We reproduce it on the backside cover of this book.

Acquisition

Living at a time when it is possible to watch a film on a mobile phone or tablet computer, it is important to recall that as recently as the 1970s a color film rental for three days could cost between $200 and $300—partly due to the 20-30 pound weight of 35mm film reels. The commercial videocassette market did not yet exist. As late as the early 1980s Universal City Studios, and Walt Disney, were still suing Sony to squelch the spread of VCR technology. They eventually wised up and were profitably selling their own videocassettes by the time the

225

Supreme Court finally ruled against them in 1984.[4] The rest is video history.

When we began collecting Iowa films, we searched for movies in video format for rental or purchase. With the proliferation of cable and then satellite channels specializing in classic films or made-for-TV movies, it became possible to see many films that could not be purchased. Some films in our collection, such as *Happy Land*, could only be seen in this way. We also took advantage of the online auction phenomenon that brought millions of rare, collectible items into the market place. Through eBay, for example, we found out-of-print videocassettes as well as rare books, magazines, and lobby cards connected with Iowa films. Amazon.com has become a gateway for videos from a variety of vendors. Amazon Instant Video, You Tube, IPTV, and other online sites allow film viewing on computers, laptops, and handheld devices. Streaming sources such as Hulu, Netflix, Vudu, Vimeo, and Roku are another source for movies. Searchers should be wary about downloading films from sources that are advertised as free but morph into viral downloads that seize control of your computer.

Through our years of building a collection of Iowa films, film directors such as Max Allan Collins, of Muscatine, and Scott Beck and Bryan Woods, originally from Bettendorf, were able to point us toward copies available to purchase or they donated copies to our project. Sometimes we have purchased films on museum or organization websites. In a few cases, we have traveled to see archived films such as the 1921 silent film *The Wonderful Thing*, only available in Iowa at the Appanoose County Historical Museum in Centerville.

Continuing Search

There are still films that remain elusive. Nearly all silent movies are unavailable. Large numbers of films have disappeared because their original nitrate-based negatives disintegrated. As a group, made-for-TV movies are especially hard to purchase, although they are sometimes shown on Lifetime and other cable channels. From the standpoint of exploring the influences of films on a national audience, this is frustrating. Made-for-TV movies sometimes reach millions of viewers in a single broadcast, surpassing the audience size for many successful theatrical releases. Unless they are recorded during their broadcast, they may not surface again for years, and then perhaps at 3 a.m. Amazon.com increasingly stocks TV movies. After more than a decade of searching, we found the TV movie *One in a Million: The Ron LeFlore Story* for sale on Amazon. Documentaries can also be a challenge because they get a single showing on television or at a festival and are not always packaged for distribution. Recently Iowa Public Television has been exemplary in streaming much of its older library of films that explore Iowa topics.

Preservation and Archiving

We have collected an impressive, but incomplete, group of Iowa-related films during the past two decades. We found more films than we ever suspected we could acquire—many of which seemed lost forever. Our film collection of videotapes and DVDs has been donated to the archives of the Sioux City Public Museum and is available for viewing at 607 4th Street, Sioux City, IA 51101 [(712) 279-6174].

Endnotes

[1] See the Birthplace Society website for details about the memorials and Miller's life: www.glennmiller.org/history.

[2] See John Carlson, "Iowa the Attraction for Movie Enthusiasts in San Diego," *Des Moines Register*, 10 October 1999, 5M. Print.

[3] See "Movies filmed in Iowa," blogs.desmoinesregister.com/dmr/index.php/2009/09/18/movies-filmed-in-iowa.

[4] The defense of home copying was delivered in the case Sony Corp. of America v. Universal City Studios, 464 U.S. 417 (1984).

Chapter 4: Iowa Film Festivals

With improving mobility, and quality and falling costs for digital video and sound recording equipment, cinematography with professional production values has become increasingly possible for young filmmakers. They also have options to learn in the filmmaking courses at regional community colleges, colleges, and universities. But where can these independent films find their audiences? One venue has been the film festival. Premier locations for independent films are Tribeca in Lower Manhattan, South by Southwest in Austin, and Sundance in Park City, Utah. Those venues have become sites for the gathering of celebrities, politicians, and deal-inking agents of the major film distributers. The opportunities for significant audiences naturally stimulate thousands of submissions, only a fraction of which can be screened. The frustrating experience of most filmmakers has been documented in the film *Official Rejection* (Shut Up and Shoot Pictures, 2009).

The past decade has seen the growth of Iowa's film festivals. They share a common pattern of running for a limited period, being friendly to students with very short films, and bestowing numerous awards. Feature length films are shown at most of them. Although Iowans are well represented among the filmmakers screened, submissions are not limited to Iowans. We list below the Iowa festivals and their websites.

- **Iowa Indie Festival**. Music Man Square in Mason City: www.Iowaindie.org.
- **Iowa 4-H Film Festival**. Iowa State Fair: www.extension.iastate.edu/4h/statefair/filmfestival
- **Julien Dubuque Film Festival**. Dubuque: julienfilmfest.com
- **Landlocked Film Festival**. Iowa City: www.landlockedfilmfestival.org
- **Oneota Film Festival**. Decorah: oneotafilmfestival.com
- **Siouxland Film Festival**. Sioux City: siouxlandfilmfestival.org
- **Snake Alley Film Festival**. Burlington: snakealleyfestivaloffilm.com
- **Wild Rose Film Festival**. Des Moines: www.wildrosefilmfest.com

Chapter 5: Iowa Film Archives

There is no central archive maintained by the state for Iowa films as our book has defined them. Neither the Iowa Film Office nor its successor, Produce Iowa, maintains an archive of films shot in Iowa. Nonetheless there are some video and film collections around the state.

- **Iowa Public Television.** IPTV has accumulated a collection of *Iowa Stories*, many of which can be streamed from its website. www.iptv.org.
- **Iowa State University Special Collections Department**. This collection of films and videos, many quite short, are focused on activities and programs at ISU. There are numerous "campus scenes," Veishea celebrations, debates, and informational descriptions of particular majors. www.add.lib.iastate.edu/spcl/collections/film.html.
- **State Historical Society of Iowa Labor Film Collection, 1940s-1980s**. The archives contain 137 films (over 41 hours) dealing primarily with labor unions in Iowa, their issues and political campaigns. The SHSI website collection offers a detailed overview of its holdings: http://www.iowahistory.org/libraries/collections/iowa-city-center/iowa_labor_collection/IowaLaborFilms.htm.
- **Sioux City Public Museum**. We have donated videocassettes, DVDs, books, and posters acquired in collecting since 1996. There are currently more than 300 items listed in the Past Perfect database under the heading "Marty Knepper's Iowa Films and Books." Items are available for viewing at the Research Center, 607 4th Street, Sioux City, IA 51101 [(712) 224-5001].
- **The University of Iowa Collections Supporting Television and Film Studies**. The collections are principally oriented to national and international cinema. There are a few sources that reflect Iowa-based filmmaking, or films about Iowa. They include the Max Allan Collins papers, Phil Stong's scripts for *State Fair* (1933, 1945, 1962), and the Twentieth-Century Fox Script Collection—1500 titles for the years 1929-1971, several of them with Iowa aspects.

231

Appendix A: *The Strange Woman* (1918): Reviews of the first film with an Iowa setting

The Strange Woman was the first feature length film with a fictional Iowa setting. We transcribe here reviews from *Variety* and *Moving Picture World*. Note that *Variety's* reviewer makes the familiar Ohio for Iowa substitution, while getting the town's name "Delphi" right. *Moving Picture World* gets the state of Iowa correctly, but changes the name to "Delhi." No copy of this film has survived.

Variety 27 Dec. 1918.

"The Strange Woman" is a production made by Fox and used as a vehicle for Gladys Brockwell. It is an adaptation from the dramatic play of the same name by William J. Hurlbut, which was seen several seasons ago. A very successful film version has been made by J. Grubb Alexander. The story of the picture is familiar to most theatregoers. The theme deals with the practicability of a sort of free love or temporary or trial marriage. Inez de Pierrefond is an advanced young person who has spent most of her life on the Continent, imbibing the ideas of the most "emancipated" and evolving a few of her own. At this juncture she meets John Hemingway, an ambitious and rising young man who hails from a small town in Ohio, rejoicing in the name of Delphi. The two become engaged and Inez goes back with John to his hometown. The results are amusing and make for a capital plot. Among these small-town ladies blossoms Inez, smart in her Parisian frocks and worldly manners, and creates a furor. She is the subject of all conversations and the object of all thoughts. But as she begins to express her views she causes horror among the good women. When they find out that she has written a book on free love they can stand no more and set out to boycott her and bring her to shame. John's mother, however, refuses to aid them, divining the real worth of the girl, and finally things work out to a normal and satisfactory conclusion. Aside from the excellent work of Miss Brockwell as Inez, a part which suits her admirably, the best part of the picture is the work of the various types of women who make up the highly respectable society of Delphi. These different bits are remarkably realistic and amusing. William

The Strange Woman (1918), lobby card.
In the film's pivotal scene, Inez Pierrefond (Gladys Brockwell), a sophisticated woman from Paris, shames the gossipy, malicious and hypocritical small towners who turned up to humiliate her.

Scott as John Hemingway and Ruby LaFayette as his mother stand out. The picture is remarkably well put on, the direction good and the photography adequate.

The Moving Picture World 12 Oct. 1918, 272.

"The Strange Woman" Gladys Brockwell, Star of the Fox Production Made from the Stage version of William J. Hurlbut's Work.

Reviewed by Walter K. Hill.

When Ruby LaFayette, a kindly old lady of the earlier days of stage accomplishments, took to the films to spend her declining years of entertainment usefulness there was a great gain for the screen. It was Miss La Fayette's work that held true and good in "The Strange Woman" as screened in the Fox projection room, with Gladys Brockwell playing the star role—a part created by Elsie Ferguson in the original stage version of William J. Hurlbut's work. It was this kindly old lady that lifted her part into such idealism that it saved from entire disregard the whole story as scenarioized [sic] by J. Grubb Alexander.

More years ago than is necessary to here record, Ruby LaFayette was heading her own company in the Middle West, after being graduated from the supporting ranks of numerous stars of other days. In her stage schooling, Miss LaFayette secured a touch of art, a hold upon the natural-ness and realities of the drama that makes her work in pictures essentially a delight—a natural sequence of thorough schooling.

"Never again will I put on the manacles of accursed, wicked marriage" is the keynote of the play—the plot undertaking to enforce the motto this sub-title nails at the masthead of the screen craft in which Miss Brockwell stars.

From a small town in Iowa a young man goes to Paris, meets the woman who has arrived at "free love" conclusions because her matrimonial ship had once been wrecked. Sailing now in the craft that has been hauled off the rocks of disappointment and restored to seaworthiness the woman in the case admits her love of the young American, and is willing to voyage without a pilot's license.

Back to Iowa comes the young man with his Parisienne love, and would start instanter [sic] to convert his mother to the acceptance of "free love" faith.

This matter of social "salvation" is taken out of his hands by the women folks who constitute the villagers. Their ideas do not quite coincide with the Parisienne view of matrimony, and they all have read a copy of the French woman's book on the subject. For, when a small town starts upon its mission, we are led to believe that they go through with it, whether the job be knitting for soldiers or ripping up the frail reputation of a Parisienne society matron.

Through this concerted movement on the part of the villagers the French woman is able, in due season, to tell the natives of Delhi [sic], Iowa, what she thinks of them, and then speeds home to tell the good old lady, the supremely trustful old lady, the abidingly loyal old lady—who believes In her son and believes In the woman who loves him because he is her son. As a matter of fact the mother is shown to be turning over to the "free love" faith (a trick of this particular mother love) that finishes off the story by opening the eyes of the Parisienne to the better and more substantial uses of the marriage bond.

Gladys Brockwell has a thankless role.

Appendix B: *The Wonderful Thing* (1921): Reviews of the first made-in-Iowa film

The Wonderful Thing was the first feature length film shot in Iowa. The events were a source of great excitement during the three days of May 1921 that actors and film crews were present. (Lisa Eddy, "Going Hollywood," *Iowa Living Magazines, Appanoose County Living,* October 2012: 11.

In our long filmography we list citations for reviews from the *New York Times* and *Variety* as indicators of contemporary critical opinion. Both of these reviews can also tell us something about the state of reviewing at the beginning of the film industry. Note the complaint of the *Times* reviewer that "the picture is excessively talky" and the desire for more than "flashes of pantomime." In a time when popular stage plays were transitioning to screen, there seemed to be a preference for more difference, in this case physical gestures that would move the narrative forward.

Review from *The New York Times,* 7 Nov. 1921, 20.

Of course, there's no denying that Norma Talmadge is one of the American screen actresses who can really act and that Herbert Brenon is a director who can make vividly expressive moving pictures so it is readily admitted that any production to which they jointly devote their efforts can hardly be without something to recommend it, but—

How do such competent persons come as close to concealing their talents as they do in "The Wonderful Thing," the photoplay at the Strand this week? Except for a few scenes, and, perhaps, its consistently good photographic quality, it might be the work of almost any of the many mediocre actresses and directors in the numerous studios between the Atlantic and Pacific Coasts.

For instance, the picture is excessively talky. There is almost no scene in it which means anything without its accompanying, and interruptive, subtitles. In fact, the story is told in words. If all of the pictures were taken out of it, it would still be fairly complete

237

and intelligible. Yet Mr. Brenon has shown in other productions that he can make expressive moving pictures that do not need the verbal crutch. Why hasn't he done so here? When it is reported that his scenes are well composed, except those in which the frame is allowed to clip off the tops of the players' heads, and that the photograph, as a rule, is soft yet clear, the most that may be said by way of recommendation for his work has been put down. Of expressive kinetic photography there is practically nothing in the picture.

Miss Talmadge is a pantomimist. In other pictures she has shown that she can make her thoughts and feelings known by silent acting, by facial expressions, gestures, postures and movements of her body. Yet, in this picture she does little besides talk. In a few scenes there are flashes of pantomime, but most of the time she just moves her lips as if, when she was making the photoplay, she thought the motion picture camera was a phonograph. And she's no better at moving her lips on the screen than hundreds of other actresses. But she's a far better pantomimist when she chooses to be.

Nor do the others in the cast do anything special. Most conspicuous among them, because of her social prominence and the publicity that attended her entrance into motion picture work is Mrs. Lydig Hoyt, who is programmed as Julia Hoyt and has a minor role in the photoplay. Whether Mrs. Hoyt is a screen actress of the first rank remains to be seen. She hasn't much chance in "The Wonderful Thing," and, with the others, does little besides talk.

The story of the production can be accepted only as a fairy tale. It is billed as an adaptation of the play by the same name by Lillian Trimble Bradley, but how closely it follows its original the present writer cannot say. In its screen form it makes free use of the "Peg o' My Heart" idea, with the Frenchified daughter of a wealthy American hog raiser playing the role of despised benefactor in a snobbish English home. The story is kept going by all sorts of complications, any one of which would have been straightened out in two minutes by the exercise of a little common sense by any of the persons involved; but, then, the story would not have been kept going.

Review from *Variety*, November 11, 1921

"The Wonderful Thing" is a screen adaptation of the play of the same name, written by Lillian Trimble Bradley and Forrest Halsey. It was scenarized by Clara Beranger and directed by Herbert Brenon as a vehicle for Norma Talmadge, a First National release. On the stage it was far from a success, but serves as a breezy "society play" for the screen star. The role is a relatively light one for Miss Talmadge, being mostly comedy, with a smattering of emotional display.

She plays the daughter of an American hog raiser who has amassed millions in the middle West, falls in love with a titled young Englishman, learns from his sister that he hesitates to propose because he is poor; she impulsively pops the question to him and they are married.

The young bride hears her husband married her for her money and is heartbroken, but cannot understand why he won't use any of her wealth. It develops he did marry her for her money in order to save a younger brother from jail for forgery, but even then would not make use of his wife's fortune. In the end it all comes out right and the titled family which had sneered at her is humiliated by her generous impulses and anonymous financial assistance.

The production is high class in every respect—the technical details, direction, lighting and uniformly excellent acting by the entire company. There is but one glaring error of direction—a scene showing the familiarity with which an English serving maid conducts herself in conversation with a member of the titled English family. Director Brenon knows, or should know, enough about England not to permit such a faux pas. It is the one wrong note in an otherwise acceptable photoplay feature.—*Jolo*

Appendix C: World War II and Iowa: Hollywood's Pastoral Myth for the Nation*

This essay discusses a brief period in Iowa cultural history and film history—1941 to 1946—when Hollywood turned to pastoral concepts of rural Iowa to help sell the war to the American public. The rural Midwest, with Iowa as its most representative state, assumed the role of "the steady heart of a nation at war," a *Life* magazine correspondent proclaimed.[1] Illustrating this heartland theme, the cover of the April 18, 1942, *Saturday Evening Post* asks, "For What Are We Fighting?" The cover's image, an idealized painting of a small rural town by Iowan Grant Wood[2], answers the question. Several modest homes surround a church. One man plants a garden. Another mows a lawn. A third climbs a ladder held by another man to reach a roof, to repair it. A woman hangs a quilt on the line to dry. A child plays by a tree. These people work hard, cooperate, and live simply—inspired by religious faith and surrounded by beautiful nature lovingly cultivated. Americans fight World War II, the cover art implies, to defend a romantic concept of agrarian democracy tightly woven into the fabric of our patriotic thinking since the time of Washington and Jefferson. And in the movie houses, prior to the Pearl Harbor attack on December 7, 1941, Hollywood used entertainment movies such as *One Foot in Heaven* and *Cheers for Miss Bishop* (both 1941 releases based on books by Iowa authors) to promote democratic ideals, glorify sacrifice, and indirectly promote intervention in the European War.

After America declared war, Hollywood voluntarily cooperated with the U.S. military and propaganda agencies. *Happy Land* (1943), about an all-American Iowa boy killed in the war, and *The Sullivans* (1944), based on the true story of five Irish Catholic brothers from Waterloo who died on the same ship, represent the sentimental movies made during the war that aimed to tell—and sell—the story of "why we fight" and to reconcile the public to the inevitable loss of life. *The Best Years of Our Lives*, about veterans returning to a transformed rural heartland, appeared in 1946 when Hollywood no longer worked hand

* This is a book chapter reproduced from *Representing the Rural*, edited by Catherine Fowler and Gillian Helfield (Detroit: Wayne State UP, 2006, 323-40). It is published by permission of the Wayne State UP.

241

in hand with the government. This "coming home" film is far more realistic than the other WWII Iowa films—and yet it also draws on pastoral concepts.

Understanding this period when myths about rural Iowa joined the war effort requires exploration of historical context—in particular, Iowa's pre-war image, traditions of pastoralism and agrarian democracy, and the aims of the wartime film industry. Studying these five films—along with their marketing and reception—illuminates not only the period 1941-46 but our own era as well.

Iowa: Forever Rural

With a fourth of the grade A farm land in the United States, with soil yielding in some years more wealth than all the gold mines of the world, Iowa is a modern Promised Land.

Sixty percent of the two and a half million people of the state live on farms or in small towns, and even the largest cities . . . are a part of the rural scene, deriving their prosperity and most of their dwellers from the farms.

— August, 1939 *National Geographic* article on Iowa[3]

Films have a part to play in the fight for freedom. As the beneficiary of freedom, the motion picture recognizes its debt to democracy. The people's entertainment is enlisted for the duration in this people's war.

—*Movies at War*, a 1942 report on Hollywood's War Activities Committee[4]

Throughout the twentieth century—despite Iowa's increasing urbanization, industrialization, and population flight from its small towns and farms—the nation has pictured Iowa, and Iowa has identified itself, as a rural state, with virtually no other competing imagery. Ask bicoastal people today for their images of Iowa, and they will mention corn, pigs, tiny towns with ma and pa stores, pickup trucks, and barns. Virtually no one mentions urban or industrial images. Iowans themselves sell postcards perpetuating the misleading rural iconography.

In *The Middle West: Its Meaning in American Culture*, cultural geographer James R. Shortridge confirms that in the twentieth century Iowa emerged as the representative rural Midwest state, a symbol for the region.[5] According to Shortridge, the rural heartland was admired by the nation from 1900 to 1920 for its "pastoral traits of morality, independence, and egalitarianism."[6] In the urbanizing 1920s and into the 1930s, Sinclair Lewis and others painted an unattractive picture of rural Americans as old-fashioned, moralistic, and culturally backward.[7] The rural Midwest reached a nadir of popular opinion around 1950 with no mitigating shift in attitude until rural nostalgia emerged in the later decades of the century as a reaction to the stresses of urban life.[8] Iowa and the agricultural Midwest, however, did experience a brief return to respect just prior to WWII, exemplified by the work of Midwest regionalist painters such as Iowa's Grant Wood.[9]

Nothing better demonstrates this short period of Midwest glory than a long, illustrated *National Geographic* article celebrating Iowa that appeared in August 1939.[10] Leo A. Borah reports on the state after a twenty-year absence from his rural Iowa hometown. He admires Iowa's prominence in agricultural production, innovation, and policy-making; he evens claims that all Iowa is rural, including its towns and cities. He is impressed by the numerous churches and church colleges, many founded by 19th-century immigrants or their descendents. "Hardly an outpost of civilization," he claims, "has not felt the influence of earnest Christians from the 'Bible Belt.'"[11] Of the landscape he writes, "I have seen places of far more spectacular beauty than the rolling prairie farms of Iowa but nothing to surpass them in appearance of prosperity and contentment."[12] He waxes eloquent about the bucolic pleasures of his childhood. In short, rural Iowa provides wholesome values as well as nutritious food.

Borah's kind of pastoralism—with its idealistic association of rural life with food production, virtue, and civic duty—is older than Hesiod, whose works date from the 7th century BCE. Ancient agricultural societies such as Crete worshipped life-giving goddesses and gods and venerated the arts of peace, not war,[13] since raising crops and animals requires hard work and a stable, cooperative community. In time, however, ancient cultures—and particularly Rome—came to celebrate war, and a tradition linking rural life and military valour emerged. Cincinnatus (5th century BCE), a stalwart farmer appointed dictator of Rome during an emergency, in a single day of fighting rescued the empire's consular forces. He then astonished grateful Rome by immediately resigning so that he could return to farming.

This theme of agrarian martial virtue recurred in Revolutionary War America when George Washington was described as a selfless agrarian like Cincinnatus who, unmoved by fame or power, served his nation. The State of Virginia memorialized this idea in Jean-Antoine

Houdon's statue of Washington titled "Cincinnatus" (1788), a figure still standing in the capitol at Richmond.[14] The traditional English ideal of the sturdy yeoman farmer as backbone of the nation had crossed the ocean and no doubt influenced Thomas Jefferson's articulation of the agrarian mythos in his *Notes on the State of Virginia* (1800). There he expresses profound mistrust for urban culture, his confidence lying instead with the yeoman as the foundation of American democratic life. With these traditions, it should not surprise us to find American military virtues associated with rural people, especially during World War II, when attitudes toward pastoral ideals had begun to shift back from contempt to respect.[15]

As the World War II generations disappear, their experience is increasingly conveyed by nostalgic slogans. That era's adults were "the greatest generation" (Tom Brokaw) who fought "the good war" (Studs Terkel). Current generations, with horror images of the holocaust in mind, assume that creating the consensus to fight the war was a rapid, unquestioning process. The historical record documents more contention. President Franklin Roosevelt struggled from the mid-1930s to persuade citizens and legislators that national interest demanded direct military assistance to Great Britain and the Soviet Union.

Countering such initiatives was air hero Charles Lindbergh, a prominent member of the America First Committee, which believed that FDR's administration was engaged in a secret conspiracy to bring the U.S. into war partnership with England. Lindbergh could see sinister Jewish propaganda in Hollywood's creative output. Speaking to 8,000 Iowans at an America First rally in Des Moines on September 15, 1941, Lindbergh's speech with the title "Who Are the War Agitators?" warned against Jewish influence in Hollywood: "Their greatest danger to this country lies in their huge ownership and influence in our motion pictures, our press, and our government."[16] It was certainly true that Roosevelt, a movie fan, worked to enlist the talents of Hollywood to market the war through entertainment films.

Persuasion was needed since, in the mid-1930s, the Production Code Administration (PCA), which self-censored movies for the industry, muted criticism of fascism and approved some films that presented fascism positively. It had the commercial goal of preserving European markets regardless of the political situation there and did not want "to depart from the pleasant and profitable course of entertainment to engage in propaganda."[17] But apart from the profit motive, there was also some flirtation with the romance of fascism itself. Columbia Pictures' encomiastic *Mussolini Speaks* (1933) carried the studio's own tribute: "To a man of the people whose deeds will ever be an inspiration to mankind—Benito Mussolini."[18] The PCA sanitized the screenplay of Robert Sherwood's Pulitzer-winning, anti-fascist play *Idiot's Delight* (1936) in order to make it inoffensive to Italy, a major European export market, even though the Italian government by then had invaded Ethiopia and had begun harmonizing its anti-Jewish policies with those of Germany.[19]

By 1940, however, the PCA gave the green light to films that supported intervention in the European war. It recognized the British sympathies of the American people and the drift toward war that was partly propelled by films that kept naming European enemies.[20] *Blockade* (1938) tilted against the fascist-themed Falange regime of Franco in Spain. *Confessions of a Nazi Spy* (1939) portrayed German subversives in America. Charlie Chaplin's *The Great Dictator* (1940) mocked Hitler and Mussolini as "Adenoid Hynkel" and "Napaloni," dictators of "Tomania" and "Bacteria" respectively.

So many interventionist films began to flow out of Hollywood that Burton Wheeler (D-Montana) and other isolationist senators responded in mid-1941 by using the Interstate Commerce Committee for hearings on Hollywood's bellicose foreign policy. These hearings were disbanded the day after Pearl Harbor. Hitler's tactical mistake in aligning himself with Japan's war on America had finally given FDR a license to engage directly in the war against Germany. But the protracted wait had taught Roosevelt that large tasks of persuasion remained.

A December 18, 1941, memo from FDR defined the war role for the film industry. "I want no censorship of the motion picture," he insisted, but then enjoined newly created bureaucratic agencies to "consult with and advise motion picture producers of ways and means in which they can most usefully serve in the national effort."[21] These new agencies included the Office of War Information (OWI), the Bureau of Motion Pictures (BMP), the Office of Censorship, and the Office of Inter-American Affairs. Films containing combat scenes typically coordinated additionally with one or more of the military branches for equipment and to avoid disclosing tactical information.

By mid-1942, BMP had released guidance for American filmmakers in a publication titled "Government Information Manual for the Motion Picture Industry."[22] The manual conveyed themes from FDR's "Address to Congress" on January 6, 1942. It told Hollywood that propaganda films needed to address these urgent topics: (1) Why We Fight,

(2) The Enemy, (3) The United Nations,† (4) The Home Front, and (5) The Fighting Forces. Rural Iowa films during WWII fall mainly into the categories Why We Fight and The Home Front.[23]

Pre-War Fictional Films of Patriotism and Sacrifice

The 1941 movies *One Foot in Heaven* and *Cheers for Miss Bishop*—about building schools, churches, and democratic spirit on the Iowa prairie—defined democratic principles and portrayed characters willing to sacrifice their dreams and pleasures to practice these principles. The two films indirectly advocated intervention and anticipated *Happy Land* and *The Sullivans*, which more explicitly insisted on wartime sacrifices abroad and at home.

Nominated for a Best Picture Oscar and widely reviewed, *One Foot in Heaven* was adapted from a memoir by Iowa native Hartzell Spence about his determined, charismatic father, William Spence.[24] The film stresses sacrifice throughout. Will Spence gives up a potentially lucrative and intellectually stimulating career as a doctor to become a Methodist pastor serving growing Iowa prairie towns at the turn of the twentieth century. Reverend Spence and his family learn to live with poverty, abysmal parsonages, and disputes among parishioners. Spence's wife leaves a life of comfort and affluence for one of little privacy, frequent moves, and unending, unpaid work. The children must forego forbidden but popular pastimes such as dancing, card-playing, and movie-going. For Spence, democratic ideals and Christian ideals are intertwined, for all persons are equal in the sight of God. To live and preach these ideals of serving God and a democratic nation, Spence and family make personal sacrifices.

The film's World War I scenes show Spence ministering to injured soldiers in Sioux City, while his wife works as a Red Cross nurse. When crowds cheer the Armistice, Spence offers a prayer for 1918 that anticipates the intervention debates of 1941. After thanking God for bestowing peace, Spence prays that war may never return. But, he continues, "If it is thy will that we must ever again in this imperfect world defend our democratic way of life, give us the strength to do so with courage and determination." Spence implies that the time to fight for democracy may come.

---

† As soon as the war began, 26 allied countries designated themselves as "the United Nations." The post-war international organization we know as the United Nations grew out of this alliance.

Cheers for Miss Bishop, based on a novel by Iowan Bess Streeter Aldrich, is a fictional film about a patriotic spinster English teacher at "Midwestern College" (now University of Northern Iowa).[25] Like *One Foot in Heaven* and the popular *It's a Wonderful Life* (1946), the film glorifies relinquishing individual dreams and personal happiness to serve community and nation. When young, Ella Bishop's patriotism is sparked by the college president's declaration that an educated citizenry is the foundation of democracy. Ella faithfully teaches immigrants and their descendants for decades, never fulfilling her youthful dreams of marriage, children, and travel. The emphasis on immigrant students suggests an important principle of American democracy: the United States is a refuge and a land of opportunity for those who seek freedom and success through hard work.

A turning point in the film—and a lesson in democratic principles and democracy in action—is a moment when young Ella refuses to spend the evening with her fiancé so that she can testify at a hearing. A Swedish student, Mina, who possesses a remarkable memory, stands accused of cheating. While Mina recites much of the Declaration of Independence from memory and clears her name, Ella's fiancé is seduced by Ella's scheming cousin Amy, and they later marry. Ella's participation in a democratic process has cost her dearly—and yet Mina goes on to realize the American dream by becoming a distinguished historian, thanks to Miss Bishop.

These heroic Iowa characters in 1941 movies surrender self interest entirely to establish prairie churches and schools and promote concepts of agrarian democracy held sacred by Americans, foreshadowing the sacrifices the nation soon must make to fight fascism. The sentimental films *Happy Land* and *The Sullivans*, released during the war, replay the idea that democratic and Christian principles define Iowa (and America) and expand the idea of sacrifice to giving one's life, or accepting the death of loved ones, in time of war.

"Why We Fight": *Happy Land*

MacKinlay Kantor, author of the 1942 *Saturday Evening Post* story "Happy Land" adapted for the 1943 film,[26] grew up in rural Iowa and worked as a journalist before writing popular fiction. During WWII, he participated in combat as well as aiding propaganda efforts, serving as a gunner in the U.S. Air Force and a war correspondent for the British Royal Air Force.

247

The opening scene of the movie *Happy Land* links pastoralism and patriotism. Choral voices hail the "happy land" and sing of freedom and liberty, while the camera closes in on a small town surrounded by fields and pastureland. A boy sitting atop a load of hay symbolizes the film's theme that it is worth fighting and dying to protect the wholesome rural culture of Iowa that grows fine boys as well as fine crops.

While the appropriately named "Hartfield" has a population of 6000, pastoral imagery characterizes the town scenes. We see Victorian homes with porches, tree-lined streets, churches, a park, a cemetery, and a popular picnic spot, Briggs Woods, with a creek. The social center of Main Street is the pharmacy with soda fountain owned by Lew Marsh. Looking out from inside the pharmacy, we see trees across the street, sometimes in sunlight and sometimes in shadow. Few scenes in the film do not have trees, bushes, grass, house plants, flowers, hedges, or bouquets of flowers. The plant imagery establishes the film's central metaphor that Iowa is "a place to grow," as a former state slogan put it.

Early in the film Lew and his wife, Agnes, receive the heartbreaking news that their only child, Rusty, was killed in Pacific combat. This blow renders Lew bitter and depressed; he avoids church and work; he is unmoved when the minister point outs that Rusty died for his country. Lew grieves that Rusty never lived fully.

In a plot turn that looks back to Dickens's *Christmas Carol* while anticipating *It's A Wonderful Life* and *Field of Dreams*, the ghost of his own dead grandfather who raised him visits Lew. Dressed in a Civil War uniform, Gramp strolls with Lew through scenes from the past. Gramp evokes images of Lew marching in a parade as a returning WWI soldier and of his meeting and marrying Agnes. Lew sees newborn Rusty at Gramp's deathbed. Flashing forward to a Memorial Day cemetery visit, the child Rusty stands fascinated by the Grand Army of the Republic flag on Gramp's headstone. When Rusty asks his parents whether he will someday have a flag, Agnes impatiently interjects that there will be no more wars. Gramp-as-ghost comments approvingly about the right way to raise boys—"not thinking about battles and conquests" but immersed in "homely simple things right here."

The film then takes us into a cornfield where young Rusty plays Indians. After his first day at school, he brings two poor children from the Dakotas to Marsh's for ice cream. As he grows, we see his companionship with his dog, his progress through the Boy Scouts, his participation in the church youth group, and his work at the family pharmacy. He plays football and runs track, learning to be a "good loser." Rusty sacrifices his savings earmarked for a Boy Scout axe so a customer can get needed medicine.

When older, Rusty falls for a glamour girl who inappropriately wears high heels to a picnic, but he eventually finds romance with a local girl who appreciates, and dresses sensibly for, picnics in Brigg's Woods.

When Hitler's forces invade Poland, Rusty's friends join up with the Canadian Air Force, while Rusty trains as a pharmacist so that he can join the family business—or, if needed, enter the service with a skill. After success in pharmacy school, Rusty joins the navy before Pearl Harbor, following family military tradition.

The flashbacks make Lew realize that Rusty did have a good, full life and that Hartfield gave him solid moral character. Gramp observes that Hartfield provides the best possible nurturance for any young man. After the stroll through the past with Gramp, Lew participates in life again, but comments, "Rusty was my boy. I will miss him every day of my life." Though still grieving, Lew comes to believe, as Horace put this film's message nearly 2000 years previously—"Dulce et decorum est pro patria mori" ("It is sweet and fitting to die for one's country").[27]

"They Did Their Part": *The Sullivans*

While *Happy Land* works out an imaginary script about heartland rearing and national service, *The Sullivans* depicts the tragedy of a real family from Waterloo, Iowa. The Sullivan family had six children, five of them boys—George, Francis, Joseph, Madison, and Al. The father worked for the railroad; the mother was a busy housewife. When the Pearl Harbor attack was announced, the boys immediately decided to enlist in the navy, insisting to recruiting officers that they would join only if allowed to serve on the same ship. After wrestling with the implications and trying to dissuade them, the navy relented, and the five Sullivans began their tour of duty on the *USS Juneau*. Having accepted the brothers as a group, the navy capitalized on their presence by using them for publicity pictures.

The *Juneau's* task group was called to the fierce battles at Guadalcanal in the Solomon Islands. With four of the brothers trapped below deck in a massive explosion, the *Juneau* sank on November 13, 1942. The fifth brother, George, drifted for several days on a raft: he died of exposure and starvation after deliriously surrendering himself to sharks.[28] The film omits several communication lapses known to the navy that resulted in neglecting the rescue attempt for the ship's survivors until far too long a time had passed. The movie also fabricates the death scenario, showing four brothers on deck when the torpedo hit and suggesting they might have escaped if they had not attempted to rescue the fifth brother, George, below deck. In the film, all five die on the ship, inseparable in death as in life

Waterloo in the 1930s, when the boys were children, had a population of over 70,000 and major farm industries. The film, however, visually gives Waterloo a more rural/small town feel. Near the Sullivan house, with its garden out back and its clothesline waving the boys' pants, is a river where the boys like to fish. As they grow up, we see the boys in all seasons enjoying the outdoors and getting into scrapes. Though the Sullivan family on screen is not rich, the father has a steady job as a freight conductor and the family has money for their needs—unlike many Iowans in the Great Depression. John Satterfield's history of the Sullivan episode characterizes Waterloo in much the same way as the movie does:

> Waterloo and other "average" places form the keel beams of the ship of state. From such places stem the values and the outlooks that determine the American character. These sensibilities—a sense of justice and fairness, a belief in the value of individuals and a willingness to work for the common good—are the last legacy of towns like Waterloo stretching to every corner of the United States.[29]

In Satterfield's praise, one hears Grandpa Marsh extolling Hartfield as a site for cultivating patriotic virtue.

The film portrays the Sullivan boys as a band of scalawags. The youngest, Al, almost drowns when the boys launch a boat they found and attempted to repair with mud. They almost destroy their mother's kitchen when they cut through the plumbing to install a port for passing firewood through the wall. They brawl with one another and outsiders, confirming the stereotype of the American-Irish as hot-tempered fighters.

The Sullivans' devout Catholicism pervades the film, suggesting a link between religious faith and patriotism. We see Al's first confession, conversations with a priest, and Al's church wedding. We see that although the boys have a wild streak, they have also learned family loyalty, a sense of duty, and patriotism from their parents. Al's wife recognizes the importance of these values in the family and urges Al to enlist with his brothers, even though, unlike them, he has a wife and child.

After the boys enlist, the patriotic pathos begins when the family receives the devastating news that "all five" are dead. Iowa stoicism in the face of loss is revealed when Tom Sullivan puts his hand briefly on his wife's shoulder to console her and then immediately leaves for the railroad, having never missed a day of work. The film ends with Mrs. Sullivan christening the ship *USS The Sullivans*. She remarks, "Tom, our boys are afloat again"—and we see all five, with Al tagging behind as usual, marching in their sailor suits off into the clouds to heaven, while the musical score plays "Anchors Aweigh."

Once Americans went to war, the nation needed to be reminded repeatedly why we were fighting and what justified home front austerity and the monumental number of injuries and deaths. (Some 300,000 Americans died in the war; nearly 700,000 were wounded).[32] *Happy Land* and *The Sullivans*, made with government approval, did not show heroic battle, the evil enemy, or real Iowans' war activities. Instead, by celebrating fallen heroes and stoical families from rural Iowa, the films declare that we are fighting to preserve agrarian life, the foundation of American democracy, and that Americans must do their duty, like Lew Marsh and Tom Sullivan, and carry on the war effort in spite of grief.

WWII Vets Return to the Heartland:
The Best Years of Our Lives

The Best Years of Our Lives (which swept the 1946 Oscars, winning in eight categories) had its unlikely origin in Kantor's long narrative poem, *Glory for Me*.[31] The setting, Boone City, is not identified as Iowa in the film, but Kantor's Iowa background and textual references in *Glory for Me* suggest Des Moines. The film presents three servicemen who meet on the plane as they return to a changed heartland. Their stories interweave in the film. An infantryman and former Cornbelt Bank employee, Al Stephenson returns to a loving wife and family, and to a good job—but drinks excessively and knocks heads with bank executives who won't risk loans to deserving vets. Former medal-winning flyboy Fred Derry can't find a job or keep the unfaithful wife who earlier married him only because of his glamour in uniform. Sailor Homer Parrish returns to a devoted family and fiancée, but is ashamed and embarrassed, with her, about the hooks that replaced his hands.

This highly acclaimed movie portrays a less than pastoral view of the home front after the war. Boone City seems tired of the war and deprivations, now more enthusiastic about materialism than patriotism. The bank wants to make profits, not help vets re-establish themselves. Some people resent the returning servicemen.

Yet, despite its honesty and realism, the movie ultimately reinforces the core heartland values expressed in earlier WWII Iowa films. In the tender final scene, Homer marries the faithful girl next door in a Christian ceremony. Fred, his best man, has finally found a job converting airplane scrap metal into suburban housing. Now divorced, he will marry Al's admirable daughter. Al has spoken his views to the bank executives, and his wife has loyally stood by his side during his difficult adjustment. Life will go on after the hardships and sacrifices of the war. The title of the film may be ironic, but the heartland values that people embraced during the war are real, even if threatened by postwar politics and consumerism. Despite a much better script, direction, and acting than *Happy Land* and *The Sullivans*, *Best Years*, too, has its propaganda message: support the veterans who fought and suffered during World War II.

What can we learn from the Hollywood-U.S. government promotions of *Happy Land* and *The Sullivans* and the response of critics and audiences to the films? Ironically, the films of the war period fell flat with critics and audiences. Perhaps this reveals the creative limitations of propaganda films and a serious misjudgement regarding the appeal of films about death and grief.

The Office of War Information was especially enthusiastic about the filmed version of *Happy Land*. One OWI reviewer remarked that "it was 'the most effective portrayal of straight Americana viewed to date.'"[32] Exploiting the film's rural themes and Kantor's status as the state's most popular author, Twentieth Century Fox arranged for the film's premiere at 62 Iowa theatres on 2 December 1943.[33] A *Des Moines Register* ad trumpeted "the World's First Showing of a truly great motion picture about Hawkeye courage and just plain Iowa folks!" Kantor appeared at a Des Moines theatre with Iowa's Lt. Governor, who praised Kantor for "bringing honor to the state." Kantor remarked that "this story is about an Iowa boy of the current generation who did not return from the war"[34]—a statement that was true for nearly 8,500 other Iowans who died in the war.[35] Despite OWI's enthusiasm and the PR stunts, *Happy Land* made a tepid splash as home front propaganda.

In attempting to lure audiences, Iowa newspaper ads for the film were mum about the theme of mournful sacrifice for the "happy land." One ad finessed the issue with vagueness, by proclaiming—"HAPPY the land that can give us such a story! HAPPY the people who can live it! HAPPY are you who can thrill to it!" The ad conveyed the rural paradise motif without hinting at the plot's grim reality: "A picture as American as an ice-cream soda at the corner drug store! A story as stirring as marching behind a band down Main Street! A romance as thrilling as the first love light in a woman's shining eyes."[36]

Critics greeted *Happy Land* with condescending tolerance. *Time* found it a "tender, folksy elegy" but added that the novel "is hard to picturize without being mawkish."[37] *Variety* called it "a strong tear jerker" that achieved iconic status as a "story of a typical Iowa country town and a typical family."[38] The *New York Times* also commended its "well intentioned effort . . . to get somewhere close to the feelings which agitate the heart of the ordinary man, in a plain American town and to reach a simple conclusion as to why we are fighting this war."[39] While *Variety* predicted that the film would be "a highly prolific grosser, with holdovers in most locations," we found no evidence of commercial or propaganda success. Like much wartime propaganda, *Happy Land* passed quickly into obscurity.

The government realized immediately after the deaths of the Sullivans that there was the potential for a patriotic film and propaganda campaign. Tom and Aleta Sullivan served as advisors for the film, visited defense plants for pep talks to war workers, and sold war bonds. Aleta's steady refrain was that "they did their part"—which became the slogan for the Sullivans war bond poster reproduced here—and that they want us all "to keep our chins up." The *Waterloo Courier* quoted Aleta: "Everyone should work harder to turn out more ships, and to help win the war. Mothers should pray for their boys and, above all, be brave and keep their chins up."[40] When she christened the destroyer *USS The Sullivans*, Aleta said:

> "I only wish that my boys could be here to see this warship. But I know that they must be watching us today from up in Heaven, and I know they must be happy that this ship is ready to go out there to carry the fight."[41]

When *The Sullivans* premiered in early 1944, the nation had known of the family tragedy for a year. The *New York Times* reviewer noted that the filmmakers had "adorned the film freely with clichés" of the "family film" and that the Sullivan parents had sold war bonds in the lobby for the premiere at the Roxy Theatre.[42] *Variety*'s reviewer commented, "It has been done with assumed fidelity and no doubt will be richly cherished as a documentary account of heroism of the Sullivan family of the small Midwestern town, whether or not it achieves exceptional support from the general public as entertainment."[43] In the Midwest, the reaction was muted. The *Des Moines Register*'s brief notice mentioned the genre elements without praise, calling the film "the biography of five typically American kids, their scrappy, carefree childhood, and their

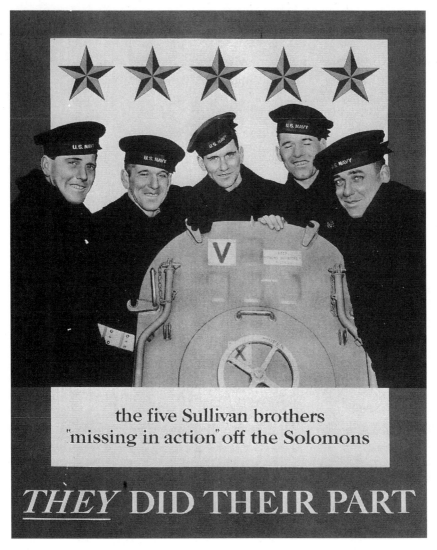

the five Sullivan brothers
"missing in action" off the Solomons

THEY DID THEIR PART

fighting, laughing manhood."[44] This was not that "exceptional support" *Variety* predicted, so the disappointed filmmakers at Twentieth
Century Fox quickly renamed the movie *The Fighting Sullivans* to stir
additional audience interest.[45] This change did not extend the film's
exhibition life. A Fighting Sullivans Memorial Fund had been established immediately following the tragedy and had raised $5500; after
the film's release, contributions dribbled in—reflecting no surge of
awareness or new enthusiasm for memorializing the Sullivan family.
[46] The nation was apparently weary of grief, sympathy, and causes.

Americans wanted future victory, not to dwell on heavy sorrows of the past. *The Sullivans* virtually disappeared from the cinematic landscape until *Saving Private Ryan* revived interest in the film in 1998.

The relative failure of the rural Iowa propaganda films, compared to the two moderately successful 1941 films, may relate to factors already mentioned: mediocre scripts and filmgoer indifference to gloomy plots. Moreover propaganda films can also weary their audiences with their character stereotyping, emotional manipulation, oversimplified issues, and silencing of dissent. Several examples can be cited to suggest why the propaganda films flopped. Unlike Gramp in *Happy Land*, who comes straight out of central casting as a warm-hearted old codger, Will Spence has intriguing personality quirks and contradictions. Though a strict adherent to the church's "Discipline" which forbids movie-going, he attends a silent western film with his son to prove to his son the moral turpitude of the movies; instead, he loves the movie and has to reinterpret the "Discipline" to justify his new passion. The best example of over-the-top emotional manipulation is the ending of *Happy Land*: the omniscient, almost Christ-like Rusty sends his parents an emotional replacement for himself—his war buddy Tony Cavrek, an orphan from Chicago who needs a good dose of Iowa pastoralism. Tony tells the family Rusty died trying to save a comrade, and then moves into Rusty's room, Rusty's job, and the hearts of Rusty's family. It is almost as though Rusty died so Tony could enjoy rural life. An example of squelching dissent comes when the main characters in the propaganda films enlist, a seemingly instinctive decision they need not justify to family or audience. Unnaturally, no one in these films— not even Al Sullivan's wife with a new baby—questions the enlistment decision or expresses any fear, doubt, depression, or anger.

Iowa's Cinematic Role After World War II

As we have seen, in 1941-1946, Hollywood cooperated with the government's need to promote the war effort. Because of timely books written by Iowans and the deaths of the Sullivan Brothers, rural Iowa— presented pastorally—became the setting for films that indirectly or directly supported the war effort and the soldiers who fought. Like *Sergeant York* (1941), which extols the WWI rural hero, these films are part of the long cultural tradition uniting agrarian character and service in war.

Though these films mostly present Iowans positively and celebrate the agrarian ethos as fundamental to democracy, this image of Iowa quickly disappeared after the war. As early as 1948, Billy Wilder film *A Foreign Affair* satirizes fictional Iowa Congresswoman Phoebe Frost who zealously investigates the morale and morals of GIs occupying post-war Germany. She is prudish, naively patriotic, unsophisticated, and unused to liquor—all these qualities too evident and ridiculous when she belts out the "Iowa Corn Song" in a German cabaret filled with war survivors.

Having done its duty during the war, Iowa had to accept a less dignified role— or no role at all—in post-war movies. The number of Iowa films decreased significantly in the 1950s, 1960s, and 1970s, and those that appeared were mainly historical, comic, or anti-pastoral.

Iowa's image might have looked better in the post-war period, and later, if 1940s films had shown real Iowa during the war: its record agricultural production, with the assistance of foreign nationals and prisoners of war; significant scientific discoveries at Iowa State University that helped produce uranium for the Manhattan Project; extensive training of women for the military; women and men working together in important war industries.[47] A more complex, modern image of Iowa is suggested here, but one that didn't suit the "Home Front" niche that Hollywood and the OWI had in mind to meet its wartime propaganda aims. Only recently has the pendulum swung back to a more pastoral view of Iowa in blockbuster films such as *Field of Dreams* (1989) and *The Bridges of Madison County* (1995). Ironically, however, the Iowa in these films reverts to Iowa of the 1940s war films: rural and old-fashioned.

In the nostalgic 1990s, films about Iowa and Iowans gained popularity again. *Field of Dreams* and *The Bridges of Madison County* both generated tourist sites that advertise Iowa as a pastoral paradise where people can find love, reconciliation, or dream fulfilment. Simultaneously, the popularity of World War II films and documentaries skyrocketed to the point that some cable channels seemed to offer World War II programming around the clock. Not surprisingly, the two threads—rural Iowa and WWII—linked again, to produce the movies *The Tuskegee Airmen* (1995) and *Saving Private Ryan* (1998). This time the war films emphasize combat, not home front, and the main characters survive the war, apparently due to their "happy land" traits. Both films replay the familiar pastoral hymn to rural Iowa, however. With widespread despair about economics, our democratic institutions, and eroding moral character, contemporary Americans seem to view the difficult World War II years as a utopian time when the country pulled together and was worth the sacrifice—and to feel mythical rural Iowa is a place that should exist. As the present drifts farther from a past that never was, a pastoral view of heartland America becomes increasingly difficult to accept as real on screen, but it seems to fill a psychic need in our citizens.

The earnest effort of the 1940s films to find a compelling rural iconography for the good America speaks to the current readiness for war. In developing a political opportunity for a declaration of war in Europe, FDR cautiously waited from the mid-1930s crises with Italy and Germany to the invasion of Pearl Harbor in 1941. Looking at the U.S. invasion of Iraq in 2003 for comparison, President George W. Bush's administration within months moved U.S. citizens away from preference for a United Nations mantle of consensus to a sense of unilateral urgency. It only seemed necessary to take aim at a coordinate on the Axis of Evil and suggest a Saddam/Al Qaeda conspiracy. Media coverage 24/7, allowing viewers to see the war as it happens, along with the increase of comic book superhero themes,[48] have changed the propaganda process dramatically. We no longer need to romanticize the people of the happy land or plead for their contributions to the national cause. Professional soldiers will root out evildoers abroad, while home front citizens are urged to use their tax cuts to shop so the world's largest economy will not falter. Even though the older films can be criticized, they help Americans especially see themselves as they are now.

Endnotes

[1] "The Middle West," *Life*, November 9, 1942, 103; cited in James R. Shortridge, *The Middle West: Its Meaning in American Culture* (Lawrence: University Press of Kansas, 1989), 61.

[2] Grant Wood, "Spring in Town," painted in 1941; the picture appeared on the cover of *Saturday Evening Post* shortly after his death on February 12, 1942.

[3] Leo A. Borah, "Iowa, Abiding Place of Plenty," *National Geographic*, August 1939, 144-45.

[4] David Culbert, Foreword, *Film and Propaganda: A Documentary History*, vol. 2, *WWII*, part 1 (Westport, CT: Greenwood Press, 1990): vii.

[5] Shortridge, *The Middle West*, 100.

[6] Ibid., 8.

[7] Ibid., 12, 44-45.

[8] Ibid., 39.

[9] Ibid., 60.

[10] Borah, "Iowa, Abiding Place of Plenty," 143-82.

[11] Ibid., 161.

[12] Ibid., 159.

[13] Riane Eisler, *The Chalice and the Blade: Our History, Our Future* (San Francisco: Harper and Row, 1987), chap. 3.

[14] See Gary Wills, *Cincinnatus: George Washington and the Enlightenment* (New York: Doubleday, 1984), 225, 240.

[15] Further evidence of pastoralism's return before the war is the popularity of the much Oscared film *Mr. Smith Goes to Washington* (1939), which contrasts the naive patriotism of Smith, raised in the West, with the corruption of Washington politics.

[16] Quoted in A. Scott Berg, *Lindbergh* (New York: G. P. Putnam's, 1998), 427.

[17] From correspondence related to *Confessions of a Nazi Spy* (1939), quoted in Colin Shindler, *Hollywood in Crisis: Cinema and American Society, 1929-1939* (London/ New York: Routledge, 1996), 208.

[18] Thomas Patrick Doherty. *Pre-Code Hollywood: Sex, Immorality, and Insurrection in American Cinema, 1930–1934* (New York: Columbia University Press, 2013), 76.

[19] Clayton R. Koppes and Gregory D. Black, *Hollywood Goes to War: How Politics, Profits, and Propaganda Shaped World War II Movies* (Berkeley: University of California Press, 1987), 22-23.

[20] See the chapter "Hollywood Turns Interventionist," in Koppes and Black, *Hollywood Goes to War*, 17-47, for the step-by-step interplay between American politics, the MPPA, and the creative film community.

[21] James M. Myers. *The Bureau of Motion Pictures and Its Influence on Film Content During World War II: The Reasons for Its Failure* (Lewistown, NY: Edwin Mellen Press, 1998), 208, 209.

[22] Koppes and Black, *Hollywood Goes to War*, 65.

[23] This essay does not discuss every Iowa film made during the World War II years. Others include *Don't Get Personal* (1942), *The Major and the Minor* (1942), *Orchestra Wives* (1942), *Double Exposure* (1944), *Blonde from Brooklyn* (1945), *Bud Abbott and Lou Costello in Hollywood* (1945), the musical *State Fair* (1945), and *Johnny Comes Flying Home* (1946).

[24] Hartzell Spence, *One Foot in Heaven: The Life of a Practical Parson* (New York: McGraw, 1940).

[25] Bess Streeter Aldrich, *Miss Bishop* (New York: Appleton-Century, 1933).

[26] MacKinlay Kantor, "Happy Land," *Saturday Evening Post*, 28 November 1942, 9-11 (complete). Kantor expanded the story into a novel with the same title (New York: Coward-McCann, 1943).

[27] Horace, *Odes*, Bk 3, Ode 19, line 2.

[28] John Satterfield, *We Band of Brothers: The Sullivans and World War II.* (Parkersburg, IA: Mid-Prairie Books, 1995), 139-55.

[29] John Satterfield, *We Band of Brothers*, x.

[30] "Casualties in World War II," *Time Almanac* (New York: Information Please, 2000), 399.

[31] MacKinlay Kantor, *Glory for Me* (New York: Coward-McCann, 1945).

[32] Koppes, *Hollywood Goes to War*, 162.

[33] *American Film Institute Catalog of Feature Films: 1893-1970, Happy Land* entry.

[34] "Iowa Views 'Happy Land,'" *Des Moines Register*, December 3, 1943.

[35] Dorothy Schwieder, *Iowa: The Middle Land* (Ames: Iowa State University Press, 1996), 279.

[36] Advertisement, *Des Moines Register*, December 3, 1943.

[37] *Time*, December 13, 1943, 92.

[38] *Variety*, November 10, 1943, 34.

[39] *New York Times*, December 9, 1943, 33.

[40] Satterfield, *We Band of Brothers*, 183.

[41] Ibid., 190.

[42] *New York Times*, February 10, 1944, 19.

[43] *Variety*, February 9, 1944, 12.

[44] *Des Moines Register*, March 12, 1944.

[45] *AFI Catalog*, entry for *The Sullivans*.

[46] Satterfield, *We Band of Brothers*, 192.

[47] Schwieder, *Iowa: The Middle Land*, chap. 15.

[48] See Robert Jewett and John Shelton Lawrence, *Captain America and the Crusade Against Evil: The Dilemma of Zealous Nationalism* (Grand Rapids, MI: Eerdmans, 2003), chap. 3.

Appendix D: A Short Bibliography

I. Portrayals of Iowa and Other Midwestern States

The American Midwest: An Interpretive Encyclopedia. Ed. Richard Sisson, Christian Zacher, and Andrew Cayton. Bloomington and Indianapolis: Indiana UP, 2007. Print. The section "Images of the Midwest" (55-126) includes relevant overview essays on "Flyover Country," "Genuine America," "Heartland," "Movies," "Television," and "Yeoman Farmer." There are individual entries for "Phil Stong's *State Fair*," "Meredith Willson's *The Music Man*," "*M*A*S*H*'s Radar O'Reilly," and "*Field of Dreams*."

Knepper, Marty S., and John S. Lawrence "Iowa Filmography: 1918-2002." *Annals of Iowa* 62.1 (2003): 30-100. Print.

—. "Visions of Iowa in Hollywood Film." *Iowa Heritage Illustrated* 79.4 (1998): 156-69. Print.

Lostetter, Timothy Lee. *Iowa in the Movies.* Monroe, WI: Flatbridge Media, 2013. Print.

Prasch, Thomas, ed. "From Projections of the Past to Fantasies of the Future: Kansas and the Great Plains in Recent Film." *Kansas History: A Journal of the Central Plains* 36.2 (2013): 104-08. Academic Search Premier. Web. 25 May 2014. This is the most extensive biennial film review section that *Kansas History* has published since 2001. These reviews cover classics, contemporary films, and documentaries.

Rasmussen, Chris. "Mr. Stong's Dreamy Iowa." *Iowa Heritage Illustrated* 79.4 (1998): 147-55. Print.

Shortridge, James R. *The Middle West: Its Meaning in American Culture.* Lawrence: UP of Kansas, 1989. Print.

II. Portrayals of Other States and Regions

Cox, Karen L. *Dreaming of Dixie: How the South Was Created in American Popular Culture.* Chapel Hill: U of North Carolina P, 2011. Print. This book emphasizes the scant knowledge of the South in Tin Pan

Alley and Hollywood, both contributing to national perceptions of race and The Lost Cause.

Campbell, Edward D. C., Jr. *The Celluloid South: Hollywood and the Southern Myth*. Knoxville: U of Tennessee P, 1981. Print.

Davis, Mike. *Ecology of Fear: Los Angeles and the Imagination of Disaster*. New York: Vintage, 1998. Print. The story of how Los Angeles— with its history of drought, wildfires, floods, earthquakes, and riots—became the preferred setting for the disaster and dystopian genres.

Fienup-Riordan, Ann. *Freeze Frame: Alaska Eskimos in the Movies*. Seattle: U of Washington P, 1995. Print.

Graham, Don. *Cowboys and Cadillacs: How Hollywood Looks at Texas*. Austin: Texas Monthly Press, 1983. Print.

Kirby, Jack Temple. *Media Made Dixie: The South in the American Imagination*. Baton Rouge: Louisiana State UP, 1978. Print.

Springwood, Charles Fruehling. "Farming, Dreaming and Playing in Iowa: Japanese Mythopoetics and Agrarian Utopia." *Tourism: Between Place and Performance*. Ed. Simon Coleman and Mike Crang. New York: Berghahn Books, 2002. 176-90. Print. An account of how a Japanese baseball fan recreated a *Field of Dreams* site in rural Hiroshima, in effect "translating" Iowa into a different culture.

Williamson, J. W. *Hillbillyland: What the Movies Did to the Mountains and What the Mountains Did to the Movies*. Chapel Hill: U of North Carolina P, 1995. Print.

III. General Reference

American Film Institute Catalog of Motion Pictures Produced in the United States. Vol 3. Berkeley: U of California P, 1993. Print.

American Film Institute Catalog of Motion Pictures Produced in the United States. Vol 4. Berkeley: U of California P, 1999. Print.

American Film Institute Catalog. American Film Institute, 2014. Web.

New York Times Film Reviews. New York Times, n.d. Web. This source is extensive but not complete for all reviews that have appeared in its pages. According to the *Times*, the listing "contains all reviews since 1960, and selected reviews going back to 1910."

New York Times Film Reviews, 1913-1968. New York: New York Times and Arno, 1970. 6 vols. (1-5: Reviews; 6: Appendix, Index.) Print. The reproduction of reviews is comprehensive, and thus includes many that *The Times* did not select for the electronic archives. This publication has been supplanted by the web version.

"Film Reviews." *Variety.com*. Variety, n.d. Web. In 2010, *Variety* started opening a subscription-based access to page images of its entire archives at varietyultimate.com. Some reviews are available only through varietyultimate.com.

Variety Film Reviews. New York: Garland, 1983. Print. Issued in ten volumes, these reviews are comprehensive from 1907 to 1996. This publication has been supplanted by web versions.

About the Authors

Marty S. Knepper is professor of English and chair of English and Modern Languages at Morningside College in Sioux City, Iowa. She is a past president of the Popular Culture Association and serves on the editorial board of the international academic journal *Clues*. She has written numerous articles on detective fiction, film, and women's studies. John Shelton Lawrence is Professor Emeritus of Philosophy at Morningside and co-author of *The Myth of the American Superhero* (2002). In addition to a filmography for *The Landscape of Hollywood Westerns* (2006), he also created filmographies for the Film and History Association books *Hollywood's White House* (2003), *Hollywood's West* (2005), and *Why We Fought* (2008). Before his retirement, he and Marty regularly team taught an interdisciplinary seminar in American Popular Culture.

Index of Iowa Films